THE LAST RISING: THE NEWPORT INSURRECTION OF 1839

THE LAST RISING

The Newport Insurrection of 1839

DAVID J. V. JONES

CLARENDON PRESS · OXFORD

1985

Oxford University Press, Walton Street, Oxford OX2 6DP

London New York Toronto
Delhi Bombay Calcutta Madras Karachi
Kuala Lumpur Singapore Hong Kong Tokyo
Nairobi Dar es Salaam Cape Town
Melbourne Auckland

and associated companies in
Beirut Berlin Ibadan Mexico City Nicosia

Oxford is a trade mark of Oxford University Press

Published in the United States
by Oxford University Press, New York

British Library Cataloguing in Publication Data
Jones, David, 1941–
The last rising: the Newport insurrection of 1839.
1. Chartism—Wales—Newport (Gwent)
I. Title
322.4'4'0942991   HD8396
ISBN 0-19-820076-5

Library of Congress Cataloging in Publication Data
Jones, David J. V.
The last rising.
Bibliography: p.
Includes index.
1. Newport Uprising, Wales, 1839.
2. Labor disputes—Wales—Newport (Gwent)—History—19th century.
3. Labor and laboring classes—Wales—Newport (Gwent)—History—19th century.
4. Social conflict—Wales—Newport (Gwent)—History—19th century.
5. Chartism—History. I. Title.
HD5366.Z9N495   1985   942.9'91081   84-20601
ISBN 0-19-820076-5

Typeset by Joshua Associates, Oxford
Printed in Great Britain
at the University Press, Oxford
by David Stanford
Printer to the University

Preface

THIS book has been some time in the making. Over a period of ten years I have been collecting information on the rising. Some of the evidence was used by my old teacher, Professor David Williams, in 1939, but much of it is new. I have looked at a number of files and boxes of material which, so far as I know, historians have neglected or ignored.[1] The main difference from other studies, however, lies in the interpretation. I am especially interested in the ordinary people who made the rising, and I have described them and their society in some detail. This is not a history of John Frost and the other radical leaders. I am also interested in the Chartist movement throughout Britain, and this has helped me to understand that moment of time in November 1839.

Although the rising was only one of many popular disturbances in the nineteenth century, I hope to show that its nature and significance deserve attention. 'Nov. 3, 4 & 5th. ought not to be indeed cannot be soon forgotten', wrote William Phillips of Whitson. 'The events of that time will give to our county a conspicuous part in English history.'[2] In a sense much of the history of industrial South Wales is encapsulated in the affair. For a while we can peer into a unique class society and catch a glimpse, too, of the relationship between the people and the machinery of state. Not everything, of course, is revealed. The rising was a secret business, and some of the more intriguing questions will never be answered. Of one thing I am certain: there is more to be discovered. Finally, this book is dedicated to the miners of South Wales, whose story this is.

November 1983   DAVID JONES

Acknowledgements

I WISH to acknowledge the financial help of the University College, Swansea, and of the Leverhulme Trust. I am also grateful to the Librarian at Windsor Castle for his assistance, and acknowledge the gracious permission of Her Majesty the Queen to use the material in the Royal Archives. Finally, I wish to thank the following for advice on, and permission to reproduce, the illustrations: the British Steel Corporation (Dowlais Works); the Glamorgan Archive Service; Richard Keen of the Industrial and Maritime Museum, Cardiff; E. Jones and T. Rowson; the National Library of Wales; and Keith Thomas.

Contents

Maps

Illustrations

Abbreviations

BL	British Library	NPL	Newport Public Library
CPL	Cardiff Public Library	NS	*Northern Star*
GRO	Glamorgan Record Office	PP	Parliamentary Papers
HO	Home Office	RA	Royal Archives
MG	*Merthyr Guardian*	TS	Treasury Solicitor
MM	*Monmouthshire Merlin*	WV	*Western Vindicator*
NLW	National Library of Wales		

Introduction

ON 4 November 1839, in the early morning of a cold and wet Newport day, soldiers of the 45th Regiment shot and killed some twenty Chartists and wounded many more. The event, and even more the secrecy and planning behind it, shocked contemporaries. 'I hope now that this will go no further,' wrote Prime Minister Melbourne two days later; '. . . Such a mode of proceeding is a thousand times more dangerous than unions and great meetings which are always known beforehand. . . .' The Whig government, which had dealt severe and apparently successful blows to the Chartist movement in the summer months, and which was now involved in other weighty matters, suddenly found itself face-to-face with the spectre of revolution. Lord Normanby, at the Home Department, was dragged from the theatre to meet the first refugee carrying the sad tidings from South Wales, and even then he and Melbourne found it hard to accept his message. 'It is but a few days since the Attorney-General made his foolish and insolent boast of having put down the Chartists and extinguished Chartism,' mocked one newspaper, revelling in the government's embarrassment. 'He is answered in a terrific voice from the Welsh mountains.'[1] In London, Paris, and New York during the early days of November people waited expectantly for news from the Principality, and all over Britain political militants, prophets, and fanatics came to life.

At the subsequent court hearings, the last mass treason-trial in modern times, the prosecution correctly emphasized the exceptional nature of the Newport affair. In scope and potential the proceedings of that November weekend were much worse than Peterloo, the Pentridge rising, and similar clashes with authority. 'The outbreak, as it is called, is of much greater extent than I had a conception of', ran a typical comment, '& had it succeeded at Newport, murders and burnings would have annihilated men and property. . . .' 'Wales . . . the hitherto most peaceful part of the kingdom has been rendered . . . as volcanic as Ireland. . . .'[2] *The Times*, Macaulay, leading spokesmen for religious and business groups, and a wide range of political and police reformers, all saw the Newport rising as perhaps the greatest challenge to the integrity of the

United Kingdom and to the growing confidence of early Victorian society. 'In the history of the civilised nations I can find nothing like it—nothing to be compared with it,' said Thomas Prothero, lawyer and industrial capitalist; 'the only thing to which it bears a resemblance, is the irruption of a horde of American Savages upon some hostile village.'[3] Newspaper correspondents, legal counsel, and government officials came to realize, sometimes slowly and reluctantly, that this rising of miners had to be seriously investigated and taken into the wider debate on the future of the British working class. Euphoria at the Chartist defeat, captured for ever in the triumphant army lithographs of dead bodies outside the Westgate hotel, lasted for only a brief period.

In Wales the debate over the Newport rising took on a particular significance. 'It has often been asserted', wrote Sir Thomas Phillips, a decade later, 'that the insurrection of 1839 was Welsh in its origin and character, and carried on with more secrecy, because contrived by persons who communicated with each other in a language not understood by authorities.'[4] 'I do not believe', added Lady Charlotte Guest, 'that any but Welshmen could be brought up to such a pitch of enthusiasm.'[5] The rising was quickly set in the context of the Scotch Cattle, the Merthyr insurrection of 1831, and the Rebecca Riots, and it was commonly believed that industrial South Wales was the last place in Britain where a popular revolution could be planned and executed with secrecy and success. 'The system, arrangement & great secrecy amongst these deluded people is, & will be the source of constant alarm,' said the agent of the Marquis of Bute on 6 November 1839, '& we feel that we are not safe for a moment.'[6]

The Newport rising highlighted the contradictions and divisions in Welsh society. Many of those who participated in the Chartist affair knew only that it was an expression of class solidarity and an experiment in popular politics. 'I went up to the road to them & spoke to a few of them on the folly of their conduct', reported John Lewis, a tin-plate manufacturer of Tydu near Newport. 'They told me', he continued, 'that it was useless for me to talk to them in that way, that they were kept out of their rights, & that they were determined to have the Charter. I then said, supposing that as you say your rights *are* withheld from you, this surely is not the way to obtain them. One of them, who appeared to be a kind of leader said in reply, it was by such means that the people obtained their rights

in America & in France.'[7] Although this bid for workers' democracy and independence soon ended in death and martyrdom, the
rising itself became an important part of class mythology and consciousness. Generations in the mining towns were brought up on
stories of that November day. 'The Newport Riots' became a popular theme of ballads, verse, and peep-shows, and for many decades
the picture of John Frost hung on cottage walls.

For other members of South Wales society the images and legacy
were different. Some viewed the coalfield as a colony to be won and
conquered.'It requires some courage to live amongst such a set of
savages', said Reginald Blewitt of Llantarnam Abbey, Member of
Parliament for the Monmouth boroughs.[8] 'I am sorry to say that I
believe the ranks of the Chartists to be rapidly on the increase,'
wrote his fellow industrialist James Brown of the Cwm Celyn and
Blaina ironworks three months before the rising, '& am anxiously
looking to the newspapers for a satisfactory report of the Military
being call'd out & 2, 3 or 400 slain and then (but not before) shall we
have peace at home.'[9] Such people later crammed into the court-
rooms at Newport and Monmouth, and led the municipal and
national celebrations of victory.

Of course, the significance of the Newport rising for the middle
and upper classes did not end there. 'The Chartists are coming' was
a cry which echoed through the century. It concentrated the mind
wonderfully on issues of poverty, progress, and policing. Later Parliamentary Papers show clearly that a considerable amount of
employer paternalism, religious education, and liberal politics
began about this time. The rising confirmed middle-class preju-
dices about the brutality and ignorance of the Welsh 'gwerin'.
Representatives of central and local government constantly
reminded themselves that many of the rioters were ignorant of 'our
[English] language' and 'our [Established] religion'.[10] The need to
change this situation led directly to the three official examinations
of Welsh education, culminating in the infamous Commission of
Inquiry of 1847. In all these reports the memory of the Newport
massacre helped to direct the leading questions on the violence,
intemperance, immorality, criminality, and ignorance of the
people of the valleys. Ironically, Thomas Phillips, the mayor of
Newport who was knighted for his services to Queen and country
during the rising, later produced a long and reasoned defence of the
Welsh character and culture. For this, and for his subsequent efforts

in the cause of Welsh education and religion, Phillips has gained a prominent place in the story of the Welsh identity. So, in a more curious way, has Dr William Price of Pontypridd, and a few others associated with the Chartist conflict. In one way or another, therefore, much of the history of modern Wales and modern Welshness began on that November morning 144 years ago.

What remains unclear, however, is the nature of the rising itself. In 1840 Edward Dowling, proprietor of the *Monmouthshire Merlin* the leading local newspaper, predicted that 'this insurrectionary movement will . . . be a subject of utter astonishment to the future historian of the county, when, like ourselves he looks in vain for an adequate or palpable cause'.[11] Some of the actual participants were ignorant of the objectives of the Chartist leaders, whilst others had notions 'vague in the extreme'.[12] A few brave souls, who openly set themselves the task of discovering the secrets of the rising, retired baffled and confused. Opinions, even of sympathetic radicals, changed daily as new details emerged from court examinations and newspaper enquiries. Sadly, for government prosecutors and future historians, much of the vital evidence on the intention of the rioters was destroyed just before or after the march on Newport. At Coalbrookvale, Ebbw Vale, Gelligaer, Blackwood, Newport, and Bristol secret documents were burnt, and police searches proved quite unsatisfactory. Even more galling for the authorities was the fact that most of the delegates at the secret and decisive conferences prior to the rising were killed at Newport or managed to escape. Others who knew what was at stake on 4 November 1839 chose to remain silent, or, like Zephaniah Williams and Dr William Price, have left us only fragmentary and elusive reminiscences. Frost, after his return to Britain in 1856, promised to write a full account of his role in the affair, but died when he was just about to complete the task.[13]

The first historians of Chartism were intrigued by the rising but were hardly illuminating in their comments. R. G. Gammage, who deeply admired the spirit of the Welsh, relied mainly on newspaper reports for his inconclusive survey, while a few years later, Robert Lowery described the insurrection as 'a mad and foolish affair'.[14] William Lovett, in his autobiography, provided some additional information on the discussions that preceded November 1839, but his account is largely an attack on his rival, Feargus O'Connor. Thus the pattern was set for the next generation of historians. The

Fabians, with their dislike of 'projects of futile violence', were rather dismissive of the whole event.[15] Julius West, writing in 1920, reduced the rising to a fairly innocuous gathering of 200 people. G. D. H. Cole, a much better historian, concluded, after a long investigation, that 'the "Newport Rising" was a small affair; and its leader was a small man, not only in stature, but in importance too.'[16] Amongst Marxist historians the rising was seen from two very different standpoints: for Reg Groves it was a genuinely revolutionary cry by a leaderless and frustrated proletariat, whilst for Theodore Rothstein it was the outcome of a plot partly conceived by those in authority. All these early writers, however, were agreed on the necessity for more research and the 'well-nigh impossible' task of uncovering hidden motives. Then, on the centenary of the rising, Professor David Williams published his *John Frost*, a brilliant and detailed account which is still the standard work on the subject.[17] During the next twenty years Professor Williams discovered some exciting new material on the Newport affair, but in his chapter for *Chartist Studies* in 1959 he reiterated his typically cautious opinion that the rising had no violent or revolutionary intent. 'The only reasonable explanation of the Newport riot', he declared, 'is that it was intended as a monster demonstration.'[18] It is the purpose of this book to re-examine his claim and to set the rising in the context of a unique industrial society.[19]

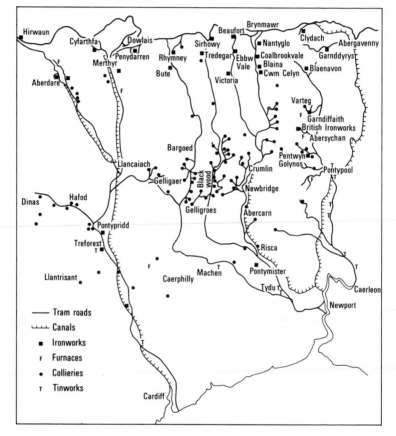

MAP 1. The Ironworks and Collieries of South Wales in 1839

A Unique Society

ANY analysis of the events of 4 November 1839 must begin with a survey of the South Wales coalfield and its people. The government itself recognized this point, and commissioned several private and official surveys of the mining population. Within a matter of months Seymour Tremenheere, schools' inspector, Sir Edmund Head, assistant Poor Law Commissioner, and Col. Considine, commander of the armed forces in the district, had all presented reports on the background to the Newport troubles. They discovered a geography, an economy, and a society which had few parallels and fewer precedents. 'The localities in which the vast populations of the hills are congregated are remote and peculiar', Tremenheere reflected a few years later. 'From the central chain of high moorland, separating the counties of Monmouth, Brecon and Glamorgan, numerous valleys run off at right angles towards the south.'[1] These valleys, from the Taff and Rhondda in the west to Afon Lwyd in the east, produced a substantial share of Britain's industrial wealth. By 1839 well over a third of the pig-iron in Britain came from the 122 working furnaces on the coalfield, and the total coal output of the region was some 4 m. tons per year. Much of this iron and coal was sent by canals and tramroads to Newport and Cardiff, the premier ports of the region.

Although South Wales had good mineral resources, it was only in the last four decades of the eighteenth century that large-scale exploitation began. By 1790 four of the greatest ironworks in the world were in operation at Merthyr Tydfil and Dowlais, and within a short time the heads of the Monmouthshire valleys had been transformed into an industrial heartland. Initially, Blaenavon set the pace, but in the 1820s the works at Nantyglo, Ebbw Vale, and Tredegar emerged as Merthyr's closest rivals. By 1839 the leading iron concerns on the coalfield were those of Guest at Dowlais, Crawshay at Cyfarthfa and Hirwaun, the Harfords at Ebbw Vale and Sirhowy, the Baileys at Nantyglo, Thompson at Penydarren, the Rhymney Iron Company, Homfray at Tredegar, the Hills at

Plymouth, the Blaenavon Company, the Varteg Iron Company, the Pentwyn and Golynos Company, and the British Iron Company at Abersychan. In all, there were at least fifty ironworks, and, at the time of the Newport rising, new sites were being developed at Victoria, Rhymney, and Abercarn. The scale of operations varied considerably, some of the forges and furnaces on the roads between Aberdare and Pontypridd and between Risca and Tydu producing no more than a few thousand tons of iron per year.

Situated as most of these works were in high and fairly inaccessible places, transport proved to be the most important aspect of their development. In the 1790s the Glamorganshire and Monmouthshire canals were cut from the hinterland of Cardiff and Newport to the mouths of the industrial valleys, the gradient being accommodated by a series of spectacular locks and viaducts. The iron and coal was brought to these canals on rough turnpikes and tramroads. Well-known hauliers like Thomas Watts of Gelligroes and Morgan Saunders were contracted to carry thousands of tons a year on their horse-drawn vehicles. In the case of the Tredegar ironworks, for example, horses pulled the wooden trams as far as Crumlin, where the ore was transferred on to barges for the last stage of the 23-mile journey to Newport. Then, in 1829, the pattern began to change; thereafter, a considerable proportion of Tredegar's output was taken via the new turnpike and railroad. It arrived, as did so much of the iron and coal trade, at Pillgwenlly, Newport's great industrial depot and marshalling yard, and from there it was a short trip to the Tredegar Wharf.

In 1841 Harry Scrivenor, who had been once a manager of the Blaenavon Coal and Iron Company, published details of the amounts of iron that were carried on the canals and tramroads of South Wales. The statistics, limited as they are, provide an interesting picture of industrial progress:[2]

Glamorganshire Canal (in tons)

Year	1817	1820	1830	1835	1839
Tons	39,497	49,382	81,548	119,858	132,781

Monmouthshire Canal (and tramroads)

Year	1810	1820	1830	1835	1839
Tons	34,070	45,462	112,647	155,317	176,346

1. The Dowlais Iron Company, 1840

These figures represented about two-thirds of the total output, as Alan Birch's more recent estimate indicates:[3]

Year	Output (*tons*)	Furnaces
1806	68,867	35
1820	154,000	—
1827	272,000	90
1830	277,643	113
1839	453,880	127
1840	505,000	163
1842	317,430	—
1848	631,280	196

Most of this output was sold in the domestic market, but towards the end of our period exports became more important, with South Wales supplying pig- and bar-iron to America, France, Russia, Italy, and several other European countries. During the mid 1830s, too, the nature of the iron product began to change, as the first railway boom promised a bright new future. In general, the later 1830s were good years on the coalfield, although there were the first signs in 1839 of another three-year depression. This was the way of things; the whole economy of south-east Wales was 'dependent upon one very fluctuating trade, with an enormous population around us . . .'.

As if to underline the point, the cutting and mining of coal in the area was, for at least the first two decades of the nineteenth century, closely related to the fortunes of the iron industry. Some four to six tons of coal were needed in the production of one ton of iron, and so the major ironworks opened their own deep-balance pits and developed existing coal patches and levels. At Tredegar, for instance, Duke's pit was started in 1806 and soon No. 1 and No. 2 pits were also in operation. In some places, as in the districts around Tredegar, Sirhowy, and Blaenavon, more coal was mined than was needed locally, the additional amounts being sent to neighbouring iron-, copper-, and tin-works or sold to domestic consumers throughout Britain and Ireland. At the bottom of the industrial valleys, from Porth in the west to Pontypool in the east, several hundred small and independent sale-coal collieries were also opened at this time. After 1820 the levels and pits near Dinas, Llancaiach, Blackwood, Risca, and Pontypool sent every week over 10,000 tons northwards to the ironworks and southwards to the sea. It has been estimated that by 1839 coal shipments amounted to $1\frac{1}{2}$ m. tons, more than a third of which was sent from Newport.[5]

This economic growth was more than complemented by the increase in population on and around the coalfield. The following table, of leading industrial parishes, gives some idea of the startling pace of change:

Parish	Year 1801	Year 1841
Aberdare	1,486	6,471
Merthyr Tydfil	7,705	34,977
Gelligaer	1,051	3,215
Bedwellty	1,434	22,413
Aberystruth	805	11,272
Mynydd-islwyn	1,544	5,385
Llangynidr	775	2,775
Llangattock	1,046	4,334
Llanelli	937	7,366
Trevethin	1,472	14,942

Within all these parishes there were, of course, localities where the density and increase of population was much greater than the above averages. Thus the hamlet of Uchlawrcoed, which contained Tredegar ironworks, had a population of 513 in 1801, 2,728 in 1811, 3,640 in 1821, 5,359 in 1831, and 13,140 in 1841. In February 1840 it was claimed that the population of Tredegar itself was just over 7,000, 1,500 of whom were under the age of 7 years, and it was anticipated that the four new furnaces being built would attract another 2,000 people.[6] In a place like Tredegar or in Blaenavon and Brynmawr, where the population was perhaps 2,000–3,000 fewer there were districts where the number of persons per house rose well above the norm of five to six, and where lodgers crowded into private houses and every available public and beerhouse. To the south the industrial communities were smaller, but a number of these, such as Blackwood and Tre-lyn (Fleur-de-lis), and the shanty villages alongside the tramroads between Crumlin and Pye Corner, grew at a spectacular speed.

At the time of the Newport rising several estimates were made of the size of the mining population of the South Wales coalfield. The best guess, which closely matched the census figures of 1841, was given by Col. Considine.[7] He indicated to the government that, in the following industrial valleys, almost 150,000 people were dependent on the iron-, coal-, and tinworks:

Valley	Works	Numbers
Clydach	Iron and coal	4,000
Afon Lwyd	Iron, coal, and tin	25,000 +
Ebbw Fach and Fawr	Iron	25,000 +
	Coal, near Crumlin	2,000
Sirhowy	Iron	10,000 +
	Coal	10,000
Rhymney	Iron	7,000
	Coal	4,000
Taff	Upper ironworks	40,000
	Lower iron- and tinworks	probably 5,000
Cynon	Iron	10,000
Small lateral valleys descending to the Taff	Collieries and other works	about 5,000

Of these 150,000 persons about one in four were industrial wage-earners, and a quarter of the latter set off to march to Newport on the morning of 4 November 1839.

In addition to this coalfield population, Considine estimated that another 25,000 people lived in towns close by, namely Abergavenny, Usk, Caerleon, Newport, and Cardiff. The figure, however, was much too low, as the following table shows:

	Year 1801	Year 1841
Abergavenny	2,573	4,797
Monmouth	3,345	5,446
Usk	1,117	2,182
Pontypool	1,017	3,708
Caerleon	667	1,174
Newport	1,423	13,766
Cardiff	1,870	10,077

The towns which played the largest part in the story of the Chartist rising were the two castle-towns of Abergavenny and Monmouth, with their muddy streets, elegant shops, theatres, courts, and prison, Pontypool, with its long main street and even longer industrial history, and Newport. Newport was the boom-town of the 1830s; as its trade increased dramatically, so its population massed in dark, overcrowded courts and pushed outwards towards the Pillgwenlly and Commercial wharves and the immediate hinterland of rail, road, and canal termini. The town was famous for its narrow streets, for its bridge over the Usk, and for the varied origins and range of occupations of its people. Considine called it 'a vile town . . . in which I think the lower classes are of the very worst description'.[8] In his eyes, their close relationship with the men 'of the hills' symbolized the uncomfortable fact that almost a quarter of a million people across South Wales were dependent for their livelihood on the continued success of two or three major industries.

One result of the Newport rising was a minute examination of the communities that had emerged to service these industries. Contemporaries, who were unable to delineate the immediate causes of the Chartist troubles, found the roots of the rising in the settlement pattern, class structure, social provisions, class relationships, and system of wage-payment on the South Wales coalfield. Seymour Tremenheere, and those investigators who followed him, divided the settlements into two main categories: the iron towns, with a typical workforce of 1,300–4,000 and a dependent population of perhaps two or three times that number, and the smaller colliery towns and villages. The former were essentially works towns, often, as at Sirhowy, Ebbw Vale, and Nantyglo, built on company land, along the valley sides and as close as possible to the works and tramroads at the bottom. The grey-black two-, three-, and four-roomed stone-terraced houses were erected by the iron companies and by private speculators, and they were occupied in distinct class, occupational, and ethnic patterns. 'The houses were graded to correspond to the industrial importance of their occupants', recalled one famous son of Rhymney, and the street names—Iron Row, Forge Row, Engine Row, Colliers Row, Staffordshire Row, Irish Street, and the Barracks—indicated other demarcation lines as well.[9]

Apart from Merthyr Tydfil, which at this time was the largest town in Wales, most iron towns were built around one centre. As the industry grew, so these communities developed, ribbon-like, up or down each valley. By 1839, for example, the Ebbw Fawr valley had a chain of mining villages and towns, stretching from old Beaufort and Rassau at the top to the newest works colony of Victoria, named in honour of the young Queen. Similarly, down the

Rhymney valley there were three communities of denser settlements, whilst in the Ebbw Fach some 15,000 people lived in the two-mile industrial belt comprising Brynmawr, Nantyglo, Coalbrookvale, Blaina, and Cwm Celyn. To the south-east, around Pontypool, the pattern was somewhat different; a considerable number of ironworkers lived in the town and travelled to work at Varteg, Abersychan, and Blaendare.

A few iron communities, like Tredegar with its rectangular street development and its market house, bank, and post office, had been planned as model towns, but most settlements were no more than mining barracks until the 1860s. The proudly named 'Newtowns', one created by Richard Johnson near Rhymney bridge, and the other built by the Ebbw Vale Company in the years 1828–34, were simply neat rows of works cottages. Perhaps the most primitive and feared of all these settlements were the sprawling suburbs of Brynmawr and Dukestown (Twyn Sirhowy), set on the northern mountainous edge of the coalfield. These were the uncontrolled open villages of industrial South Wales.

Despite a few urban improvements, the continual refurbishing of Dowlais House, Bedwellty House, and other masters' residences, and 'the clean and comfortable' interiors of miners' homes, the general impression left on visitors to the northern half of the coalfield was the lack of planning and the bleak outlook of these communities. 'Overcrowded houses, the almost total absence of the various means of decent external accommodation, and the accumulation of dirt and refuse before and between the rows of cottages, are among the most prominent of the causes', wrote Tremenheere, 'which have conspired to lower the habits and sensualize the minds of large masses of the people.' 'The whole district and population partake of the iron character of its produce; everything centres in and ministers to the idolatry of profit. . . . There are, of course, even in this black domain, some individual exceptions, but the general picture can only be drawn with truth in the colours I am constrained to use.' 'The bodies and habits of the people are almost as dirty as the towns and houses of the swarthy region in which they swarm.'[10] 'Merthyr stank in the nostrils of the world', said one informed observer, and there, as in the iron towns to the east, the death-rate was well above the national average.[11] Scarlet fever, typhus, and cholera were irregular but expected visitors, and always there was the familiar death of the very young. Jane

Ferriday (Feredy), 15-month-old daughter of Mary, whose husband was killed by soldiers at Newport, lies with her playmates in the huge cemetery alongside Bedwellty parish church. A glance at the death registers for that parish can still turn the stomach.[12]

In the southern part of the coalfield settlements were smaller, healthier, and set in a more open and green landscape. Some of the mining villages in the parishes of Mynydd-islwyn and Machen were extensions of old industrial sites, but most were new and housed the 50–150 men needed at an average-sized pit. Llanfabon had a population of some 400 people in 1841, a third of whom were colliers, and to the north-east the community centred on Manmoel colliery had 280 people. Blackwood, the only colliery town in this area, began life in 1820; it was planned as a model garden village by J. H. Moggridge, industrialist, philanthropist, and former friend of John Frost.[13] By 1829 Blackwood had a thousand inhabitants, and as it continued to grow it acquired a reputation for having the worst sanitation and drainage in the county. The town, and some of the neighbouring communities which supplied a large proportion of Newport's coal trade, were soon as black and overcrowded as any of the iron towns. Such comparisons, however, cannot be taken too far, because over much of the lower Rhondda and the countryside between Llanhilleth and Caerphilly the scattered industrial collections of country cottages, company shops, chapels, and public houses took on the character of the neighbouring rural villages. There, as in West Wales, it was common for colliers' families to work on farms, roads, and quarries for part of the year.

The journalists and government officials who travelled across this changing scenery in the aftermath of the Newport rising were greatly impressed with the class nature of Welsh industrial society. At Merthyr Tydfil, the largest and most advanced industrial town, people had congregated in well-defined districts.[14] The ironmasters, the Crawshays, Guests, Hills, and Thompsons, lived aloof in their mansions and a mock castle. Tradesmen and professional people from south-west England and the Welsh coastal towns inhabited the central urban district, the skilled ironworkers occupied Georgetown and South Glebeland, the unskilled settled close by the works, whilst the Irish, the casual workers, and the vagrants were residents of 'China' and Caedraw. Across the mountains to the east the iron towns and villages had a less complex social structure, but there also one's place of residence indicated status. Many years later Thomas Jones described the social gradations in his beloved Rhymney:

At each end [of the Terrace] was a large house standing in its own walled-in grounds with trees and garden to match; these were occupied by the manager of the Company Shop and the chief colliery manager. Then next to these came at each end a house of intermediate size, one occupied by the cashier and one by the assistant-general-manager; the rest of the row was filled in with houses half in size of the two intermediaries, for the lesser managers or superior foremen. We first moved to an ordinary and then to an intermediate, which had ample accommodation. The removal was a proof that my father's position in the Company Shop was improving. He was no longer an assistant but a manager of sorts. The inhabitants of the terrace did not form a coherent society in virtue of their proximity. We were good neighbours but we never took tea at either of the end houses while we lived in an ordinary. They were church and we were Chapel—that formed an effective social barrier. We did not then speak of the bourgeoisie and proletariat.[15]

At the head of this society were the employers. A dozen of them monopolized the production of iron in the early decades of the century: the industry was dominated by English families such as the Hills of Blaenavon, the Baileys of Nantyglo and Beaufort, the Homfrays of Tredegar, and the Harfords of Ebbw Vale and Sirhowy, the only Quakers in an Anglican profession. These families had a keen sense of their power and achievement. Crawshay Bailey, for instance, son of a Yorkshire farmer, believed fervently that their efforts alone had turned the bleak valleys of South Wales into thriving industrial communities. He warned reformers that he would 'risk my life rather than lose my property'.[16] On one occasion he met Henry Vincent, Chartist delegate, near Nantyglo, and, pointing to some furnaces, declared that the land and men belonged to him.[17] At times these employers behaved like the landed aristocrats with whom they often associated. Samuel Homfray, the rugged and blustering offspring of an industrial pioneer, even married into the leading county family, turned Bedwellty House into a country seat in the 1820s and obviously enjoyed being addressed as 'Squire' by his workmen.

Both Samuel Homfray and Crawshay Bailey were proud of the fact that they lived on the coalfield, even if they fortified their homes with guns and cannon. Other ironmasters, such as the Crawshays, Benjamin Hall, Alderman Thompson, and some of the Harfords, had bought family homes outside Wales to which they retreated, especially in troubled times. Several of the largest works were effectively put in the hands of agents like John Llewellyn of Abercarn House, Newbridge, and Richard Johnson of Rhymney. These in turn sometimes employed a score of contractors. As a result, in the opinion of Samuel Homfray, the industrial communities were denuded of proper authority and influence, and left to the Welsh and the working class.[18] The establishment of joint-stock companies in the later 1830s, with their head offices outside the Principality, only increased the separation between capitalist and community. The British Iron Company at Abersychan and the Blaenavon and Rhymney Companies brought in a large number of managers and agents from the industrial areas of England and Scotland. Thomas Brown, born at Merthyr and promoted to take charge at the Blaina works, was a rare bird, though he wished to emphasize that the respectable English-speaking, Anglican world of management was not entirely closed to the ambitious poor. 'The little property I have become possessed of, I wish to keep,' he declared at an anti-Chartist rally in April 1839. 'It was obtained by honest, industrious means, and I would now impress upon the minds of every workman that the same means which have raised me, are within the reach of every man before me. It was known that [my father] . . . came into Wales as a workman.'[19] One wonders about his chances had he been a Welsh-speaking miner.

Such was the geographical mobility of these managers and agents, and such was the omnipresence of the ironworks, that few visitors were surprised by 'the absence of a [residential] middle class'.[20] Of Brynmawr, something of a special case, it was said in the 1840s that it 'contains 5,000 people, nearly all of whom are of the lowest class, and, with the exception of one or two shopkeepers, exclusively so'.[21] The middle class that existed was composed chiefly of outsiders, 'better tradesmen' from Swansea or Bristol, a few independent hauliers and engineers, and professional people like works managers, surgeons, and Anglican clergymen. Tremenheere believed that the presence of large numbers of these people had a beneficial effect on class relationships, education, and religion in the iron towns, but like all investigators, and the prosecution in the Chartist trials, he relied heavily on them for information and value judgements. One thing is certain: the middle class on the hills were acutely aware that they were special, even marked,

2. Thomas Brown, manager of the Blaina and Ebbw Vale Ironworks, *c.*1854

people. During one industrial conflict William Wood, manager of the Abersychan works, disguised in a woman's clothes, just escaped an angry mob, and he never forgot the experience. On the eve of the Newport rising his middle-class friends scrambled off the coalfield.

In the small colliery villages the class structure was even more monolithic. Of one community close to Old Rock colliery, it was said 'we have no middle-class of tradespeople here'.[22] The prominent figures in the coal industry were usually non-resident. Initially English businessmen had opened the biggest pits in the Risca and Pontypool areas, but by 1839 the largest coalowners were iron-masters living up the valleys and merchants, legal, and landed families from Newport and Cardiff. The industry was dominated by men such as Thomas Phillips, the diminutive mayor of Newport, his fellow lawyer and coal exporter Thomas Prothero of Malpas Court, Thomas Powell, timber-merchant and alderman of the same town, Joseph Beaumont of Llanarth, and those self-made men, Walter Coffin, Martin Morrison, and Lewis and Rosser Thomas. These people were granted leases to work the coal seams by the Morgans of Tredegar Park, the Salisburys of Llanwern Park near Newport, and other prominent landowning families, and the more prosperous coalowners then sub-let their collieries to contractors and agents.

These agents were required to raise a particular amount of coal and deliver it to the ports, in return for a quarterly payment. Many of the contractors, like David Williams and David Davies, agents of Rosser Thomas and John Fletcher Hanson at Gelligaer, were Welsh people who lived in the district and had been trained as master-miners, surveyors, and clerks. At Gelligaer, Crosspenmaen, Llanhilleth, and other neighbourhoods, these agents also kept company shops and beerhouses. Their precise social status was a matter of considerable interest to those Chartists seeking to identify class friends and allies. The unpopular Aaron Brain, occupier of Hengoed colliery and contractor for the Place-Level colliery of Thomas Prothero, Hananiel Morgan, who was Thomas Phillips's agent at the Cwrtybella and Manmoel pits, and William Evans, surveyor and storekeeper to Martin Morrison at Tynygelly, Traenant, Penycoedcae, and Kendon collieries, were a cut above the working population, but at the small pits contractors were associated by background, marriage, and religion with fellow colliers.

All this influenced their response to radical and community politics, and ultimately forced employers to think more carefully about the character of colliery agents on the coalfield.[23]

Beneath the small middle class and the petty bourgeoisie of agents and shopkeepers were 'the people of the hills', the men and women who worked the iron and coal. Along the eastern boundary of the coalfield, up to 40 or even 50 per cent of the population were immigrants from England, Ireland, and Scotland. Most of these were from the nearest English counties, a social fact which was of considerable importance in the Chartist story. In general, however, the great majority of the working class was Welsh by birth and, until the 1870s, by speech. Perhaps half the industrial population of Monmouthshire had been born in the county and many others had travelled only from Breconshire and Glamorgan. Similarly, a very large proportion of Merthyr's workforce were natives of Glamorgan, Carmarthenshire, Pembrokeshire, and Cardiganshire. Most were first-generation industrial workers, who had close connections with their old rural communities, even returning for part of the year for harvest and holidays.

As they travelled, sometimes like gypsies, across the coalfield, the workmen made full use of family and community ties. The new industrial towns were settled in very pronounced cultural and geographical patterns Thus many people from North and Mid-Wales gravitated towards Twynyrodyn in Merthyr Tydfil, whilst natives of Kingswood, near Bristol, were attracted to the collieries at Risca. The Irish, too, were congregated in a few places: at Merthyr and Dowlais, where they were some 5 per cent of the population, and in the 'lowest quarters' of the Monmouthshire iron towns. Some of them had been driven by poverty to the ports of South Wales, and then encouraged to settle by ironmasters seeking cheap and pliable labour. Very soon they established their Orange and Green lodges, and a growing hostility developed between Welsh workmen and the Irish and English 'outsiders'. In June 1834, for instance, the Guests received a warning that Dowlais House would be 'scotched' if the Irishmen were not dismissed from the works.[24] Visitors to the coalfield in the economic depression that followed the Newport rising were astonished by the depth of anti-Irish feeling.[25] On a dozen occasions in the early nineteenth century this hostility turned into extensive rioting and strike action, culminating in 1853 and 1857 when attempts were made to drive all

Irish people out of the Ebbw Fach, Ebbw Fawr, and Rhondda valleys.[26]

Employers were, it must be said, not averse to sectionalism within the mining population. At the Bute, Nantyglo, and Varteg works ironmasters offered the Irish special contracts and used them for strike-breaking. Aaron Brain sacked all the protesting Welsh workmen at the Hengoed colliery in favour of outsiders in 1841, and could hardly have been surprised at the violence which ensued. After the Newport rising, excessive, and not always accurate, publicity was given to the loyalty of the Irish in South Wales.[27] It was, along with certain housing, contract, and wage policies, part of the strategy of ensuring a divided workforce. So, too, was the stress on loyalty to works and community. On a few occasions the personal, political, and economic rivalry between the Crawshays and the Guests and between the Harfords and the Homfrays spilled over into pitched battles between the workmen of the different towns. 'Valley mentality' as it has been sometimes called, was one of the main obstacles to widespread union and political action, and the degree to which it was overcome marked perhaps Chartism's greatest achievement.

For this mining population the family and the work-place were the two pivots of their existence. By 1841 the ratio of males to females on the coalfield was 20 : 17, and the average size of a household 5.8. A large number of the early settlers were young men, and the evidence indicates that they were quickly married often to younger women born in their home counties. By their early thirties, the average age of imprisoned Welsh Chartists,[28] these people had probably three children living at home, though it is worth noting that 24-year-old Thomas Kidley, 35-year-old William Williams, and several other prominent men in the rising were still bachelors. Thousands of these single men lodged in the homes of friends and relatives, and provided the women of the household with one of their main sources of income.

The women of the coalfield had a well-defined role and limited job opportunities. Their main function, in the eyes of so many contemporaries, was to be helpmates and bearers of children. Soon after marriage they retired to the family home, winning fulsome tributes for their cleanliness and obsession with rich food and warm clothing. What emerged clearly only after the Newport rising was the independence shown by, and the economic contribution of, the women of these industrial communities. Not only were they, as at Merthyr, prominent as domestic servants, shop assistants, and keepers of beer- and lodging-houses, but they were also important in the mining industry itself. In parts of Monmouthshire, notably the iron towns along the heads of the valleys, 1 in 10 of the industrial labour force was female, and most of these were young women, childless wives, and widows. Some worked on the fringes of the iron-making process, as limestone breakers, sand-girls, and coke-feeders, but most worked above or in the mines. Those under-ground filled and dragged the drams. It was, as national and local Chartist leaders protested, bitterly hard work, but for some women its advantages were just as obvious.[29] Although wage-payments were small, they still paid the rent of Hannah Hughes of the Ebbw Vale ironworks, and 19-year-old Charlotte Chiles could earn more in a month by drawing, landing, and weighing coal at Craig colliery near Merthyr than in half a year as a kitchen maid.[30]

For the children of these women horizons were similarly low. William Wood believed that half the boys under 13 years of age in the Abersychan area were employed twelve hours a day in the iron and coal industries. At Merthyr it was estimated that 4,000 male and 500 female children worked for Josiah John Guest and his col-leagues in 1841.[31] Perhaps a fifth of the employees at the ironworks and collieries of Monmouthshire were under 18 years of age, and there were few areas of Britain where children started work at a younger age. It was not uncommon in the sale-coal collieries for children of 4–6 years to be carried to work on their fathers' backs. For the first five or six years they were employed as air-door boys, and given the appalling task of filling and dragging carts in the narrowest tunnels. After the age of about twelve they graduated to being horse-drivers, hauliers, and eventually coal-cutters. By the age of seventeen years they were regarded as adult workmen, and their income rose accordingly. The reasons for this child labour were endlessly debated in the aftermath of the Chartist troubles, but the motive was a simple one. In the collieries a miner with his infant could claim an extra tram of coal. When jobs were insecure, wages low, and food-prices high, another wage-earner in the family was a necessity. No one knew this better than Edward Jenkins, the Independent minister of Bedwellty parish who kept a poorly attended school and had two of his own children down the pits.[32] The poorer the family the earlier the children began work.

3. Ironstone miners of Nantyglo, ?c.1870. Although of a later date, this is a good illustration of an early method of mining iron in use at the time of the rising

This is a useful reminder that the workforce was not a single mass. It has been suggested that perhaps 40 per cent of the industrial workers were skilled, but this tells us little. At the ironworks the men and women were sharply divided into those who laboured at the furnaces, forges, mills, and those at the ironstone- and coal-mines. At 'the works', as distinct from 'the mines', certain jobs such as puddling (converting pig- into wrought iron), refining, and rolling required several years' apprenticeship and offered higher wages and greater security. The degree of craft exclusiveness which these employees enjoyed was reinforced by a separate bargaining process, and by close companionship at home and in their social clubs. It was claimed, without too much truth, that such well-paid craftsmen held back from supporting the Chartist movement. At the mines and collieries, and particularly amongst the casual labourers and surface-workers, wages were lower, although in the iron towns these workers had greater security than the men at the sale-coal collieries to the south. There the colliers, labelled 'rough' and 'inferior' by respectable residents, worked fitfully under the watchful eye of 'gaffers' and 'doggies', the under-agents, overmen, and master colliers. In all these places, however, there was considerable pride in the men's industrial skills, remarkable control at the place of work, and a determination to enforce family rights. Contractors and stewards had to be careful about whom they employed at the pits and how working arrangements were changed.[33]

The legendary independence of Welsh labourers was hardly surprising, for this class and frontier society was marked by an absence of community care and social provisions. 'Next to nothing was done for the comfort and convenience of life among the workpeople', Tremenheere noted in his memoirs. '. . . Nearly the whole body of employers acted on Bentham's theory that the masters had no responsibility beyond paying the men their wages; everything else that they wanted the men had to do for themselves. . . . The men and their wives were astonished at the idea that the Government wanted to know all about them, and that sympathy existed anywhere towards them.'[34] Like the Home Secretary Lord John Russell, Edward Coplestone, Bishop of Llandaff, Col. Considine, and Sir Edmund Head, Tremenheere believed that the industrial population of Glamorgan and Monmouthshire were neglected and pitiably ignorant. 'His superiors are content, for the most part simply to ignore his existence, in all its moral relations', ran a typical comment a few years later. 'He is left to live in an underworld of his own, and the march of society goes so completely over his head, that he is never heard of, excepting when the strange and abnormal features of a Revival, or a Rebecca or Chartist outbreak, call attention to a phase of society, which could produce anything so contrary to all that we elsewhere experience.'[35]

For Thomas Phillips, the great hero of the Newport rising, in his reflections on *Wales* in 1849, 'Chartism is found in all its worst manifestations—not as an adhesion to political dogmas, but as an indication of that class antagonism . . . [which] originated, as great social evils ever do, in the neglect of duty by the master, or ruling class.'[36] Examples of employers' paternalism in 1839 were hard to find, even where proprietors were resident. The Whig *Cambrian* newspaper, consistently wise after the event, criticized Joseph Bailey and his son for not building a church, school, or marketplace at Nantyglo and Beaufort, but there were many like them. At only a few places, such as Dowlais and the Varteg, can one detect the faint beginnings of a conscious policy of making the works the centre of social improvement. In 1837 the first works school was opened at Tredegar, and two years later the Rhymney Company obtained a great deal of prestige by giving money to erect a church. But at Brynmawr and Beaufort, and at most colliery villages to the south, nothing was provided except employment.

It was a mark of contemporary concern that extraordinary efforts were made to convince the capitalists of South Wales that a new approach was needed. People searched through the wreck of the Chartist rising to prove that 'kindly feeling' and community involvement had been rewarded. Claims were made, at one time or another, that employers' actions at Dowlais, Rhymney, Risca, Blaenavon, and Varteg reduced the impact of the Chartist gospel and made their workmen reluctant to join the march on Newport. Although political meetings were held on the Varteg, one report suggested, incorrectly, that only about thirty of George Kenrick's workmen 'belonged to the Chartists' and none participated in the rising. The Chartists had even, it was noted, shown their respect for Capel Hanbury Leigh by not injuring his works in the Pontypool area.[37] Blaenavon, where the Hills and Hopkins had early endowed a church and helped to build a schoolroom, was widely regarded then and since as the classic case of an industrial town where the labourers consistently refused to join the industrial and political battles of their comrades.[38] In 1816, the 1820s, and again in 1834, the records, however, reveal that despite an occasional military presence, Blaenavon was not a quiescent spot. During the Chartist period the situation may have changed, although it is difficult to evaluate the evidence. In August 1839 men at work refused to join a political procession, and one militant was taken into custody by Mr R. Hopkins and a local policeman.[39] On the night of 3 November two hundred Blaenavon men assembled on the Varteg road, but only a few reached Newport. Perhaps they were influenced by their employers, but across the hills at Beaufort, Nantyglo, Sirhowy, Ebbw Vale, and Tredegar there were few signs of the workers' deference which other historians have noted in the early nineteenth century.[40]

The actual provisions for the welfare of the industrial population in 1839 were detailed by Tremenheere in his report after the rising.[41] In his survey of the five main parishes, with a population of some 85,000, he found that there were only a dozen Anglican churches and six Anglican Sunday Schools, eighty inadequate and poorly attended nursery and elementary schools, and nothing in the way of youth and adult education. Some of the churches were of very recent origin, whilst older institutions were, as at Bedwellty, sometimes sited inconveniently for the new workforce. These churches were hardly an attractive proposition for ambitious men, and so the incumbents tended to be young, poor, and—to the sarcastic delight of the Welsh *Silurian*—English-speaking. Where industrial companies made a financial contribution to the upkeep of local churches, clergymen were regarded by the workpeople as the voice of capitalism, and the radical press rightly believed that the more wealthy Anglicans on the fringes of the coalfield were pillars of the social and political establishment. Half a dozen clergymen, led by the Revd R. A. Roberts of Christchurch, attended anti-Chartist rallies in his parish and at Coalbrookvale; the Revd James Coles presided over many of the examinations of Chartist prisoners; and the Revd Evan Jenkins of Dowlais preached the most famous sermon against them.

The reforming Bishop of Llandaff had tried for years, without too much success, to convince people of the urgency of providing Anglican education for the ironworkers and colliers. The number of British and National schools was small; most of the schools visited by Tremenheere were private adventure and Dissenting schools, with ex-miners, women, and ministers amongst the teachers. These, and the first works schools were largely financed by parents. In some places, as in the vicinity of Blackwood and Gelligaer, school buildings and attendance were both poor, and altogether Tremenheere estimated that two-thirds of working-class children did not receive formal education. Those who regularly made use of existing institutions tended to be the children of the better-paid workmen and craftsmen like masons and carpenters. Even some of these were 'apt to believe that their superiors are actuated by some selfish motive in endeavouring to induce them to send their children to school'.[42] Those who provided the evidence for Tremenheere were convinced that their generation of miners and colliers were more illiterate than the one before, and the legal and prison statistics can be used in support of this argument. Those committed to gaol for their activities on 3–4 November 1839 were returned as illiterate or having an imperfect knowledge of reading and, sometimes, of writing. What examiners often failed to appreciate, however, was the Welshness and reticence of this working class. Most of them could probably read Welsh, and a number who read and wrote well in the language signed English depositions with a mark. Even the articulate and letter-writing Benjamin Richards, a boot- and shoe-maker and beerhouse-keeper of the Tredegar district, used a mark and is described in the official records as a Chartist who could only read imperfectly.[43]

Outside the day and Sunday Schools the provision of education and 'rational recreation' for the people of the coalfield was almost non-existent. Consideration was being given in 1839 to financing adult evening classes and an institute for the 'better class of workmen' at Dowlais and Newport, but only at Pontypool was a Mechanics Institute established. This had begun life in October, with Capel Hanbury Leigh, the Lord Lieutenant, as its patron, and with George Kenrick and the Independent minister John Cooper prominent as supporters. Other forms of welfare were largely missing, though some of the largest works had doctors—paid for by deductions from wages—and at Tredegar and Ebbw Vale employers had agreed with the Poor Law authorities to look after their own poor, in return for exemption from the rates.

The system of poor relief on the coalfield was both primitive and arbitrary. Poor Law guardians were often simply ironmasters in another guise, and the pauper seeking money for food and rent was sometimes offered part-time employment instead. After the passing of the Poor Law Amendment Act of 1834, new workhouses were built at Tredegar and Pontypool, and, to the delight of Samuel Homfray, tighter restrictions were placed on the granting of subsidies for wages, food, and rent. Sir Edmund Head, who noted that the Pontypool and Newport workhouses were empty enough to provide accommodation for troops, believed that 'parochial assistance' was 'a matter of no importance' to the industrial population. Yet, as we shall see, the nature of poor relief did concern Chartists right across the coalfield and, surprisingly, John Frost suggested many years later that it had been 'the principal cause' of his movement.[44] Colliers who lost their employment in these years found it hard to obtain immediate assistance; frequently they faced the choice of moving house or suffering the indignity of being returned to the parish of their birth. Local welfare services were simply not designed to cope with the results of a severe depression or long strike. Everyone was agreed that at such times the families of coal miners experienced real starvation.

Survival, like everything else in the area, depended ultimately on working people themselves. They established their own community institutions and their own forms of self-help. It was an achievement which observers never fully appreciated. 'My friends—the working classes, I congratulate you that by far the great majority of you are a church or chapel people; and I rejoice to know that you read your Bible', said Mr Every in one of the rare Wesleyan compliments to the ironworkers and colliers of South Wales.[45] By 1839 there were well over 200 chapels on the coalfield, mostly of Baptist, Independent, and Wesleyan and Calvinistic Methodist persuasions. In places like Tredegar a new chapel was erected almost every year, as different groups of immigrants arrived and as revivals and sectarian conflict accentuated the need for accommodation. Where these chapels were self-governing organizations, the ministers and language of worship came from the working-class community which they served. No one can now estimate with any accuracy the numbers who attended the Ebenezers, Zions, and Carmels scattered across the valleys, but a tolerable guess would be some 40 per cent of the population.[46] A similar proportion supported the Sunday Schools attached to meeting-houses and chapels, for in colliery villages these were 'almost the sole—. . . and most congenial—centres of education.'[47] Contrary, therefore, to the opinions of respectable observers in 1839, much of the consolation, hope, cultural ambitions, and moral perspectives of the Welsh working class was rooted in religious institutions.

What part these institutions played in the emerging working-class movements of the time has never been fully investigated. A typical comment of 1839–40 was that the Chartist movement had been planned in the chapels, and a great deal was made of the radical sympathies of some Nonconformists, especially of the Unitarians in Aberdare and Merthyr and of the Independents and Primitive Methodists further east.[48] As we shall see later, some preachers were drawn into reform because of the democratic constitution of their chapels, from personal conviction, and as a result of their vulnerable position in the working-class community. Chapel buildings on the Glamorgan–Monmouth border were probably used for the occasional Chartist meetings, and we know for certain that two ministers, the Independent Benjamin Byron and the Baptist William Miles, supported John Frost and that some enthusiastic chapel-goers joined the march on Newport.[49]

On the other hand, district and national assemblies of Wesleyans, Calvinistic Methodists, and Baptists throughout the 1830s roundly turned on workers' organizations, and threatened recalcitrant members with expulsion. It was an attitude deeply resented, especially it seems in the Abersychan and Pontypool area, where copies of the Charter were sent to Dissenting ministers with an accompanying request to join the 'gigantic world movement'. Thomas Parry, one of the Chartist leaders at Pontypool, issued several literary appeals to 'our watchmen', reminding them of their political enthusiasm in the Reform crisis, and declaring that they were out of touch with the grievances and aspirations of their congregations.[50] In reply, conservative Methodist ministers and elders at Blackwood and further up the valleys stated that Chartists were no more than 'infidels' and 'levellers', and refused to join them on the night of 3 November 1839. In fact, the only well-known rationalist amongst the Chartists was Zephaniah Williams. He believed that Jesus Christ was just a good man, but sufficiently good that had he been living at Coalbrookvale in 1839 his house would have been pulled down over his head by the 'friends of order'.[51]

Besides the chapel the other representative institutions of the new industrial population were the pub and club. Beer-drinking had always accompanied work and play on the coalfield, and it was widely believed that 'the more wages they get, the more they spend in drink . . .'.[52] One or two of the largest employers banned the building of public houses on their land and Kenrick at the Varteg ironworks presided over the embryonic total abstinence movement, but over much of Monmouthshire restrictions on the amount and character of drinking-premises were minimal. After the passing of the Beer Act of 1830 the popularity of such places increased, and within nine years there were over a thousand of them in the industrial parishes. According to John Somerset Pakington, in a House of Commons debate on the subject, there were in Dukestown alone 5 public houses and 28 beerhouses amongst the 151 domestic dwellings.[53] Some of these were owned or rented by works managers and agents, as Zephaniah Williams happily noted, but many were run on a part-time basis by work-men and their wives. Several Chartist leaders, including Williams himself and Benjamin Richards, earned extra money in this way.

The functions of these beerhouses were many, and no one who has been through the literature of the period can doubt their importance. Men, women, and children visited them at all hours of the day and night, and they provided temporary lodgings and accommodation for small meetings. Workmen relaxed there with cards, skittles, and music, and on fair days and when prize-fighting and racing occupied 'the men of the hills', the public houses and beerhouses were crowded. Every week-end, too, the miners were to be found at such places, often calling on their way to and from chapel. It was said, most frequently by Tremenheere, that week-ends and pay days were one long drunken spree, with 'people immersed in habits of sensuality and improvidence . . . wasting nearly one (working) week out of five . . .'.[54] After the Newport rising much attention was drawn to the connections between intemperance, violence, and the willingness of the industrial popu-lation to take up arms against the government, but a considerable number of Chartists were in fact noted for their sobriety. As they rightly protested, the drinking-house was about the only place where political societies and benefit clubs could meet.

The Welsh, it was said, had a passion for clubs, and in the new iron towns friendly societies blossomed as well as chapels and pubs. They were at first local societies, and their mottoes were 'Union', 'Brotherhood', and 'Friendship'. Some were clearly attached to the ironworks, or rather to sections of the works, as names like the

'Nantyglo Firemen's Society' and the 'Garndyrris Forge Society' indicate. The average membership of these, and the parallel female societies, was less than 100 people, and their chief purpose was to give a degree of security and companionship to those who could afford it. Meetings were held monthly, and a typical subscription was one shilling.[55]

During the 1830s the number of these societies grew rapidly, until there were some 400 clubs on the coalfield, representing perhaps half the workforce. Many of the new clubs were lodges of national organizations like the Oddfellows and the Welsh Ivorites. At the time of the Newport rising, for example, five new branches of the Oddfellows were being opened in the Tredegar district.[56] In some areas lodges were set up under the honorary leadership of employers, managers, and other professional people, and with the blessing of the church and poor-law authorities. Not surprisingly, these Oddfellow committees were persuaded in the 1830s to condemn trade-union and political action in South Wales. How important this was is debatable, for Oliver Jones argues, perhaps correctly, that some lodges were useful reservoirs of secrecy, money, and fraternity. A Chartist attempt to obtain Oddfellows' money alerted magistrates on the eve of the rising, and their ceremonial swords were used in the conflict.[57] For ordinary working men the appeal of such national organizations lay in their financial resources, and their extravagant forms of ritual and status. Local societies proved more vulnerable to the vagaries of the economic climate, and some of those around Gelligaer and Bedwellty collapsed when families needed them most. Sadly, admitted Tremenheere, all the clubs afforded 'only very slender provision' for the permanently disabled, aged, and widowed.[58]

In truly difficult times, the poorer families resorted to more basic forms of self-help. There was remarkable agreement, even amongst those most hostile to the working class, that 'the poor people are very kind and accommodate to each other . . . and will help each other in time of distress to an extent that would scarcely be believed, and ought to put to shame the paltry charity of those who are in wealthy circumstances'.[59] Those injured, widowed, and starving benefited from 'biddings','gatherings', and auctions amongst neighbours, workmates, and chapel-goers. Similarly, colliery villages, ravaged by unemployment and strikes, sent processions and committees to obtain money and food from up the valleys.

The extent to which the industrial population turned to crime during such periods is by no means clear. The legal evidence and criminal statistics which survive suggest that offences did increase in number during the worst economic years of the early nineteenth century. Committals for trial in Monmouthshire, Glamorgan, and Breconshire, for instance, rose gradually from 229 in 1836 to 399 in 1839, but then leapt to 572 in 1840 and 601 a year later. A large share of Petty and Quarter Session cases on the coalfield were female and child larceny of food and clothing, thefts from works, wagons, and canals, and conflicts over wages and contracts. The chief constable of Merthyr wrote, in the depression of 1842, of the workmen's determination to 'steal, but never starve', and the presence of the poor and unemployed in the courts of the district underlines his point. There was, even so, a considerable amount of non-violent crime which did not fit into this category. The police courts from Merthyr to Newport were regularly used to enforce work practices, and magistrates like Samuel Homfray, Capel Hanbury Leigh, Lewis Edwards, and the Revd R. A. Roberts often gave offending men and women the choice of one month's gaol or a return to work.[60]

In view of the comments of these, and other magistrates, after the rising it is worth examining the criminal and lawless reputation of the people of the coalfield. Samuel Homfray spoke of communities which were 'at least a stage beyond civilisation'.[61] Sir Edmund Head, assistant Poor Law commissioner, said in his report of 14 November 1839 that the coalfield now 'resembles the growth of a penal settlement as well as of a prosperous manufacturing district. Whenever a man runs away from his family or commits any depredation in Herefordshire and the adjoining counties the answer to any enquiry is, "he has gone to the Hills". There, without any police worth speaking of to watch newcomers of suspicious appearance, or control the resident bad characters, the whole mass of Welsh, Irish, runaway criminals and vagrants has fermented together, until this outbreak has demonstrated of what materials it consists.'[62] Merthyr and the largest industrial towns each had 'a set of bad characters', but the number of professional thieves, highway robbers, counterfeiters, crooked gamblers, and vagrants was smaller on the coalfield than in many other parts of Britain, and few appear to have joined the Chartist march.[63]

Sir Edmund Head was certainly correct, however, in his description of police numbers. There were no more than twenty paid policemen on the coalfield, a ratio to population twice as bad as that of London. The old system of having head constables and parish constables elected yearly from local tradesmen was hardly adequate in the newly-settled districts and, for several reasons, the works helped to fill this gap. Thomas Leadbetter, a furnace manager, and John Williams acted as Blaenavon's constables in the early years of the century, and soon the Dowlais company had its own force of watchmen and specials. At Tredegar the superintendent of police was William Walter Homan, an ex-soldier and a truly unpopular figure. He was appointed by Samuel Homfray only a few years before the rising and was paid out of the company rate. With the assistance of two other policemen, some parish constables, and the occasional company scout and special constable, Homan was responsible for the control of 7,000 people.

In the towns near the edge of the coalfield the police forces were more established and accountable to the public. Abergavenny had three paid officials, and in the parish of Trevethin Superintendent John Roberts and his three colleagues directed twenty-three parish constables. At Newport in November 1839 there was a similar arrangement, though this municipal authority had made a decision to appoint professionals from across the water. The Chartists who arrived at the Westgate hotel on 4 November were met by Superintendent Edward Hopkins, Moses Scard, and Henry Chappell, all of whom had been policemen in Bristol.[64] If newspaper reports can be believed, these men and their colleagues in the hills spent a good deal of their time establishing new standards of public order. Cases of assault on fellow workmen, women, and the police filled the calendars of Newport, Pontypool, Tredegar, and Merthyr police courts, and disorderly conduct was a very common offence at week-ends and holidays. 'Drunkenness . . . strife, jealousy, bickerings, assaults, and quarrelling—this', ran one report, 'is the constant reality' of life at 'sadly notorious Brynmawr.'[65]

Of hostility towards the police there is considerable evidence. Amongst the Chartists this became very apparent during the months and days before the rising. Benjamin Richards threatened to kill Homan, his colleague William Davies, and all other 'Tories', whilst George Shell, the young cabinet-maker of Pontypool, openly challenged Superintendent John Roberts to come and take his gun.[66] Perhaps the depth of popular opposition helps to explain why it took so long for policemen to be stationed in places like

Ebbw Vale and Dukestown. When, as at Blaina and Llanhilleth, there were also no magistrates or Petty Sessions within reach, the outlook for the respectable and the victims of criminals was a gloomy one. The greatest danger was, of course, an outbreak of popular disorder, and to combat this, temporary expedients were adopted, from the brief experiment of an armed mountain police in 1834 to the stationing of troops in the largest iron towns. At the beginning of 1839 the nearest soldiers were those in the barracks at Brecon, and the Chartists knew that South Wales was then about the least protected area in the country.

What is generally overlooked was the instinctive respect for law and order in those parts of the coalfield where the machinery for its upkeep was weakest. Nineteenth-century defenders of Wales and the Welsh made an exaggerated claim about their law-abiding character, but there is an element of truth within the myth.[67] 'The people though ignorant are of very peaceable habits as a mass' was the opinion of several informed observers from the Rhondda to Pontypool. Police chiefs were sometimes impressed by the recorded level of stealing in the worst recessions, and even in a bitter eleven-week colliers'strike in 1840 there was 'no attempt at plunder'.[68] Had, as a few people believed, 'habits' improved over the previous decade as religious, educational, temperance, and political institutions taken hold? So far as is known, comparatively few of the leading Chartists had criminal records. Those with such a background had usually been involved in disputes over contracts or had been arrested for drunken and disorderly behaviour.[69] Thomas Ferriday, for instance, whose brother was killed at Newport, was feared by his radical colleagues as a hard man who had been in trouble with the police. Possibly, as Henry Vincent always claimed, the Chartists were from the more thinking, law-abiding, and sober sections of the working population, and certainly those people who gave evidence against them in court had no better reputations.

In their search for the origins of the Chartist troubles most observers turned their attention finally, and reluctantly, to the nature of class relationships across the coalfield. The expressions most commonly used were 'control' and 'bitterness', and the perceptive observer was aware of the connection between the two. Employers and agents had an extraordinary degree of control over the lives of working people, and indeed they often insisted on the need for it.[70] Industrial leaders like Samuel Homfray, Capel Hanbury Leigh, Sir

Benjamin Hall, Thomas Phillips, and William Needham of the Varteg ironworks were landlords, shopkeepers, magistrates, and Poor Law guardians as well as employers. It was said that Crawshay Bailey, who owned the works, inns, and nearly all the houses and shops at Nantyglo, was thus able to prevent Chartism from taking hold there.[71] In fact, he failed in the attempt, but his conversation with Henry Vincent on 23 April 1839 is instructive. Bailey told the Chartist that his men were happy, defied him to get the furnacemen out, and threatened to duck him in the pond. Vincent replied that they were 'his men', as the ironmaster would see if he attended the evening meeting. In the event, Bailey sent his son and twenty clerks and agents, and a lively time was had by all.[72]

Henry Scale, the Tory industrialist of Aberaman House, Aberdare, called the conduct of some of his Monmouthshire colleagues 'very tyrannical'.[73] Reports indicate that at Varteg and Blaenavon, as well as in Rhymney and parts of the Rhondda, workmen were required to move in and out of company houses at short notice, and many were further tied to their employers by the skilful use of contracts and discharge notes. Victimization and eviction were common in some of the colliery villages, and only the demand for labour in the best years of the industrial revolution enabled marked men to secure employment elsewhere. During slumps, of course, resistance to control proved more difficult. 'There is a terrorism existing over the men', said Joseph Thomas, a blacksmith of Pontllanfraith, near Blackwood, in 1841, 'and they dare not speak out.'[74]

Thomas was referring particularly to the most notorious aspects of employer control, namely the 'long pay' and the truck system. At the turn of the century the problems of obtaining money and provisions for the new workforce were acute, and people resorted to various kinds of barter and token payments. Employers usually took charge of food supplies, buying goods from Bristol or Ireland, and selling them through their company shops. These truck shops were a special feature of Monmouthshire society, and all the major industrial concerns owned one or more of them.[75] At Rhymney and Ebbw Vale they had a large shop in the town and branch stores selling meat, beer, and all manner of provisions. Employers sometimes managed these shops themselves, but in the colliery districts it was common practice to let them out to tenants on a rent or commission basis.

'I find it difficult', wrote the son of a company shopkeeper, 'to convey to the reader the central and dominating place occupied by the Old Shop in the life of a small community like that of Rhymney.'[76] Records show that most working people used these shops, initially from necessity and later from choice or compulsion. The degree of choice was, in most areas, limited by the method of wage-settlement, Henry Scale's 'rod of iron'.[77] Workers on the coalfield were paid at monthly or at even longer intervals. Contractors and foremen gave them their wages at company offices, shops, and beerhouses. The amount of cash that changed hands was comparatively small, for perhaps two-thirds of a person's income had already been drawn in fortnightly or weekly subs. These advances were of tokens only, although after the anti-truck Act of 1831 some were made in cash on the understanding that they were exchanged for goods at shops owned or favoured by the company. Those who broke this unwritten agreement, who complained of the quality, weight, and prices of the shop goods, and who supported the Chartist call for workers' co-operative stores, knew the possible consequences of their action. At Gelligaer and Blackwood they lost their jobs.

Opposition to the truck system attracted a wider spectrum of support in the years after the Napoleonic wars. Magistrates like John Moggridge of Woodfield House and the Revd William Powell of Abergavenny, tradesmen of Merthyr and Pontypool, and the local newspaper, the *Monmouthshire Merlin*, came out strongly against this 'infamous practice', and applauded the legal cases brought against companies and agents. Workmen from Tredegar to Blaenavon also joined strikes against the payment of wages in goods, and it has been shown that the company shop was one of the main targets of the miners' terrorist group, the 'Scotch Cattle'.[78] At an important meeting in 1832 magistrates, ironmasters, and coal-owners agreed that truck had long been the chief source of discontent on the coalfield, but with the exception of some works at Merthyr and Newbridge, this system of control and extended credit proved ever more attractive to employers. After the Newport rising Sir Benjamin Hall tried to persuade his friends that Chartism had flourished in precisely those communities where the anti-truck legislation had been ignored, but fellow critics like the Revd James Coles found no evidence of this. As for employers, apart from Josiah John Guest of Dowlais and Thomas Phillips, most carried on as before, echoing Somers Harford's rebuke of Hall: 'The people are better off with very little money, than when in full possession of their earnings.'[79]

Throughout 1839 representatives of property in South Wales justified the special relationship between masters and men. They argued, as some historians have done, that certain forms of control or feudalism were both necessary and popular on the coalfield. George Brewer, manager of the Coalbrookvale ironworks, said that over the previous twenty years none of the men in his care had felt the pangs of hunger or been insubordinate, and Crawshay Bailey claimed that at Nantyglo 'we have lived pleasantly together without the interference of strangers . . .'.[80] In good times workers had been 'richly rewarded' with the best wages in Britain, and in bad times the employers had provided a safety-net of company shops, soup-kitchens, and other forms of charity. After the rising Samuel Homfray, George Kenrick, Edward Dowling, and several promi-nent Anglican clergymen launched a clever publicity campaign to prove that the people of South Wales were the best-treated and most highly paid serfs in history.

One of the objects of Tremenheere's inquiry was to establish the truth of this claim. Using figures that had been supplied by these employers, and by Sir Edmund Head, he returned the following table of the weekly income at a typical ironworks:

Furnace and mill-men	25–60s.
Miners and colliers	21–5 s.
Artisans	18–24s.
Labourers	12–18s.
Boys, women, old men, and inferior workmen	3–12s.

The investigator was told by Thomas Prothero, coalowner, and others that it was possible for a mining family to have a combined wage of £3 a week, but he found it hard to reconcile this with the evi-dent lack of working-class capital and savings. Apart from a few col-liers who built their own homes in a boom period, most workers spent almost all their income on food, drink, and renting and fur-nishing their houses. Sadly, concluded Tremenheere, the working class preferred idleness and excursions to the public house to con-stant labour and the prospect of a small fortune.[81]

It was undoubtedly true that workmen at the mines and ports of South Wales could earn more in the early nineteenth century than workers in many parts of Britain. In the late 1830s the income gap between iron- and coalworkers and the men of the cotton and hosiery trades of the Midlands and north of England was especially marked. Chartist missionaries were struck by the comparative prosperity of the coalfield, and William Griffiths of Pontypool suggested that it was one reason for the delayed growth of radicalism in the region.[82] Later, after the rising, it was established that the artisans and miners in custody were more prosperous than political prisoners elsewhere. A few of them, like Wright Beatty, a coal trimmer of Newport and John Slugg of Pontnewydd, earned only 15s. a week, but William Thomas, the Ebbw Vale miner, earned 25s., and John Lovell, the self-employed gardener, mason James Godwin of Brynmawr, and roller David Evans had a more 'comfortable subsistence'.[83] 'They are too prosperous', commented W. T. Harford Phelps, solicitor for the prosecution in the trials, '. . . they receive more money than they can, or at least, as our experience proves, more than they will, apply usefully.' On one thing, every respectable observer agreed, the Newport rising was 'not a rebellion of the belly'.[84]

This, as Walter Coffin quietly remarked, left one crucial question unanswered: why did a people so apparently controlled and prosperous indulge in such an act of folly? Gradually local residents were forced to admit that class relationships in South Wales were rather different from what Crawshay Bailey and Edward Dowling had suggested.[85] In private, and later in public, official investigators refused to accept the proffered image of a paternalist and contented community. 'Except in a few of the great works', recorded Tremenheere in his memoirs, 'the relations between employers and employees was [sic] of the worst description.' He found, on his visits to South Wales in the 1840s, much 'disaffection towards the state' and 'suspicion' of, and 'hostility' towards, employers.[86]

Tremenheere sought an explanation for this in the absence of religious and educational provisions and in the workers' ignorance of political economy, but others closer to the people of the coalfield found bitterness growing in the very conditions of life and work that employers chose to ignore. Living conditions were, as we have seen, often difficult, and illness and death stalked the valleys. Cholera and typhus killed several thousand people in the mining towns during the second quarter of the century, and those lucky enough to get beyond their fifth birthday knew that bad chests, ruptures, and rheumatism awaited them. What they resented was the additional prospect of serious injury at work, and their employers' insensitive response. Accidents were so common that no one commented on the number of Chartists who arrived at Newport on 4November without legs and arms. The worst hazards were the lack of ventilation, fire damp, roof falls, tram accidents, and burning at the furnaces. In this era before works inspection and official statistics it appears likely that the same number of people killed by soldiers on 4 November 1839 expired every month in the works and pits of the coalfield. There were, for instance, two pit deaths at Tredegar in the week after the rising, and the narrow seams to the south and east claimed a regular quota of eight-, nine-, and ten-year-old children. On 1 July 1839 a large Chartist procession from Coalbrookvale to Brynmawr was held up as the body of a man killed at Blaina was carried through on a plank.[87] No one, recalls Thomas Jones, ever quite forgot or forgave the manner of a miner's passing.[88]

Uncertainty of life on the coalfield was matched in some districts by that of work. The iron industry was subject, as the history of the early nineteenth century shows, to considerable fluctuations in demand and price, to wage-cuts in the order of 20–40 per cent, and to long lay-offs. Workmen learned to keep a wary eye on iron prices at Newport and Cardiff, and in slumps like that of the early 1830s large numbers of people were in debt to company and private shop-keepers. Only some of the skilled men at the furnaces, forges, and mills enjoyed real security; contracts for miners and colliers were often on a monthly basis, and income depended on the tonnage weighed.

In those collieries where coal was produced for use in the homes and engines of Britain the problems of obtaining regular employment were even greater. Apart from the fluctuating demand, seasonal and otherwise, there were addition complications of geology, bad weather, transport difficulties, and delays at the docks. Winter was a notoriously hard time on the coalfield. Contractors across the Mynydd-islwyn seam admitted that colliers worked for only eight or nine months in a year, changing jobs several times in that period. Real wages there were well below those published by employers like Prothero; after deductions at source for rent, medical attention, and tools, workmen found it a struggle to meet the high cost of provisions. 'They are said to have good wages', remarked Henry Vincent on his visit to Pontllanfraith in March 1839, 'but I found this far from being the case. Work is very irregular . . .'.[89] Some of the workmen who later joined the Chartist march had, at one time or another, been 'absolutely without food'. In these economic circumstances, argued magistrate Edmund Williams of Maesyrydda in the parish of Bedwellty, indebtedness was a necessary evil.[90] Almost everyone in Blackwood or Traenant knew what it was to beg and borrow. Such 'improvidence', so much criticized by Tremenheere, was not discouraged by Monmouthshire employers, for men in debt found it hard to gain a discharge note or sustain a strike.[91]

Against this background one can begin to see why the conflicts between men and employers in South Wales were some of the most bitter and prolonged in nineteenth-century Britain. 'The masters are looked upon generally as the natural enemies of the men' declared one government official in 1847; '. . . both classes imagine that they are necessarily antagonistic.'[92] The ironmasters after 1802, and the coalowners after 1830, met fairly regularly, and occasionally produced a combined policy on output, prices, and wages. In 1839, for example, there was considerable agreement between Prothero, Powell, and friends on the optimum level of coal production, and on the claims of the workforce. The most consistent of the men's demands concerned wages, the timing of wage settlements, and the iniquities of the truck system. From time to time employers were also called upon to answer charges relating to the level of food prices, the manner in which workers' payments were assessed, and the legality of wage reductions and dismissals. The workmen had a strong sense of 'rights', and particularly resented the arbitrary conduct of employers like Thomas Prothero, Crawshay Bailey, and John Scale of the Clydach ironworks. In their defence, the ironmasters and coalowners were prepared to withhold wages and parish relief, impose fines and imprisonment, and use spies and soldiers. 'Starvation produces wonders', exclaimed Scale after a successful and bruising battle over the weighing of coal.[93]

In one sense, most of the conflicts of the early nineteenth century were about control. When Reginald Blewitt, amongst others, at the time of the Chartist rising claimed that the miners wished to treat the works as their own, he touched upon one of the neglected aspects of our industrial history.[94] From the beginning men who worked closely together in treacherous conditions demanded a say in the numbers, character, and training of the labour-force. They were particularly sensitive about new methods of recruitment. When cheap labour in the form of Irish and English workers was brought into the Rhymney valley in the 1820s, widespread rioting was the result. At Tredegar, and right along the heads of the valleys, the men of works and mines jealously guarded 'the secrets of the trade'. Some of them, too, in these days of sub-contracting and piece-work put restrictions on their own productivity. Even before the arrival of national trade unions on the coalfield, the most organized working men and women made agreements amongst themselves and with employers about the amount of coal or iron that ought to be produced, and stockpiled, when prices were low.

Combinations amongst the working people of South Wales were very common. Almost certainly the first trade societies were those of the skilled and highly paid craftsmen at the iron foundries and furnaces, but after the Napoleonic Wars the miners and colliers proved equally capable of organized and sustained action. By the early 1830s the workforce of the ironworks could bring out all the sale-coal colliers, and vice versa; it was a remarkable achievement. As the strikes of 1827, 1836, and 1840 showed, the most impressive displays of solidarity were those of the men at the small pits between Dinas and Newport. Despite their economic vulnerability they were able to moderate some of the worst wage-reductions and the excesses of the truck system. On a number of occasions, notably in 1816, 1822, 1830, and 1832, the whole of the Glamorgan and Monmouthshire coalfield came to a halt, and the men and masters of Tredegar, Nantyglo, Ebbw Vale, and Blaenavon, fought each other to a standstill. Miners' leaders were imprisoned for breach of contract and regiments of soldiers kept watch on their colleagues.

The popularity of national trade unions during and after the Reform crisis added a new dimension to workers' organization and the employers' response. The South Wales lodges affiliated to the Friendly Society of Coal-Mining in 1831 began and ended their meetings with a prayer, and during their secret discussions resolved to impose a closed shop and to restrict entry into, and the output of, their industry. Josiah Guest and Anthony Hill of the Plymouth ironworks, with support from Walter Coffin, Digby Mackworth, Home Secretary Melbourne and a few shrill Nonconformist ministers, launched a counter-attack, and after eight weeks the men of Merthyr submitted. Three years later the pattern was repeated, although this time the battle front was wider, as employers, magistrates, clergymen,and officers of the Oddfellows societies confronted several thousand unionists across the coalfield. Initial thrusts by Capel Hanbury Leigh and Samuel Homfray were followed in June 1834 by one of the most impressive and unified assaults ever launched by the ironmasters and coalowners of South Wales. William Crawshay, Crawshay Bailey, Thomas Prothero, and other representatives of industry agreed to refuse employment to any person connected with trade union or Scotch Cattle activities. Only the workmen at Cyfarthfa, Hirwaun, Blaenavon, and Varteg offered any lasting resistance, and by the autumn of the year they were apparently disillusioned by the lack of assistance from English sections of the Grand National Consolidated Trades Union.[95] It would be wrong, however, to regard this as the end of all combinations. In May of 1839, for example, the men of the Tredegar ironworks called one of their many strikes, and in the summer local union activity was reported at the collieries and in the town of Newport itself.[96] The usual place of meeting for militant sale-coal colliers was Crosspenmaen, near Crumlin, and it was there on 3 February 1839 that William Jones and William Edwards, two Chartist delegates, came upon a gathering of 2,000–3,000 strikers.[97] Some of them listened to the preachers of the new political gospel, but others preferred an immediate and physical resolution of their industrial grievances.

Violence was, from the outset, engrained in the bargaining process. Rioting was a common form of protest during the years of the Napoleonic Wars, and at one point, in the late autumn of 1800, food prices were effectively controlled on the coalfield by the intimidating threat of mob disorder. In 1816 marching gangs of men, women, and children from Merthyr, Tredegar, and other places stopped almost all the ironworks and collieries in South Wales, and there were serious clashes with soldiers and talk of an assault on the army depot at Brecon. During the subsequent years of depression, recrimination, and instinctive radicalism, the pattern of industrial violence changed, and the strike of 1822 was marked by the appearance of the colliers' own terrorist group called the 'Scotch Cattle'.

For two decades the Cattle, with their 'naw mil o blant ffyddlon' [nine thousand faithful children], were regarded as the chief defenders of workers' rights. Their influence can be seen, not just in the major coalfield stoppages but also in many of the smaller conflicts at, for example, Clydach and Pontypool. The name of this Welsh colliers' organization remains a mystery, though their methods and purpose are now well established. They met at night, often to the accompaniment of the sound of drums, horns, and guns, and sanctioned the sending of threatening letters and attacks on persons and property. The tone of these proceedings was well captured by this typical Cattle threat:[98]

> To all Colliers, Traitors, Turncoats and others
> We hereby warn you the second and last time. We are determined to draw the hearts out of all the men above named, and fix two of the hearts upon the horns of the Bull; so that everyone may see what is the fate of every traitor—and we know them all.

Apart from the iron district of Merthyr Tydfil, where the Cattle were said to have been comparatively unpopular, this terrorist organization had cells in every industrial valley. As a matter of policy the Bull preferred his men to operate outside their own communities, and on the most dangerous missions promised, in the event of an accident, to look after their wives and children. Despite claims to the contrary, in the years preceding the Chartist movement every part of the coalfield witnessed Scotch Cattle activity of a serious character. Company property worth several thousand pounds was destroyed, and scores of attacks were made on the persons and property of contractors, agents, truck shopkeepers, bailiffs, and other enemies of the people. In 1822, for instance, and again in 1830, when colliers were anxious to stop supplies reaching both the ironworks to the north and Newport to the south, miles of tramroad were torn up and wagons and barges sunk or set on fire. A few years later there were similar scenes at Blaina, Clydach, and Rhymney, though on these and other occasions it is significant that the Browns and other employers escaped personal injury. The most seriously threatened was Thomas Powell, when colliers from Gelligaer broke the windows of his home in a protest against his refusal to pay wages weekly.

The main targets of the Scotch Cattle almost defined themselves. Dr Thomas Rees, the shopkeeper of Craig-y-fargoed in the parish of Bedwellty, whose home was attacked in 1834 and 1835, stoutly condemned workers' combinations and drinking habits. About the same time the occupiers of company shops at the Waterloo and neighbouring collieries had their furniture and ledgers set on fire.

John Wilks of Argoed, John Williams of Llangattock, and many other contractors, agents, and master miners were especially hated by the Bull. 'Master, put down these doggies', said a worker to the manager of the Clydach ironworks in 1833, 'and you will hear no more of the Scotch Cattle.'[99] Other victims of this organization were blacklegs, imported strike-breakers, the Irish, and the better-paid men of the ironworks who sometimes refused to join the colliers in their struggles.

The attacks on these people were conducted with measured ritual. In April 1832, for instance, between 250 and 300 of the Cattle marched down the Bute or Rhymney railroad three abreast, led by armed men with horns on their heads, and, having posted warning notices in the Blackwood area, proceeded to knock in the windows of a hundred homes. A year later the same fate befell the Dowlais workers who had refused to support a wages strike at the Bute iron-works. Those brave or foolish workmen, like William Jones of Blaencarno in the parish of Gelligaer, who continued to work despite such obvious warnings, were paid a second visit, and this time the Cattle broke down the doors of their lodgings, destroyed prized possessions, and handed out a beating. It was a pattern which was to be repeated time and again in the Chartist rising, notably in places like Ebbw Vale and Varteg.[100]

The influence of the Scotch Cattle, and the solidarity which they helped to impose on the Welsh mining communities, was quite astonishing. Despite the efforts of magistrates Moggridge and Powell of Abergavenny and despite the presence of soldiers and the firm resistance of Homfray and Edward Frere of the Clydach iron-works, no one 'of the same class' could be found 'to give the slightest information that may lead to the detection of the villains'.[101] The *Merthyr Guardian* conveys the atmosphere of fear on the coalfield in the summer of 1834:[102]

The way-faring traveller passes the scene of outrages often bordering on murder, in silence and fear; no sound escapes his pale lips, no gesture indicates the tragedy of which he is a witness; for all that he sees is a living proof, that from Dowlais to Abergavenny, TO HIM THERE IS NO LAW.

In this year the government, magistrates, and employers made a prodigious effort to break the unity and silence of the Cattle. Eventually the constant attendance of troops, the appointment of special constables, the creation of a new mountain police, and the offers of rewards and bribes produced the required result, and on 6 April 1835 Edward Morgan was hanged at Mònmouth gaol. John Owen, the lawyer and 'Poor Man's Friend' of Monmouth, claimed that in later years the workmen became more peaceful, but we know that the Cattle were still a force on the coalfield in 1836–9, 1842–3, 1847–50, and 1857–8.[103] The importance of this for the Newport rising is evident; the working class of Blaina and Ebbw Vale, of Clydach and Pontypool, and of Blackwood and Risca were not only 'rebellious and easily roused', but were also past masters in the art of organization, intimidation, and violence.

2

A World of Politics

ON one of the Scotch Cattle letters of 1832 someone had added the word 'Reform'. The interest of working people in politics was widely regarded as something new in this decade. But there were, at least on the fringes of the coalfield, signs of political awareness and militancy a generation before, and, as we shall see, some of the English leaders of the Newport rising had been notable reformers in their native towns and villages. In Monmouthshire the world of constitutional politics revolved around the two great families of the Somersets, the Dukes of Beaufort, and the older Morgans of Tredegar, and the only occasion for popular participation was a rare electoral contest. For most of the eighteenth and early nineteenth centuries the two county seats and that for the boroughs of Monmouth, Newport, and Usk were in the possession of these two houses, and it was only in the years 1816–20 that the burgesses of the first two towns made a serious if unsuccessful bid for independence. The revolt was led by an unlikely trio of the Whig industrialist John Hodder Moggridge, the pugnacious lawyer and town-clerk of Newport, Thomas Prothero, and the tailor and draper, John Frost.[1]

Frost, a man of medium height and quiet disposition, had spent his formative years in London radical circles and, after a brief spell in Bristol, settled down in Mill Street, Newport in about 1806. There he grew up alongside three other prominent reformers, Samuel Etheridge of the 'Radical Printing Office', John Dickenson, the butcher, and William Edwards, the giant baker who, on his own admission, was forced by the post-war depression to consider 'the awful condition of the working classes'.[2] Soon afterwards, Frost and Etheridge launched the first of many printed attacks on the corruption of the great county families and, of more significance for the future, on the sharp practices and selfish inconsistencies of 'so-called reformers' such as Prothero and his brother-in-law, the coroner William Brewer.[3] In 1823 Frost spent several months in gaol as a result of Prothero's libel action, and the long-running battle

4. John Frost

between the two men sharpened and distorted local politics. 'No man was ever treated with more injustice and cruelty, than Prothero treated me', the Chartist leader wrote some years later.'Indeed, I believe that it would be a sin to forget it.'[4] In his eyes, reformer and radical were different species. Frost defined the latter as 'A PUBLIC SPIRITED MAN, ONE WHO DETESTS TYRANNY, AND WHOSE PERSON AND PURSE ARE READY TO PROTECT THE WEAK FROM THE ATTACKS OF THE POWERFUL'.[5] A radical was also a supporter of universal suffrage and, should it be necessary, of a revolutionary transfer of political power. For Frost, and his closest friends in 1822, the memory of the French revolution was never far from their thoughts.

The Reform crisis of 1830–2 gave these men an opportunity to test the changing temperature of contemporary politics. In south-east Wales these were difficult economic years, and it was one of the few areas in the Principality where landowners and landowning industrialists like Capel Hanbury Leigh had property set on fire and received threatening 'Swing' letters warning them about their future conduct.[6] In the eastern half of Monmouthshire Sir Charles Morgan, his one-time agent Thomas Prothero, George Kenrick of the Varteg ironworks, and other gentlemen held meetings, formed defence associations and swore in hundreds of special constables.[7] Soon, however, politics, and in particular the new Reform Bill, took public attention, and at an early date liberal employers, Nonconformist ministers, Pontypool householders, and the Newport mob made their intentions clear. In the county elections the Tory, Lord Granville Somerset, held on to one seat, but Sir Charles Morgan withdrew in favour of the Whig, William Addams Williams of Llangibby Castle. In the contest for the Monmouth boroughs the conflict proved to be extremely bitter, with intimidation and violence the order of the day. The burgesses of Newport let it be known that they would not support Somerset's brother, the Tory Marquis of Worcester, and, to the accompaniment of breaking glass and popular rejoicing, Benjamin Hall was returned. Hall was the son of the proprietor of the Rhymney ironworks, a friend of the Nonconformists, and an advocate of the use of the ballot in elections. During Hall's successful election campaign John Frost helped to control crowd behaviour in the town, but within a few weeks the popular verdict was overturned by a House of Commons committee. In subsequent months, as rioting spread across Britain and the other House of Parliament pursued its policy of obstruction, petitions for reform were sent from several Monmouthshire towns, and Frost and his colleagues established in November 1831 a branch of the Political Union of the Working Classes, committed to manhood suffrage.[8]

The popular radicals had thus taken some time to distance themselves from leading Nonconformist and Whig reformers, but the break had now been made. 'While they make speeches and write in favour of Reform', said Frost in 1832, '[they] have their hands firmly fixed in your pockets. . . . They want to have political power, that they may use it as to their own advantage. . . . Let us depend on *ourselves*. Let the Merchant, the Farmer, the Tradesman, the Working-man look to no one but *himself*, for if he depends on those who are in superior situations he will always be disappointed.'[9] About this time moderate reformers like Digby Mackworth and Capel Hanbury Leigh, George Kenrick and the Pontypool liberals, and especially three Newport men, Thomas Phillips, Lewis Edwards of Brynhyfryd, and the Revd James Davies, were marked down by Frost as 'enemies of the people'. When the Reform Bill was finally passed, in June 1832, the disillusionment of some ultra-radicals was complete. In Glamorgan, where Merthyr and Aberdare became a separate constituency, the number of parliamentary seats was increased to five, and the industrialists made significant political advances, but in Monmouthshire the Reform Act changed very little. Despite the rise in population, representation in Parliament remained the same and the working class lost what little political influence they had. There were only just over four and a half thousand voters in 1832, and, as late as 1851, the county had about the lowest proportion of electors in Britain. 'It is now clear, as the sun at noon day,' declared Frost in 1839, 'that the Reform Bill was a humbug, and that it was intended for nothing else.'[10]

Frost, like so many other politicians and writers of the period, had for a long time ignored the people of the coalfield. During the Reform crisis future Chartist leaders like Morgan Williams, the small Merthyr entrepreneur, the neighbouring John family, and John Llewellyn, beerhouse keeper of Pontypool, emerged as prominent local radicals, and certain industrial towns and villages were openly affected by politics for the first time. The greatest centres of

the iron and coal trade demanded some form of political representation, and even the Oddfellows and the Scotch Cattle gave token
support to reform. When the Reform Bill was rejected by the House
of Lords in October 1831 there were large and angry public meetings in the parishes of Bedwellty and Mynydd-islwyn. These
demonstrations, and the crowds cheering William Addams Williams at Abersychan and the celebratory athletics and fireworks
displays at Blackwood in June 1832, were undoubtedly orchestrated by liberal reformers such as the employer John Hodder
Moggridge and the Baptist minister, the Revd Micah Thomas of
Abergavenny.[11]

In some districts of the coalfield, however, popular politics during the Reform crisis revealed a striking degree of independence
and militancy. Political Unions were established at an early date in
Merthyr and Aberdare, and also at Tredegar, where, by common
consent, the geologist and rationalist Zephaniah Williams was a
prominent figure. In the early summer of 1831 a combination of
political frustration and local economic grievances brought about a
split in the radical alliance, and for a few days Merthyr experienced
one of the few genuine working-class risings of the nineteenth century. Workers, with their red and white flags of 'Reform', took control of the town, and sent messengers across the heads of the valleys.
One by one the works were stopped and, around Pontypool, there
were several brutal clashes with the forces of law and order. Threats
were also held out against the towns of Newport and Brecon, but in
the event the action was never as co-ordinated nor as determined as
that of 1816. On this occasion, the government quickly poured eight
hundred soldiers into the area, and the first of these killed at least
sixteen rioters.[12]

The irony of this abortive rising was that Merthyr was the only
part of the coalfield that was recognized by the architects of the
revised Reform Bill. In December 1832 the first election was held
for the new parliamentary borough, and Josiah John Guest was
duly elected to a position which he held for the next twenty years.
Despite the size of the electorate—502 voters—the radicals and
the working class continued to exercise a remarkable influence on
local politics. John Thomas, schoolteaching friend of Zephaniah
Williams, and Morgan Williams brought out the Owenite journal,
Y Gweithwr/The Workman, and, along with John Jones, the radical
Unitarian minister of Aberdare, worked hard in the cause of the

new MP for Merthyr. In the election of 1835 it was the impact of exclusive dealing and mass meetings of thousands of working men which persuaded the conservative candidate, William Meyrick, to withdraw. Two years later, the position was almost reversed, for many of the workmen, still angry over Guest's support for the Poor Law Amendment Act, offered temporary assistance to his political rivals. In a confusing and riotous contest the Dowlais ironmaster steered about on the radical wind and won by a comfortable 174 votes.[13]

In the Monmouth boroughs the story of these years was also one of growing independence and violence. Having captured the seat in 1832, Benjamin Hall was faced three years later by the Tory land-owning industrialist Joseph Bailey, who was given the support of the houses of Beaufort and Tredegar. Most of Hall's support came from the reforming burgesses of Newport, and during a very close contest there was serious rioting in that town. Two years later Bailey stood again, but this time his opponent was Reginald Blewitt of Llantarnam Abbey. This lawyer-friend of Thomas Prothero promised franchise reform and those who spoke on his behalf were James Hunt, proprietor of the Pentwyn ironworks, the Revd Thomas Morris of Tabernacle, Pontypool, Martin Morrison and Thomas Phillips of Newport, and an enthusiastic crowd of employers and ministers. At his victory appearance, before the Westgate Hotel in Newport, several thousand people cheered Blewitt to the echo. Lewis Edwards, on that occasion, claimed that Blewitt had 'for ever freed us from the fangs of Toryism', and the resident of Llantarnam Abbey did hold the seat for another fifteen years.[14] In the eyes of Frost and the ultra-radicals, however, Blewitt at Westminster proved to be almost as reactionary as the county MPs Somerset and Williams. His Whig government passed the Irish Coercion and the Poor Law Amendment Acts, sanctioned the assault on the trade unions, increased the size of the standing army, and created a new county police. 'They have had power for eight years,' said Frost in 1839, 'and every impartial man must admit, that in the history of our country we cannot find an account of men in authority, who made a more tyrannical use of it than the present ministry.'[15]

The general election of 1837 was an important turning-point in the pre-history of the Chartist movement. It marked in south-east Wales the political recovery of the Conservative party and illustrated the tenuous relationship between reformers and radicals. In the largest towns on and off the coalfield, Benjamin Havard, John Llewellyn, and other artisans were now clearly unhappy in the company of Guest, Thomas Phillips, and other careful champions of reform. On the very day of Blewitt's triumphant appearance at Newport, Mr Reynolds of Pontypool annoyed Phillips by demanding sweeping changes in the constitution.[16]

Reynolds was perhaps the very first spokesman for a radical association which had just been established in Pontypool.[17] It was only the second of its kind in South Wales, a fact of which it remained intensely proud. Initially the number of association members was no more than fifty, but it had a fertile mixture of young and old people, and of native radicals such as William Griffiths and outsiders like Samuel Shell, who signed one of their first addresses and whose son was killed in the Chartist rising. Perhaps the most articulate of the leading Pontypool radicals was the 49-year-old John Llewellyn, a hatter, trade-unionist, and beerhouse-keeper, whilst the most flamboyant character was unquestionably 30-year-old William Jones, a travelling actor who had arrived from Bristol in 1833. The association met at the Bristol beerhouse, which belonged to Jones's wife. From the beginning Jones and his friends were noted for their militant stand and one of their most popular debates concerned the extreme forms of extra-parliamentary pressure that could be placed on an obstructive government.

The growth of radical associations in other parts of the south-east was slow. Although there were radicals in Cardiff, Monmouth, and Chepstow, for instance, they were less organized than some of their comrades in Mid and West Wales. The reasons for this are obscure, though in Newport, at least, much of the interest and energy of Frost and his friends was directed towards local politics. The Municipal Corporations Act of 1835 brought a touch of democracy to corporation life, and radical representatives like Edward Thomas, Thomas Turner, and Thomas Wells now faced William Brewer and Thomas Powell across the council floor. In 1836 Frost became a magistrate, and in November of that year was elected as mayor of the borough. He was now able to defend more vigorously the interests of the poor and of the burgesses against the schemes of the corporation, Thomas Phillips, Thomas Prothero, and Sir Charles Morgan. However, the electoral triumph of Blewitt in the summer of 1837 was followed some months later by council victories for the

5. William Jones

Whig reformers, the desertion of some of Frost's friends, and the appointment of Lewis Edwards and Thomas Phillips as successive mayors. Somewhat dejected, the Newport draper gave himself to reading and, with one eye on Blewitt's parliamentary seat, began to consider an alternative political strategy.

The formation, some time in the summer of 1838, of a Working Men's Association in the town provided Frost with a unique opportunity. Its founding members were William Edwards and 'a few working men', and these were soon joined by old Samuel Etheridge and young William Townsend, the son of a wine-merchant.[18] They met on Tuesday evenings at the Bush Inn, in Commercial Street, and within a few months had a membership of some 150. Their rules were similar in spirit, and even word, to those of the parent body, the London Working Men's Association. In October 1838 a public meeting was convened at the Parrot Inn, and there Frost was asked to explain the points of the People's Charter which had been published by William Lovett. At the end of November the Working Men's Association organized another public meeting, this time at Devonshire House, and on this occasion Frost was appointed delegate for Newport, Pontypool, and Caerleon to the forthcoming National Convention of the Industrious Classes in London.

By January 1839 there were 430 card-carrying Chartists at Newport, and soon they were meeting in a number of public houses including the Royal Oak, which belonged to Frost and was run by another radical, Charles Jones.[19] Officers of the Association were changed regularly, but prominent amongst them in the early days were the grocer Edward Thomas, who was a fine Welsh speaker and poet, John Dickenson the pork-butcher, Thomas Wells the corn-merchant, and James Horner the shoemaker. These were soon joined by other officers—Charles Waters a ship's carpenter, John Lovell a gardener and Sunday-school teacher, Jenkin Morgan a 40-year-old self-employed milkman with three children, Robert Alexander a shoemaker from Bristol, and Richard Rorke a veteran Irish Whiteboy. By the spring there was also a lively group of female Chartists, with the militant Mary Brewer to the fore, and a complementary association of juvenile Chartists, in which Charles Groves (a Pentonville painter), Frost's son Henry, and Thomas Wells's son Frederick were particularly active.

One of the impressive aspects of these radicals was their missionary zeal. For weeks William Edwards and Samuel Etheridge, together with John Llewellyn and some Pontypool friends, travelled along the road between Newport and Abergavenny, giving lectures and encouraging people to establish associations. On 12 November 1838 a meeting was held at the George Inn, Caerleon, for this very purpose, and a local tradesman, John Ablatt, was elected to the chair. A radical society was formed as a result, with Mr Newberry as secretary and thirty-five founder members.[20] Up to this time few contacts had been made with Chartists on the Glamorgan side of the coalfield. In fact, Merthyr radicals like David John, pastor of the Unitarian Church, his two sons, David and Matthew, and Benjamin Havard and Morgan Williams had closer personal and political ties with areas to the west. It was only after the visit of William Jenkins, a prominent Carmarthen missionary, that an association was established in the iron town in October 1838, with Williams as its secretary. On Christmas Day, when the first mass meeting of industrial workmen on Aberdare mountain elected Hugh Williams, the Carmarthen solicitor, as their delegate to the National Convention, Charlotte Guest estimated the number of Merthyr Chartists at 700, a figure which she tripled five months later. At the end of the year a reliable estimate placed the number of enrolled in Merthyr and Aberdare at 7,000.[21]

Until the winter of 1838–9 the character and ideology of the new political gospel in south-east Wales can best be described as 'artisan'. The first Working Men's Associations were dominated by tradesmen and artisans. At Merthyr and Aberdare, where a number of ministers and schoolmasters were leading Chartists, it was said that every other shopkeeper and most men of small property were radicals.[22] Samuel Etheridge claimed that when he withdrew from the association at Newport, amongst the members were some fifty tradesmen 'and merchants as well'.[23] Thomas Wells, the corn merchant, and Edward Thomas, grocer and draper, often chaired the first Chartist meetings in that town, and the Dissenting ministers Byron and Miles, together with a few radical councillors, gave their support. Radical butchers, grocers, saddlers, and publicans were to be found in every large town across south Wales, and a few of them, like John William Phillips, the Trowbridge man resident in Pontypool, Thomas Havard of Blackwood, and John Thomas of Pontypool, were to be active in the last days before the rising.

In his first visits to the area Henry Vincent, the young Chartist lecturer from London and Hull, was impressed by the interested presence of the 'middle classes' at his meetings. Almost all of these belonged to the petty bourgeoisie, and it was reported that their attendance had been requested by the working class. 'I am', complained Jacob Thomas, a shopkeeper from Maesycwmmer, 'incessantly applied to by the Chartists to assist them.'[24] 'We were not Chartists,' echoed Sarah Edmunds of the Greyhound, Pontllanfraith, 'but we were afraid to say so to the colliers.'[25] Even so, there can be little doubt that a considerable number of agents, preachers, tradesmen, and prosperous freeholders were radical by instinct as well as from fear or convenience. William Shellard, master shoemaker and neighbour of William Jones at Pontypool, Zephaniah Williams, and Thomas Thomas of Llechwan in the parish of Llanfabon were men 'of considerable property'. David Lewis, the 37-year-old proprietor of the King Crispin, was, like Jenkin Morgan and Morgan Williams, a small businessman, and once employed more than ten men. Vincent called this master shoemaker 'a famous fellow'. 'There is no mistake about him. He says what he means and he works hard to spread our principles.'[26] The appearance in the treason-trials of persons of such respectable appearance and status as David Stephens of Crosspenmaen, Edmund Edmunds, mine-agent, William John Llewellyn, a farmer's son, William Davies, son of a Blackwood shopkeeper, John Llewellyn of Pontnewydd, and of course, Frost himself, caused contemporaries some anxiety, and, in Pontypool, urgent requests for the use of bail.[27] It also prompted a speaker at a London trades' conference to question the validity of giving assistance to prisoners Frost, Williams, and Jones, because they were not working men.[28]

The first working men to join the radical associations were shoemakers, blacksmiths, masons, carpenters, and other craftsmen, who made up a large share of the first working class in the established towns. At Pontypool, for instance, leading members included watchmakers and cabinet makers, as well as Thomas Parry the shoemaker and Evan Emanuel the turner. In Newport, a workshop of fourteen or fifteen shoemakers was well known for its radical sympathies, and even further afield, at places like Blackwood, Tredegar, and Merthyr, artisans often made the early running in the Chartist movement.[29] Benjamin Richards the Tredegar boot- and shoemaker, John Davies the Pontnewydd carpenter, and John Williams the weaver of Aberdare, were prominent lodge officials. A number of them even followed the example of Frost,

Zephaniah Williams, and William Edwards, and became full-time missionaries in the radical cause, a clear sign that these people had more time, independence, and literary skills than other groups of working men. Only a few of the latter joined the Chartist movement at the beginning, though miners at Merthyr and Pontypool, and dock-, metal-, and pottery-workers of Newport soon developed an interest in the new politics. Most of these workmen, however, joined the associations in large numbers in the winter months and spring of 1839. At Newport Thomas Wells recorded that they crowded into the Prince of Wales in lower Commercial Street, listening to lectures and enjoying the readings of newspapers brought to them by James Horner, shoemaker.[30]

In the early days the ideas that pervaded the radical speeches and publications can be loosely termed 'traditional'. After all, Frost, Etheridge, and Edwards had been involved in radical politics for some twenty years before the Chartist movement began, and their thinking did not change significantly throughout the 1820s and 1830s. The ideology, built on Tom Paine and William Cobbett, was essentially political, and the points of reference historical and philosophical. 'History teaches, and experience convinces us, that the principal object of men has been and still is, to acquire and to retain political authority,' wrote Frost in his first letter *To the Working Men of Monmouthshire*, 'and the sufferings of the mass of mankind shew us, but too clearly, how the power is exercised.'[31] The ancestors of the Morgans and other landed aristocrats had, it was claimed, seized power about the time of the Norman Conquest, and had reimposed their political and economic authority after the reign of Henry VI, during the Reformation, and in the counter-revolution of the seventeenth century. They maintained their hold on the nation in many ways, especially by corruption, the manipulation of currency, trade legislation, and heavy taxation.[32] The aristocracy controlled the church, education, and the law, and, so it was believed by the Chartists, they were boosting the military and police strength of an increasingly centralized state. Ultimately, as both the Whig and Tory leaders had recently shown, this privileged section of society clung to power by depriving 'the people' of their just economic, social, and especially political rights. Welsh radicals estimated, for example, that the income of the Privy Councillors alone was equivalent to half the total wages of the unrepresented working men of Monmouthshire and Breconshire.

It was axiomatic for popular radicals that labour created wealth and property. In this respect Frost and his friends directly confronted Crawshay Bailey and Samuel Homfray. 'The working classes raise all the food, make all the raiment, cut canals, build ships, construct steam engines, and do all the work, and yet we are told they have not sense enough to choose members of Parliament', declared the Newport Chartist in October 1838.[33] In one of the few surviving addresses of a South Wales Working Men's Association, it was argued that 'the wealth producer is made the slave to the possessors of that wealth that he has laboured to create; power is transferred from labour to capital, and the producer sinks into a mere instrument to be used as needed, and thrown aside as soon as a more efficient one is presented'.[34] There was considerable debate in the Chartist associations of the district over the merits of lower taxation, cheaper food, and a fairer distribution of property. This was not, as Walter Coffin and Thomas Powell of the Gaer proclaimed, 'communism', but a claim for a better return on labour, a more equitable exchange.

In industrial South Wales the early radical analysis of 'aristocracy' versus the 'industrious classes' was obviously more applicable in a political than an economic context. Initially, at least, the main targets of the leading Chartists were the Somersets and Morgans, though when industrialists and lawyers like Crawshay Bailey and Thomas Prothero deferred to, worked for, and joined the great landed families they also became part of 'them' against 'us'. Nothing surprised Frost more than the willingness of ironmasters, coalowners, and other 'men of talent and information' to embrace the political *status quo*.[35] Their rivals, 'the industrious classes', were, in the ideology of the artisan radicals, an amalgam of the lower middle and the working classes, and there were frequent appeals to tradesmen, small farmers, and the like to accept their vulnerable position and join the common political battle. If they assisted the radical movement, argued Frost, 'no class would benefit in a greater degree', and their property would be immeasurably safer.[36] When, in the late spring of 1839, some of the liberal middle class and Nonconformist reformers attended anti-Chartist rallies, Frost was extremely concerned at the historical wrong-turning. They were, in the eyes of radicals, only increasing the likelihood of revolution, a theme that was taken up again after the rising.[37] In the final radical analysis, when those in authority refused to reform themselves the people had the right to resist by force. Welsh Chartists took a special delight in reminding the great families of past events in America and France.

To the industrial working men of South Wales some of these radical ideas, and even more perhaps the phraseology, might have appeared a trifle esoteric, but the analysis of their social and economic ills struck a chord. During the late 1830s support grew for the radicals' assertions that people's discontent could be attributed to their lack of political power and that their main remedy was a different form of industrial action, the seizure of the state. Only in that way, argued William Edwards, John Llewellyn, and Frost, could labour be protected and financial and social burdens lifted. 'If the People's Charter was the law of the land, the People would elect a good House of Commons', wrote Edwards in typically lyrical fashion, '. . . England would be herself again; and happy would the working classes be. . . .'[38] In the opinion of the *Merthyr Guardian*, and some less hostile observers, the common existence of this political philosophy was the greatest achievement of early Chartism. Even men on comparatively high wages were seeking something else—their political rights. As John Lewis of Tydu later testified, this was a new world.[39]

We know precisely when the industrial workmen began to join political organizations in large numbers. In the early winter of 1838 radical artisans were still concerned by the small number of Chartist associations in South Wales, especially in view of the decisions to hold a people's Convention in February and to present a National Petition to Parliament. 'Let not a single parish, hamlet, city, town or village be without its association', was the cry from Pontypool early in 1839.[40] In fact, colliers from Blackwood and elsewhere had already, in December, invited leading ultra-radicals of Pontypool and Newport to visit them and explain the points of the Charter. By the beginning of February Frost could report to the West London Democratic Association that some twenty new branches had been opened in Monmouthshire in the previous months, and that there were 15,000–20,000 men 'determined upon having their rights'.[41]

Some of the responsibility for this sudden flowering of Chartism rests with political missionaries, both English and Welsh. In December 1838 the London Working Men's Association appointed the young printer, Henry Vincent, as a roving missionary. He was, by general agreement, one of the most eloquent and persuasive lecturers of his generation, and when he was invited to speak at Pontnewydd on 1 January well over a thousand people packed into the ground behind John Llewellyn's beerhouse. William Edwards of Newport took the chair and introduced the visitors, amongst whom were John Frost and William Carrier, a young working-class radical from Trowbridge. Edwards began, as speakers often did in those early days, by describing the points of the Charter, and warning that lives would probably be lost before it was granted. Frost, newly elected as their delegate to the National Convention, followed in satirical mood, scorning the extravagant expenses of the aristocracy and royal household. But it was Vincent, as usual, who stole the show. He promised that the men of Yorkshire, Lancashire, Bristol, Bath, Trowbridge, and London were determined to have the Charter and called upon the people of Wales to join the radical alliance. They had, he declared, been held down long enough, and when the word was given the whole rotten superstructure of crown, army, government, lawyers, and parsons would come crashing down. The soldiers would not resist the workers, for half of these were as radical as Vincent himself.[42] A few hours later the message was repeated at Abersychan, although there, according to a hostile source, the crowd was considerably smaller and the tone more violent.[43] On the following day Vincent was at the Bush Inn, Newport, and he then set off with Frost on a brief tour of the eastern border of the coalfield, lecturing on the immorality of the aristocracy and the iniquities of the Poor Law. Then it was time to retrace their steps, before leaving at the beginning of February, for the opening ceremony of the Convention in London.

At this very moment, local Chartists began to answer requests for assistance from deep within the coalfield. In the second and third week of February representatives from the oldest radical associations in South Wales visited the mining villages. The usual procedure was to advertise meetings by posters and criers, and the most popular times for public gatherings were mid-afternoon and evening. Speeches were in both Welsh and English, and sometimes spliced with familiar hymns and prayers. On one occasion, at Blackwood, missionaries from Pontypool and Newport addressed several hundred colliers in the cold open air, and on another, at the Greyhound Inn, Pontllanfraith, Edward Thomas spoke on the Charter for an hour and Edwards followed with another mammoth lecture. During and after this meeting the signatures of men and women were collected for the National Petition.[44]

According to Sarah Edmunds of the Greyhound, William Edwards brought many new recruits to the Chartist lodge at their inn. The Newport baker was the most enthusiastic and hard-working of all the local speakers. On 4 February he promised a meeting of Chartist delegates at Bath that he would 'go upon the Welsh hills, and . . . illuminate all the country around'.[45]During the next few months he claimed to have established eight associations and collected 10,000 signatures. His stamina was astonishing, as we can see from this account of one of his tours of the coalfield. On Sunday, 31 March, Edwards left Newport for a meeting at Pontypool, and on the next day journeyed to Nantyglo with John Llewellyn as his companion. There, as so many other visiting speakers were to do, they made contact with two local leaders and publicans, David Lewis of Brynmawr and Zephaniah Williams. At 3 p.m. Edwards talked to several hundred workmen at the Royal Oak in Blaina and persuaded them to sign the Chartist petition. Four hours later Edwards and Llewellyn were at Beaufort, and in the next two days held further meetings 'on the hills'. On Friday they were back at Pontypool, where Edwards was the chief guest at a meeting which neither Vincent nor Frost could attend.[46] In fact, the absence of the Newport draper from so many of the coalfield jamborees helps to explain the ignorance which he sometimes showed about developments there.

Both Frost and Vincent had commitments outside Wales. The former took his seat at the National Convention on 4 February and was one of the most assiduous of Chartist delegates. His position as a magistrate gave him a unique status, and on the third day he was elected chairman, a position he was to occupy on a number of occasions in the next eight months. He developed, along with Vincent, a reputation for colourful language, and both argued that the Convention should be regarded as the authentic parliament of the people. They welcomed discussion of 'ulterior measures' to obtain the Charter, and Frost was one of a very small number of delegates who defended the right of George Julian Harney to express militant thoughts outside the conference hall. On 16 March Frost was actually chairman of the famous Crown and Anchor meeting, where Londoners were given reasons for the delay in presenting the Chartist petition and where open threats were held out against the government. The Home Secretary was at last stung into action, and five days later Lord John Russell carried out his promise to remove Frost's name from the commission of the peace. This brought upon the Newport draper the welcome mantle of martyrdom and a carefully organized outcry in Pontypool and his native town. In anticipation of Russell's decision, councillors and fellow radicals had sent a memorial to the Home Secretary, praising Frost as the best magistrate in the history of Newport, and Benjamin Byron, Independent minister, added the codicil that if his chapel member was too heated at times, it was only the high spirit of the self-educated and passionate reformer.[47]

At the end of February the Convention chose several of its members to act as missionaries in search of more signatures for the Chartist petition. Frost declined to act in this capacity but Vincent, together with William Burns, a Dundee shoemaker, was appointed for the districts of Somerset, Gloucestershire, Herefordshire, and South Wales. After a fortnight's intensive canvassing on the English border, the two Chartists crossed into Monmouth on Saturday, 16 March. Three days later, after a difficult experience in that 'Toryridden', Beaufort-dominated county town, Vincent travelled to Newport, whilst Burns and George Payne, the Bristol publisher of the *Western Vindicator*, journeyed to Pontypool. At Newport four meetings were held in two days, and at one of them perhaps 3,000 people were present. On the following day Vincent met the radical ladies at the Bush Inn, where the daughter of John Dickenson took the chair, and in the evening addressed male members of the association and closed the day with a musical rendering of 'The Democrat'.[48]

Five days later, after a brief sojourn in the west country, Vincent was back at Newport in time for tea with the ladies and a procession through the town. In the evening he addressed another huge crowd from an upturned wagon, and heard Dickenson say that if the police attacked Chartists they should be treated like mad dogs.[49] On Tuesday William Edwards escorted Vincent up the line of the Crumlin canal towards Pontllanfraith. At midday the Convention delegate spoke to several hundred workmen from hustings erected at the side of the Greyhound, and then, still apologizing for his lack of Welsh, he turned his attention to a society of female Chartists. After tea Vincent was proceeded up to Blackwood by a hundred flag-waving girls, and there, in front of the Coach and Horses, he participated in another large meerting chaired by one of the local secretaries, John ('Jack') Barrill. Most of those present, including many women and a few tradesmen, signed the petition, and some returned with the speaker to the Greyhound for an evening of *penillion* singing. After breakfast on the following day William Davies, the radical son of a local shopkeeper, took Vincent, Edwards, and three female Chartists to Gelligroes, where, in a large barn, the Londoner was informed that scores of local colliers were joining associations and signing petitions.[50]

Invitations to speak were now pouring in from every mining valley, but Vincent told his hosts that he was obliged to return to Newport. Each entry into this seaport town had become an excuse for a radical celebration, and on this occasion Edwards was seen persuading people to link arms and join the processions in his honour. After another meeting with his favourite society of female radicals, Vincent was prevailed upon to address the large crowd that had been marshalled outside. Continuing a theme begun at a similar gathering eight days before, he warned that the people of Newport were not prepared to try another petition. If their National Petition were rejected by Parliament on 6 May, every hill and valley of Wales should send forth its army. According to prosecution witnesses at a subsequent trial, the crowd shouted 'We will, we will' and Edwards threw up his arm, shouting 'Here's the stuff'. As for the mayor, Thomas Phillips, who had already voiced his contempt for such displays of public power, Vincent said that he wished to see him and his partner, Prothero, hanging from the lamp-post behind him.[51] Contemporaries later regarded this demonstration as a turning-point in the history of Monmouthshire radicalism, but Vincent himself was unaware of such historical niceties when, on the following morning, he set off in the company of William Davies to meet Frost at Stroud. Stroud was the constituency of Lord John Russell, and the Newport Chartist had already been nominated as its radical candidate in the next general election. Vincent appeared tired, and had every reason to be so; he had spoken on average at least two hours per day for the previous thirteen months, and had covered six thousand miles.

When Vincent and Frost held their discussions in Stroud they knew that Chartism in Wales and the west was already a mass movement. 'There is now more of political feeling in this country than ever existed, perhaps, in any nation in the world', ran the editorial in the *Western Vindicator* of 30 March. 'It would seem that every man has become a politician.' Frost claimed that the great families of Monmouthshire were now unable to call a public meeting, and even the reforming Anti-Corn Law League found it impossible at this time to proceed without Chartist interruptions.[52] At Newport, where mayor Phillips presided over a League gathering, Edwards and Dickenson annoyed the organizers by proposing a successful amendment for universal suffrage. 'The labouring classes of Monmouthshire', wrote one Blackwood collier in this spring, 'have their eyes open and know from what quarter they are oppressed. . . .'[53]

The rapid success of the Charter on the coalfield provided the radical movement with a new and formidable constituency. 'There will soon be created in Wales the finest democratic army in the world', commented the *Western Vindicator* on 4 May. Unfortunately, no one could be sure of the size of this army, for the respectable and radical press fought a running battle over the number of people who could be regarded as genuine Chartist recruits. The signs of growth were unmistakable: over 15,000 people signed the National Petition at Merthyr and Blackwood in a few days, meetings were attended by hundreds of men and women who could no longer be accommodated in inns and beershops, and James Horner, Edwards's wife, Thomas Parry of Pontypool, and Mr Woodman of Cardiff sold a large number of political publications. The most popular newspapers were Feargus O'Connor's *Northern Star* and the *Western Vindicator*. The latter was first produced on 23 February 1839 by George Payne of Bristol, veteran of the War of the Unstamped, and it included articles by the colliers' heroes, Vincent, Edwards, and Frost. The authorities in South Wales were particularly concerned about the spread of this 'seditious literature', and Phillips and his friends warned the government that, in one way or another, the size and militancy of ultra-radicalism were increasing day by day.[54]

Estimates of the number of Chartist adherents are unreliable. Frost stated, at the beginning of February, that twenty Working Men's Associations had been formed in Monmouthshire, and that 15,000–20,000 men were 'determined upon having their rights'.[55] By the summer the number of Chartist lodges had probably doubled, and Zephaniah Williams indicated that at the end of the year there were some fifty associations in Glamorgan and

Monmouthshire, each with anything from 100 to 1,300 members. At the height of the movement's popularity in 1839 there were over 25,000 enrolled or committed Chartists in the district, perhaps one in five of the total population.[56] Such a mass movement was unprecedented and, for the propertied classes, a matter of grave concern.

Although more than that number signed the National Petition, it was, as the trials later revealed, membership of the associations which distinguished the 'out and out Chartist'. Amongst the first lodges to be founded on the coalfield, just before and after Christmas 1838, were those at Blackwood, Pontllanfraith, Tredegar, Ebbw Vale, Beaufort, Blaina, Brynmawr, Dukestown, Abersychan, and Llanhilleth. Soon afterwards other organizations were established, some of which were really cells of the earlier institutions. For example, several Chartist groups met in the Tredegar district, whilst in a two-mile radius of Blackwood, lodges appeared at Maesycwmmer, Gelligroes, Fleur-de-lis, Argoed, Crosspenmaen, and four other places.[57]

Despite requests to ministers like William Morris of Pontypool for the use of chapel buildings, and despite the advice of Vincent, the temperance reformer, most Chartist associations in South Wales were held in public houses and beerhouses. The latter had the great advantage of being outside the control of the licensing authorities, and they were, especially in more remote mining communities, the natural meeting-places for friendly societies, trade unions, and clubs of all kinds. Some drinking-houses, such as the Star in Dukestown, the Miners Arms near Nelson, and the Navigation Inn at Crumlin, where the radicals John Morgan, David Price, Richard Pugh, Morgan Morgan, and Richard Williams were in charge, had won deserved reputations as centres of popular protest. As we have seen, Chartist leaders like David Lewis of the King Crispin, Brynmawr, Zephaniah Williams of the Royal Oak in Blaina, and John Llewellyn of Pontnewydd, mixed business with politics, and accommodated radical lecturers and associations. Rooms were reserved, and new ones quickly built to meet the demand. At first Chartist lodges were held there once a week, often on a Monday or Wednesday night, and the keenest supporters attended more than one society. Membership usually cost a penny a week, and as the number of committed Chartists increased so cards were issued and greater care taken over lodge administration.

6. Zephaniah Williams

Offices in the associations rotated amongst the members, though it was common practice to appoint the innkeeper as treasurer.

As the Chartist movement gathered momentum in the winter of 1838–9, so men of the collieries and ironworks flocked into the new lodges, and began to take positions of responsibility alongside artisans and tradesmen. Esther Pugh, of the Coach and Horses at Blackwood, described the process:

> About 8 or 9 months ago a lodge was opened at the large club room in the house which will hold about 60 people. There were a few shoemakers who began it first—Owen Davies. They were strangers to me. They said their object was to collect a few pence to buy some papers. By degrees people joined. The colliers of the neighbourhood were the principal ones.[58]

Samuel Roberts, Richard Rorke junior, and Thomas Llewellyn were just a sample of the industrial workmen who joined saddlers and shoemakers in the newspaper room at the Coach and Horses, and who pressed their hard-won pennies into the hands of William Barwell, secretary of the association and Richard Pugh, treasurer. Nearby at Pontllanfraith, John Barrill, a collier, became secretary of both the male and female Chartist societies, whilst at Tredegar, John Rees, a mason and ex-military man, and his collier friend, the sandy-haired comedian David Jones, were making their presence felt. Other miners and colliers who became officers of their associations were William Harris of Abersychan, Lewis Rowland at Maesycwmmer, 53-year-old Thomas Giles of Gelligaer, and the fat and balding William Owen of Llancaiach. Not far away, in the lower Rhondda, Dr William Price, a company surgeon, William David, a Dinas shopkeeper, and a weaver named Francis were still urging colliers to join the radical cause, but the general impression in these months is of a flowing mass of black faces and of a small army of new and determined leaders.

By the spring of 1839 Chartism in South Wales had become a political movement based firmly on the family, workplace, and community. At Newport all the members of the Frost, Edwards, and Dickenson households were involved in radical activities, and popular Female Political Union and Boys' Clubs were in existence. The *Monmouthshire Merlin*, aghast at such developments, mocked the presence of the 'lowest ladies' of Mill Street and Friars' Field at Chartist meetings, and the vocal leadership of several women in later disturbances was a source of much respectable anger.[59] On the coalfield the pattern was repeated; female radical associations were established at Blaina, Pontllanfraith, Abersychan, and possibly Pontypool, and women organized money-raising tea-parties, signed petitions in large numbers, and welcomed lecturers to their Dukestown or Blackwood homes.[60] These women, to whom Frost made a special appeal at the beginning of March 1839, knew the loyalties and pressures of mining communities. Ann Thomas, wife of a Coalbrookvale collier, claimed that she attended meetings of female Chartists at the Royal Oak 'to please my husband', and Zephaniah Williams, her host at Blaina, called upon those yet unmarried to choose only Chartist husbands.[61] In the opinion of Williams's counsel at the Special Commission set up to try the Newport rioters, the women of the coalfield were as much Chartists as the men, and the Revd James Coles, chairman of the examining panel of magistrates, declared that 'it is owing to the advice of a great many of you women that we owe all this'.[62] His words were directed at Mary Ferriday, whose husband was killed alongside Abraham Thomas at Newport. 'I used to quarrel on Mondays with my husband about his going to the Chartists Clubs at the Coach and Horses at Blackwood', she later admitted. 'I was known to be against the Chartists. The woman [sic] used to mob me because I would not join them and called me a Tory and abused me whenever I met them.'[63]

There were on the coalfield, as outside, certain well-known Chartist families: the Battens and Fishers of Gelligroes, the Britons of Pontypool, the Johns of Merthyr Tydfil, and many more. It was the Battens, for example, who organized Vincent's meeting at Gelligroes, and when father and son subsequently appeared in court, Coles grieved at this common radical phenomenon.[64] As we shall see later, family connections were one of the networks that made a secret rising possible. The same was true of the work gangs, for these contained some of the closest relationships in industrial society. Capel Hanbury Leigh, the Lord Lieutenant of Monmouthshire, complained at this time that most of the men in the coal- and ironworks around Pontypool had been obliged to join the Chartist lodges, and those workmen who had been persuaded by George Kenrick to sign up as special constables were now afraid to sleep in their homes.[65] At Blackwood and Blaina, miners who refused to sign a Chartist petition and take a card could not expect to win or keep a job. Weeks later, when the plans for a rising were set in motion, small groups of workmen formed natural classes in the Chartist lodges. Virtually all the men from coalfaces at Waterloo, Fleur-de-lis, and Blaina collieries travelled to Newport together.[66]

In these communities working-class organisations and attitudes imprinted themselves on the new political movement. Evening classes, festivals, and processions, common aspects of contemporary religious and self-help institutions, were used to sustain Chartism in Tredegar and Blackwood. Similarly, in the manner of union and Scotch Cattle clubs, many radical meetings on the coalfield began and ended with Welsh prayers, and, as the rising drew near, traditional forms of workers' solidarity appeared. Secret oaths were taken in the Chartist lodges, well-rehearsed threats were issued, and Zephaniah Williams reiterated an old promise that the families of those who fell in the battle would be taken care of.

There was, as John Davies, a Blaina collier, explained, no room for doubt. He went to sign Chartist petitions at the Royal Oak because everyone else had, and people would look 'black at me if I did not do so as well'.[67] Samuel Homfray explained to bemused outsiders that respectable persons in the heart of the coalfield were too insecure to act as specials, and that terrified shopkeepers, anxious to retain miners' custom, could not bring themselves to ask for military help.[68] In such communities, resolutions in favour of exclusive dealing, as recommended by the National Convention, were hardly necessary. As we saw earlier, publicans and shopkeepers like Sarah Edmunds and Jacob Thomas gave regular assistance to the Chartists, and William Edmunds, blacksmith and preacher of Argoed, who stoically refused to join the lodges, was warned that he should seek the proper way of enlightenment.[69]

In the late spring and early summer of 1839 the scale and vigour of the Chartist movement in South Wales seriously worried the authorities. The Marquis of Bute, Lord Lieutenant of Glamorgan, now received regular reports of radical activities at Merthyr and along the border, whilst in Monmouthshire Capel Hanbury Leigh fed the government a diet of alarms and requests for assistance. The visit of Frost and Vincent to Stroud on 28 March gave the Welsh magistrates a brief respite, though the physical injuries which the latter speaker received at a Devizes meeting on 1 April led to another surge of popular anger. Vincent's treatment at Devizes confirmed his opinion of the British aristocracy, and underlined

the importance of seeking new methods of protest and organization. In future, he argued, people should appear in public marching five abreast, under the command of captains and marshals, and
in Blackwood and Newport there was also talk of defensive arming
and giving Tories 'a dose of physic'.[70]

Frost was at home for a few days early in April, but on the sixth of
that month he returned to London, where he expressed concern at
the timorous attitude of Birmingham delegates to the Convention.
In his absence, William Edwards resumed his role as leading Chartist missionary. According to several reports the tone of his speeches
had become more vituperative. On 5 April he attended a meeting at
the King's Head, Pontypool, which was chaired by William Jones,
now emerging as the dominant voice of the local radical association.
Edwards read an account of the Devizes affair and then, to quote the
reporter from the *Monmouthshire Merlin*, he declared that 'every
Whig and Tory ought to have a nail driven through his b——y heart
to a platform'. 'If the Charter was not granted on the 6th of May,' he
continued, 'he would not answer for the consequences.' Edwards
claimed that he had at Blackwood 5,000 followers who could be
called together simply by the sound of a horn.[71]

As he journeyed across the coalfield in the next few days,
Edwards encouraged people to prepare a special welcome for Vincent on his return to South Wales. On the morning of 9 April the
Newport baker arrived back in his home town, and immediately
called a public meeting at the Ship and Pilot. The meeting was
attended by many dock-workers and was chaired by a ship's carpenter, Charles Waters. Two resolutions were carried unanimously,
one expressing confidence in the National Convention, and the
other promising to defend Vincent when he arrived at Newport,
even at the expense of their lives. The only debate concerned
charges of violent language and drunken conduct brought against
Edwards, and on this matter the missionary had a comfortable
majority. On the following day a large crowd, which included some
miners, collected to give Vincent a triumphant reception, but their
hero was not on the steam packet, and so once again Edwards said a
few words. After a further day of collecting signatures for the
National Petition, he set off towards Pontypool. There he delivered
two addresses, one from the window of a private house, and a
second, denouncing the *Merlin* newspaper, to a huge gathering of
ironworkers and colliers at Abersychan.[72]

Meanwhile Vincent, who had been recuperating in Bath, travelled to Bristol on 15 April, and three days later crossed the estuary
to Newport. Samuel Etheridge, secretary of the Working Men's
Association, Edwards, and several hundred sympathizers were
there to greet him. After lunch at Edward Thomas's house in High
Street, Vincent was taken to the Bush Inn, but the number of
people present was so large that it was decided to hold an open-air
meeting. In the evening several hundred people marched five
abreast up to a house at Pentonville, and there the radical printer
lectured on the evils of the aristocracy, the manner in which people
were deprived of their property, and the prospect of a sudden and
sweeping change in the political representation of the country. He
declared his contempt for 'a fellow in this town called Phillips',
comparing him to the Devizes 'scoundrels'. On the following evening, another meeting was held above Mill Street, with William
Townsend junior again presiding, and even hostile sources estimated the number present at one thousand. Most of them—shipwrights, sawyers, smiths, masons, and plasterers—had come from
the Pillgwenlly area, and some of them carried large sticks in their
hands.

Vincent's speech on this occasion lasted all of two hours and was
interrupted only once, when a shout rang out that someone was
about to fire a gun at him. The content of his speech was to be
recalled many times at Vincent's trial in the summer. Apparently,
he talked much about the Charter, the right to resist oppression
and take up arms, and the likely support of the military. 'We will',
he promised, 'assemble on a certain day in thousands and tens of
thousands like the Jews at the Feast of the Passover.' He concluded
with these words: 'When the time for resistance arrives, let your cry
be, "To your tents, O Israel!" and then with one heart, one voice,
and one blow perish the privileged orders! death to the aristocracy!
up with the people, and the government they have established!'[73]
The mayor of Newport, arriving home from Gloucestershire on
that day, suddenly realized that his town was effectively in the
hands of 'the mob', and his urgent letter to the Home Secretary
reminded the government that there were no special constables or
soldiers within miles.[74] Vincent was also aware of this fact, and on
several occasions urged the people of the seaport town to behave in
a peaceful manner.

After a whirlwind visit to Pontypool, where this message was repeated, Vincent returned to Newport, and joined several hundred Chartists at a service in St Paul's church. The minister, the Revd James Francis, had announced that he intended giving a sermon 'to the working classes', and had made a point of inviting the leading radicals. In his sermon, soon to be published, Francis admitted the right of the people to pursue democratic politics, but deprecated the manner in which it was done. For this clergyman, the established powers were ordained of God, and in seeking to change this by force the Chartists were dividing society in a most dangerous way. Even if the Charter were granted tomorrow, it would not signal any moral or religious progress; seek first, said Francis, the kingdom of God.[75]

On the following day Vincent and Edwards accepted another invitation, and set off for a lunchtime meeting outside the Greyhound, Pontllanfraith. About 2.45 p.m., the audience lined up five abreast and, escorted by 200 children carrying flowers and flags, moved up to Blackwood. There the committee of the Working Men's Association had erected hustings and a crowd of perhaps 2,000 heard the chairman, Dr Price of Pontypridd, make the first speech in Welsh. After Vincent's address and tea, it was time to return to Pontllanfraith and an even larger evening meeting in front of the Greyhound. In the morning the missionaries travelled to David Lewis's beerhouse at Brynmawr, where another radical celebrity, Thomas Guttery, introduced the Devizes hero to the men, and many females, present. Then it was off along the tramroad to the Royal Oak at Blaina, and on the way, as we have already seen, Vincent and Edwards came upon Crawshay Bailey. He regretted that they had not been thrown into a nearby pond. The ironmaster defied the Chartists to make any impression on his furnacemen, to which Vincent replied that 'they are my men, as you will see in the evening if you attend the meeting'.[76] In the event, Crawshay Bailey's son, Joseph, candidate for the Monmouth boroughs, attended the gathering, with about twenty clerks, and heard Vincent call upon the people of Wales to stand by him and the Convention. If they were not given their rights, he announced, they would have to fight, but in the meantime he appealed for order and discipline.

The next few days can be regarded as one of the critical periods in the story of the Chartist rising. After further meetings at Pontypool and Blaenavon, Vincent arrived back at Newport on Thursday. Two hundred leading inhabitants had taken the opportunity of his absence to request an improvement in the forces of law and order. On 24 April the borough magistrates, Thomas Phillips, William Brewer, and Lewis Edwards, issued a notice, declaring recent assemblies in the town illegal, cautioning people from holding meetings and processions, and warning publicans against allowing Chartists to use their premises for this purpose. On the following day over a hundred specials were sworn in, a reserve force for the soldiers who were expected shortly.[77]

The battle lines had thus been drawn and Vincent's first act on entering Newport was to cross them. A radical address was quickly printed, defiantly calling people to attend a meeting on the evening of 25 April. After a parade through the streets to cries of 'Britons never will be slaves', several thousand people waited impatiently for Dickenson, the pork-butcher, to introduce the star attraction. Vincent mocked the mayor's proclamation, and defied the magistrates to arrest him. He urged the working class of Newport—'Citizens of the British Democracy'—to behave well, but his own words stirred the emotions. These extracts printed in the local newspaper two days later, may contain inaccuracies but the tone is authentic:

The men of Newport have declared they will adhere to the principles of the Charter. Were you honest when you said so? ('We are') Then I understand you; you should all join arm in arm—you should unite so as not to be separated. I shall go to London next week and I will know what to say to the Convention. . . . If circumstances were to occur in London which will deprive me of my liberty, you must not be discouraged, but hold two meetings where you now hold one. I do not mind temporary imprisonment, . . . show your enemies that you will meet when you please, where you please, and how you please. If your rights are not conceded, then the people must commence a movement; you must shake yourselves about— . . . Because they [the aristocracy] will not come down, they will be brought down, to their sorrow. . . . I will conclude by asking you a question. Will you keep the peace, in the event of a disturbance in the town? ('We will!') Will you protect the life and property of all individuals of whatever political creed? ('We will!') I shall then consider you as special constables. If your magistrates will not keep the peace, . . . lay hold of them, and put them in a coal-hole. If Lord John Russell or Lord Melbourne will not keep the peace, you must take them into custody.[78]

On the following day the normal life of the town continued to be interrupted by crowds eager for more of the same, and, after a speech from the window of Frost's house, Vincent was taken by Townsend down to the quayside. There he made another speech, taunting magistrates, specials, and yeomanry, and, according to his own version, the shipwrights cheered and delighted sailors ran flags up the ship bound for Bristol.[79] After his departure all afternoon long the people roamed the streets.

For several days Townsend and Dickenson organized a series of open-air meetings at Newport, and such was the intensity of popular agitation that shopkeepers closed their doors and business activity was much reduced. According to the *Merlin*, the tension of this period also affected the Chartist leadership. It seems likely that a split had developed between Samuel Etheridge, the elder statesman of Newport radicalism, and the fiery, heavy-drinking Edwards. On 7 May the secretary of the Working Men's Association issued a circular condemning violence and reiterating Chartist respect for persons and property. A reporter for the *Merlin* also suggested that William Jones had repudiated Edwards's violent rhetoric at Dukestown and Risca meetings on 1 and 2 May.[80] On the former occasion Edwards and other speakers arrived in a four-wheeled chaise, decorated with a Union Jack and two radical flags. They were met by four magistrates and over 800 people who had marched behind bands and banners from all parts of the coalfield. In the Star Field they listened to speeches in Welsh and English from half a dozen people, and officially appointed Frost as Convention delegate for 'the Monmouthshire hills'. Five days later the exercise was repeated, although this time the venue was Blackwood, and the gathering even larger.[81]

The sixth of May had originally been chosen for the presentation of the People's Charter to Parliament, and the authorities were extremely sensitive to any activity at this time. At Pontypool all the shops were closed, 1,500 specials were sworn in, and the respectable watched nervously as more than 600 people paraded the town before setting off to join their comrades to the west.[82] At Merthyr Tydfil there were similar anxieties, whilst Thomas Booker and Capt. Howells informed the Marquis of Bute that Dr Price, William David, and others were stirring up the men of the Rhondda valleys.[83] Another prevalent fear at this time was that the railway navvies, canal boatmen, and colliers in the Swansea valley might join any demonstration planned in Monmouthshire, but on 6 May comparatively few Glamorgan men travelled to Blackwood. In a sense it did not matter, for the great petition with its 1,280,000 signatures was not presented to Parliament, and on the following day the government resigned. The 'day of reckoning' had therefore come and gone, and another chapter in the history of Chartism had begun.

As the Chartists rightly claimed, the speeches and atmosphere of these demonstrations in late March, April, and early May cannot be appreciated without a close knowledge of the psychology and actions of the authorities in South Wales. A few weeks after the government had removed John Frost from the commission of the peace, the propertied classes in the area began their own assault on the radical movement. It was a calculated policy which they were later to recommend to magistrates across Britain. In its early stages the assault involved pressure on radicals at every point of their personal and political life. One aspect of this was the decision of Capel Hanbury Leigh, Crawshay Bailey, and Thomas Powell to refuse employment to known Chartists. David Lewis of the King Crispin, Brynmawr, claimed that Bailey sacked three workmen for being avowed radicals and for reading the *Western Vindicator*. With the blessing of the Nantyglo ironmaster, 'a band of ruffians' also entered the Royal Oak, tore a copy of the National Petition to shreds, and declared Zephaniah Williams's beerhouse out of bounds to Bailey's men. Similarly, at Newport, John Matthews openly admitted sacking one of his shoemakers because of his loud condemnation of magistrates and constables.[84]

At the same time landlords, publicans, and tradesmen were forbidden to deal with Chartists or to provide accommodation for them. On 12 April, for instance, William Edwards found that no publican in Pontypool would let him a room, and, like other speakers in that town and in Monmouth, he was obliged to speak from the windows of a friendly householder. Samuel Homfray was proud of the fact that no beerhouse was built and no radical meeting held on his land, and, when he learnt of the planned demonstration at Dukestown on 1 May, he ordered publicans and beerhouse-keepers to close their premises for half a day.[85] The threat of losing their licences persuaded many publicans in the summer of 1839 of the wisdom of acceding to the magistrates' requests. The same can be said of several clergymen who, from self-interest and conviction, now added their weight to the campaign of exclusion and intimidation. The sermon by the Revd James Francis on 21 April was followed in the next three months by a series of outspoken denunciations of 'Levellers' by Anglicans and Wesleyans at Blackwood, Varteg, and other places. This concerted religious attack included threats of excommunication and the sending of a loyal address to the Queen from the Baptist Association meeting at Risca.[86]

The policy of making life as difficult as possible for Chartists was accompanied by attempts, notably in the second half of April, to harass and even prohibit their meetings. Crawshay Bailey's strong-arm tactics, blunt messages from managers to Pontypool workmen, the banning of the use of town criers and premises, the presence of magistrates and note-taking policemen, and the physical intimidation of some special constables were all intended to limit the exercise of a popular right. The Newport proclamation of 24 April, issued with the full consent of the government, and later extended to some of the mining towns, was the ultimate weapon, and nothing caused more annoyance than this. In the opinion of Feargus O'Connor and John Frost the denial of a right which the Home Secretary had espoused only eight months previously was a major contribution to subsequent conflict, and it certainly identified Phillips, Brewer, and Edwards as enemies of the people. On 27 April Frost published a letter to the Working Men's Association in his town, describing the proclamation as 'a declaration of war!'

It is a declaration of war against your rights as Citizens, against your liberty, against your property; it is an attempt, a bare-faced impudent attempt to prevent you from endeavouring peaceably and constitutionally to change a system founded on bribery, drunkenness, and perjury!!! It is an attempt to uphold a disgraceful system because it suits the purpose of the signers. ... Are they aware that PEACE, LAW, AND ORDER is the motto of the Chartists? Are they aware that from the great meeting at Birmingham, to the Tory attack at Devizes not a single breach of the peace was committed at any Chartist meeting? ... Let the magistrates and constables beware how they act. Their proclamation does not carry with it the force of Law, though it is given under their hands. If they exceed their power, they must take the consequences.[87]

At meetings in the next few weeks Frost quoted the lawyer Black-stone in defence of the right to hold public meetings, and feared that Monmouthshire magistrates were setting an example for the rest of Britain.

In the considered judgement of both Frost and Vincent the only illegal meetings and activities in South Wales had been those of the propertied classes. Leading gentlemen in Monmouthshire, recall-ing their experience in the years of Captain Swing and the Reform crisis, once again established associations for the 'Protection of Life and Property'. Led by an enthusiastic Thomas Phillips, over a hun-dred people with some Yeomanry experience met on 12 April at Christchurch, a village three miles outside Newport. Amongst thóse present were the three borough magistrates and Thomas Prothero, the Revd A. A. Isaacson, and the Revd R. A. Roberts, clergyman of the parish. The last, one of Frost's declared enemies, was virulent in his condemnation of the Chartists, and it was he who proposed a loyal address to the Queen. For his part, Thomas Phillips insisted that it was time for them to make a stand against people of violence, and he moved a second resolution offering to enrol themselves in any form suitable to the government. The chairman, William Phillips, concluded by recommending them to 'keep your powder dry, and to make your horses stand fire', a remark which incensed the local Chartists. Some weeks later other defence associations were formed at Monmouth and Pontypool, and the latter had four divisions for the town and surrounding min-ing districts. William Needham was elected as its captain com-mandant, and other officers included George Kenrick, John Laurence, Edmund Edwards, and C. H. Croft. To the annoyance of some county gentlemen these associations were initially only disciplined and permanent bodies of special constables, but the Chartists correctly surmised that the Home Secretary was supply-ing them with arms. Those intended for the Newport association were placed in the depot of the 29th Regiment on Stow hill.[88]

The 'Christchurch Yeomanry', as it was popularly known, was hated by the Chartists. They claimed that it was not, as portrayed, a collection of anxious farmers, but a respectable front for Thomas Phillips and his Newport colleagues. Frost appeared genuinely sad that a number of old reforming allies and potential middle-class friends had joined such an organization, and its prominent mem-bers were constantly mocked in the radical press.[89] John Lovell insisted that the men armed by this association were brutal in their crowd control, and this message captures the perceived spirit of the recruits:

The time is approaching when you may have to show yourselves. Chivalric soldiers, should Vincent ever make his appearance in Newport again, we'll do for him. When Frost returns home we'll have him.[90]

This evoked memories of Vincent's treatment at Devizes, and brought warnings from Blackwood and other lodges that similar conduct would not be tolerated in South Wales. On the occasion of Vincent's departure for Bristol on 25 April the mayor and town clerk of Newport had to rescue a horseman who had hit someone in the crowd.

At the end of April and beginning of May the intentions of the gentlemen of the county were made plain in words and deeds. At few other times in Welsh history have class differences and ideology been so stark. On 29 April several hundred people gathered in the heart of Chartist country, at Coalbrookvale. The chairman of the meeting was Crawshay Bailey, and alongside him were ministers of religion, both Anglican and Dissenting, works managers, agents, and tradesmen and publicans who were about to lose their Chartist custom. According to Bailey's son this was 'not a political meeting', simply an opportunity to express their loyalty to the Queen and constitution. Many of the speeches were, nevertheless, a concerted attack on radical missionaries in general and Vincent in particular. 'I have known some of you upwards of twenty years', said the chairman, 'and we have lived pleasantly together without the interference of strangers. . . . Will Vincent, or the Newport baker, or any other Chartist, come among you and lay out capital, thereby giving you employment? . . . I owe all that I have to my own industry and I would risk my life rather than lose my property.' 'Who is Vincent?' asked the next speaker, George Brewer. 'Is he a Cymro?—No. Is he a resident in this country?—No. Is he a gentleman?—No. To you he is a stranger.' John Brown, an industrial colleague, also attacked Vincent, the debtor William Edwards, and the infidel Zephaniah Williams, whilst the Revd Benjamin Williams denied that the Chartists were religious people, and proffered the gentlemen on the platform as the workmen's true friends. Thomas

Brown had a special role; he was one of the few native entrepreneurs present who could, with any conviction, call the Chartists 'outsiders'.[91]

The determination of the authorities, so openly expressed at this Coalbrookvale gathering, was fuelled by an awareness of defensive measures taken and planned around the coalfield. Besides the ban on meetings and the formation of associations, special constables were being appointed, pensioners had been alerted for possible duty, and arms were being collected. In addition, Capel Hanbury Leigh was pressing the government to send policemen and soldiers to aid the civil power, and, by the second week of May, Newport, Abergavenny, and Monmouth had a military presence.[92] On 2 May 120 men of the 29th Regiment arrived in Newport, under the command of Major Wrottesley, and on the following day many of them were billeted in a ward of the workhouse at the top of Stow hill.[93] On their arrival the Chartists greeted them with three cheers, but their appearance in the town was a new source of discontent and reinforced Frost's prejudice against Thomas Phillips, Lewis Edwards, and parson Roberts. It was a matter of deep Chartist irony that an institution for the poor should be used to house troops, and, at a meeting of the Poor Law authority, Frost protested vigorously about this to Sir Digby Mackworth, the chairman, and to his fellow guardian Phillips. Major Wrottesley replied that he was afraid of people 'tampering' with his men if they were billeted in public houses, a fear fully justified during the 29th's six-month stay in the town.[94]

Within a matter of days of the soldiers' arrival at Newport the borough magistrates took a further initiative. On 1 May, after some important preparatory legal work by Thomas Phillips, the Home Office gave approval for proceedings to be started against Vincent, Edwards, Dickenson, and Townsend, and promised to reimburse any expenses. As in other parts of Britain, it had been decided to take certain Chartist leaders out of circulation. Warrants were issued on 7 May, but Edwards was in Bristol and Vincent a further hundred miles away. William Homan, superintendent of police at Tredegar, was given the task of finding and arresting the Englishman. In London Homan had interviews with Lord John Russell and Sir Frederick Roe before apprehending Vincent on his return from a Chartist meeting in the city. The policeman refused to let the missionary see a legal adviser, and on 9 May they set out for Newport.[95]

What happened then was almost a rehearsal for the November rising. News of the arrests had leaked out, and hundreds of people, including miners from Blackwood and even further afield, filled the streets. The soldiers of the 29th Regiment were on alert all day but deliberately kept out of sight, and the daunting business of controlling the milling crowds was put in the hands of 300 special constables. At the King's Head, Capel Hanbury Leigh, Reginald Blewitt, Thomas Phillips, William Brewer, Lewis Edwards, and half a dozen other magistrates began the examinations, and all was fairly peaceful until Edwards arrived by boat from Bristol and was arrested in front of a jeering crowd in High Street. When, about three o'clock, Vincent also appeared, a pitched battle broke out. The special constables were pelted with stones, and in turn were accused of hitting women and children. Several people were arrested for trying to rescue the Chartist leaders, and one of them, Thomas Llewellyn, who lived near Fleur-de-lis colliery, we shall meet again on the day of the rising. Others secured during the rioting were two prominent radicals John Lovell and Charles Waters, one William Williams, and Thomas Davies, who attacked the mayor. A woman who led the assault on special constables in front of the King's Head was also apprehended, and so was Joshua Davies, who made a valiant attempt to rescue her.

Inside the hotel the case against the four Chartists continued, and it was decided to send them for trial at the next assizes on charges of conspiracy and illegal assembling. Much to the anger of Vincent, bail for him and his three friends was set impossibly high, but for the moment his and the prosecutors' attention was distracted by the noisy mob outside. It was said that the printer failed to persuade the authorities to give him the opportunity of pacifying his supporters, and the task was taken in hand by John Frost, who had just returned from the National Convention. From the window of his house in Mill Street he urged people to be peaceful and to return home. Despite the mayor's hostile version of Frost's role, the draper made great efforts then and on later occasions to damp down the anger of rank-and-file Chartists.[96] Like Zephaniah Williams, he compared his position in the summer of 1839 to that of the moderate men in eighteenth-century France who were pushed into revolution by a stubborn and aristocratic government.[97] An anonymous letter, sent to Thomas Phillips at this time, declared that Frost had done much 'to sooth irritated minds' and warned that his arrest, which the Newport magistrates favoured, would 'prove fatal to the town'.[98]

It is perhaps easier for historians than it was for Chartist leaders to appreciate why the gentlemen of South Wales had become so aggressive. A reading of private correspondence and government papers for the spring and early summer of 1839 indicates some of the reasons for tension. First, the authorities detected a change in the audience and speeches at radical meetings. At Newport, for instance, many of the processions began in the dockland area of Pillgwenlly, and elsewhere there were fears that navvies, canal boatmen, the unemployed, and even criminals were beginning to be affected by Chartist propaganda. William Edwards seems to have had a particular affinity with the poorly paid, and, like William Jones and Thomas Guttery, he attacked workhouses and the treatment meted out to paupers. In one speech at Varteg, Edwards claimed that those offered indoor relief were being poisoned, and, at the beginning of May, the Poor Law Guardians at Newport offered a reward of £10 for the prosecution of the person who had circulated rumours that a pregnant woman had died because of 'gross cruelty' in their workhouse.[99]

Many of the Chartists' speeches in Newport or Pontypool still turned on the evils of the aristocracy, but on the coalfield, as an address from Merthyr Tydfil noted, radicalism increasingly reflected the antagonism between employers and workmen. In the Chartist lodges there was much talk of the atrocious working conditions, the employment of women and children underground, the truck system, the tyranny of some employers, and the lack of insurance for the injured and the old. Vincent, speaking at the King Crispin on 23 April, offered the prospect of a six-hour day once the Charter had been obtained.[100] Perhaps, however, it was the radical discussions of the problems of the trade cycle and the need to defend the rights and property of labour which caused most anxiety amongst employers. Crawshay Bailey, like the manager of the British Iron Works at Abersychan some months later, had heard talk that his employees wished for a stake in his company, and there were even suggestions that those employers who criticized workmen should dig the coal themselves.

The second source of tension was yet more alarming. In the first half of 1839 the Chartists, and especially Henry Vincent, brought the mining communities closer to each other and to the outside world. As we have seen, national unions and local attempts at workers' combinations had foundered on the rock of valley mentality, and there were, even in these months, villages which were slow to take up the Chartist challenge or to share the pride of Merthyr and Blackwood in their political collections and petitions. Yet this great movement, with its ideology, organization, newpapers, and missionaries, did create for a time the spectre of united class action. In February the many personal contacts between South Wales and the west of England were formalized by a delegates' conference at Bath and the establishment of the *Western Vindicator*. 'We shall', said Vincent to a Pontypool audience in April, 'be linked together as one man.'[101] On another occasion he exclaimed:

I shall tell them [the Convention] that I have brought with me the hands of the Bristol men, and the Monmouthshire men, and the Berkshire men, and so on all the way up to London. In the Convention I shall meet Feargus O'Connor who will bring in the hands of the men in the North of England; and then will come in Bailey [*sic*] Craig from Scotland, and all the other delegates from the east and west, with the united hands of the people.[102]

Soon communications were established, for example, between Pontypool, Birmingham, and Sunderland, and the sympathy expressed in South Wales for the plight of the cotton-workers and for Irish independence illustrates the widening horizons. Frost lectured all over Britain and, like Hugh Williams, Charles Jones, and other leading Welsh Chartists, he had a European and even world vision.[103] This in itself produced a few gasps of surprise from the propertied people, although as the Coalbrookvale rally indicated, what really concerned the authorities was the growing pride of industrial workmen in being part of a national movement. To understand the story of the rising it is important to realize that ordinary Chartists treated the National Petition and the requests of the Convention with the utmost seriousness.

The final source of anxiety on the part of the propertied classes were the physical expressions of this political commitment. In the spring workers from Tredegar to Newport echoed Vincent's warning that the National Petition was the first and last of its kind. Moreover, if, as a Blackwood collier feared, Convention delegates were arrested when the time came to present the great document, 'we intend to take the petition up ourselves, and sign it in their presence in characters too legible to be misunderstood'.[104] About this time notions of a people's army, as recommended in Col. Macerone's *Defensive Instructions for the People* (1832), began to circulate. Rumours abounded in South Wales that, in case of difficulties on 6 May, weapons were being stockpiled and industrial action contemplated. According to Thomas Phillips, guns and muskets had been sent from Birmingham to Pontypool and Tredegar, arms clubs had been formed, and there were exaggerated claims that William Townsend junior and Chartist hawkers were involved in the gun trade.[105] Captain Howells, investigating such matters for the Marquis of Bute, also suggested that workmen on the Glamorgan side of the border had obtained firearms, and there was some vague talk of pikes being made in the foundries and smithies of the ironworks and dockyards.[106]

As 6 May approached so the tension mounted. In the vicinity of Tredegar, Dukestown, Blackwood, and Varteg there were familiar signs that workmen were willing to use their industrial muscle.[107] Some of the ironworkers, and all the men at the collieries to the south, gave a month's notice that they intended to stop work on or about 1 May, and some of them held nightly meetings thereafter. William Jones and Thomas Parry certainly expressed opinions in favour of strike action, and the mayor of Monmouth believed that it was their intention to make 'a movement' on about 6 May and 'to march in conjunction with other forces to London'.[108] William Needham of the Varteg ironworks was one of several industrialists who made considerable efforts to stop their men from joining the Chartists at this time, but with very limited success. In his neighbourhood a kind of general panic spread in early May, and 'neither orders nor money could be had on account of the excitement'.[109] Eventually, however, the local Chartists decided to follow the instructions of Frost and the Convention, and postponed action until a later date.

In the meantime the matter of the petition had been overtaken by news of the arrival of soldiers in the district and of Vincent's arrest in London. A glance at the neglected Treasury Solicitor's papers reveals the extent of hostility which the authorities faced in executing this aggressive policy. The Chartists made considerable efforts to influence the 29th Regiment, and more than a dozen soldiers deserted. Some went up to Tredegar, and perhaps one of these was killed at the Westgate hotel on 4 November. In the government papers there are also copies of anonymous letters warning Phillips and Prothero in particular that 30,000 armed men from Merthyr, Blackwood, and Pontypool would descend on them if Vincent were placed in custody.[110] After Vincent's arrest fears grew of an outbreak 'on the hills', whilst at Monmouth a troop of the 29th Regiment, half a dozen London policemen, and 150 specials defended the gaol in which he was incarcerated.

The irony of all this was not lost on the Welsh Chartists, who had behaved with exceptional restraint up until 10 May. The authorities had pre-empted the use of physical force and potential middle-class allies had deserted 'the people' at a crucial moment. 'The time is come,' wrote Edwards from his prison cell, 'those that are not for us are against us.'[111] Frost, sent down from the Convention on 9 May to prevent the kind of spontaneous combustion that had occurred in Mid-Wales, knew who was to blame. The Newport magistrates 'are brave men to be sure, and when the hour of trial arrives, which cannot be very distant, they will be found at their post, and that post, let me tell them, will require quite as much courage as they possess'.[112] Like other Chartist leaders, Frost found it hard to control passions in the world of politics which he had helped to create.

The Tide of Revolution

On 15 May John Frost wrote to William Lovett, one of the founders of Chartism, telling him of his fears that the people would become either totally dispirited or rebellious and that both moods could prove fatal to the cause.[1] Amongst the authorities at Newport the notice against public meetings and the committal of the Chartist leaders produced much satisfaction. It was claimed that, for weeks afterwards, the streets of the town were free of the sound and disturbance of processions. Other political meetings, however, continued to be held, and right across South Wales preparations were put in hand for a great Whit Monday gathering at Blackwood on 20 May. As this day, nominated by the National Convention for simultaneous meetings, approached, William Jones and eight other householders of Pontypool and Abersychan astonished Capel Hanbury Leigh by asking him to take the chair, whilst at Dowlais, Pontypridd, and Dukestown Chartists met nightly to choose guest speakers and plan the route and time of their marches. On 13 May, hearing of a recent meeting at Morlais and concerned at the outcome of that at Blackwood, Sir Josiah John Guest sent for Dr Price and warned him of the dangers of proselytizing amongst the colliers of Dinas and Llanfabon. 'He owned being favourable to Chartism', Charlotte Guest noted in her diary, 'but disclaimed all idea of physical force, which he said had almost determined him to abandon the doctrine altogether.'[2]

On the day of the Blackwood demonstration the Guests decided to stay at home, as did many other of their friends. Charlotte believed that the families from her district were unlikely to be riotous, but William Thomas of Merthyr, Samuel Homfray, and two other magistrates attended the meeting. Estimates of numbers present varied from the *Monmouthshire Merlin*'s figure of 4,000–5,000 to some 30,000. Most of William Crawshay's workmen, and some of those from Dowlais, were in the crowd, and the hundreds that came from as far as Pontypool and Newport brought with them the two principal speakers, Jones and Frost. With its flags, bands, and stalls, the meeting had something of a carnival atmosphere, but the political objectives were grave. The people had assembled to adopt a radical address to the Queen, which expressed their anger over the treatment of imprisoned Chartists. They also renewed their faith in delegate Frost, and considered the 'ulterior measures' drawn up by the National Convention. Frost, after reading from Blackstone to prove the legality of their proceedings, gave his own views of the following proposals:

(1) withdrawing savings from banks

(2) converting paper money into gold

(3) supporting a 'sacred month', at the same time abstaining from intoxicants

(4) preparing themselves with arms to defend the laws

(5) adopting Chartist candidates at the next election, who would be considered the people's representatives

(6) dealing exclusively with tradesmen who favoured Chartism

(7) agitating for nothing less than the Charter

(8) obeying all the just and constitutional requests of the majority of the Convention.

Although there was some concern at the hesitancy and confusion which had characterized the national movement at the beginning of May, all eight of these Convention proposals were adopted. The meeting concluded, as it had begun, with a prayer, and cheers rang out for William Crawshay and Somers Harford, who, it was hoped, had some sympathy with the workers' political ambitions.[3]

What happened to the Chartist movement in the next few weeks cannot be fully reconstructed. In at least some parts of the coalfield the story was one of growth, inspired as elsewhere by the Birmingham Bull Ring riots. The respectable inhabitants of Pontypool estimated on 19 July that there were at least 4,000 known Chartists in the vicinity, and warned the Lord Lieutenant of the dangers of a 'Birmingham' outbreak. 'I am sorry to say', wrote James Brown of the Cwm Celyn and Blaina ironworks at the same time, 'that I believe the ranks of the Chartists to be rapidly upon the increase. . . .'[4] A report in the *Silurian* on 6 July stated that over 1,000 men and women had already joined the associations at Dukestown and Rhymney, and a few days earlier Dr Price, William Jones, and William David had addressed several hundred eager listeners in Pontypridd. The Working Men's Association in Merthyr was also expanding at the rate of 100–120 members a week after the excitement of the Blackwood gathering, and it was suggested that members of the middle class were at last sympathetic to the radical cause.[5]

The last comment probably referred to the fact that a subscription for the political prisoners, popularly known as the Vincent Defence Fund, had been set up, and considerable numbers of tradesmen in the iron towns were persuaded, or intimidated, into contributing.[6] The Fund acted as a catalyst for renewed energy and organization, especially amongst the female radicals, and by the end of July several hundred pounds had been collected. The districts of Merthyr, Blackwood, Pontypool, Newport, and Tredegar were, as usual, at the top of the lists.[7] It was said later that, in some areas, the division of Chartist associations into sub-groups began in connection with this activity. William Griffiths, one of Capel Hanbury Leigh's colliers, remembered being called before the Pontnewydd committee and having his name entered in a long book.[8]

About this time, too, a number of large meetings were held in South Wales, often with the expressed intention of addressing the Queen or supporting petitions against government Bills.[9] The first of these was held at the Rhymney ironworks early in June, and within a fortnight crowds of 5,000–8,000 had gathered at Hirwaun and Penrheolgerrig, and smaller meetings took place at Nantyglo, Blackwood, and Pontypool. John Frost, William Jones, and Morgan Williams were amongst the chief speakers, and the Newport Chartist devoted much of his lectures to the need to support the Convention and to prepare for the coming financial crisis. Frost was also advertised as one of the principal speakers at a Chartist rally on 1 July, but was unable to attend because the Convention was reassembling at Birmingham.[10]

This meeting, at Coalbrookvale on 1 July, was so typical in size and character that it is worth looking at it in a little detail. By 3.30 p.m. on that Monday as many as 10,000 people from the industrial valleys had reached the spot, and above them flew a dozen Chartist banners with the motto 'Peace, Law and Order—Union is Strength'. The chair was taken by the elderly, bespectacled Tredegar shoemaker, Thomas Davies, and the meeting began with William Williams reciting a prayer in Welsh. After speeches in Welsh from Richard Jones and Daniel Williams of Rhymney, it was the turn of William Jones, who had now firmly stepped into the lecturing shoes of the imprisoned William Edwards. He explained the Charter to the crowd, attacked the reporting of the *Monmouth-shire Merlin*, and denied that Chartism was dying a natural death. For one and a half hours he criticized ministers of the crown, high taxation, the church establishment, union workhouses, and Sir Digby Mackworth. Then, as the meeting was about to close, 'a man jumped up and said, that the Chartists now in Monmouth and other gaols, were prisoners not in their own but the people's cause'.[11]

William Jones's comment about the anticipated death of the radical movement is an interesting one. In spite of these obvious signs of political agitation on the coalfield, and the spread of Chartism to Cardiff and Swansea, Pryce Pryce, Charlotte Guest, and others described the movement as 'a dead letter'.[12] In July those with the task of judging the state of popular feeling reported that trouble was not expected. Captain Howells, visiting Merthyr, Rhymney, Bute, Tredegar, and Caerphilly in those days found the ironworks 'in full employ' and the outlook decidedly peaceful. As a precaution, he asked policeman Homan to contact him immediately should the need arise.[13] Howells, and Edward Dowling of the *Monmouthshire Merlin*, were especially pleased by the conviction of the Chartist prisoners at the county assizes, and the spirit with which the sentences were received. 'The most perfect order reigned in Monmouth, Newport, and the other towns', recalled the editor. 'The months of August, September, and October passed over, without alarm, and all were lulled into fancied security.'[14]

This confidence of the leaders of South Wales society, so severely criticized in the inquests after the rising, is easy to comprehend. Defensive measures, notably the organization of special constables and of the West Monmouthshire Association for the Protection of Life and Property, proceeded apace, and there was much satisfaction that magistrates across Britain were following the example of this industrial county. Chartist leaders were harassed and arrested, and the Convention decimated. Some of its leading members were arrested in July and August, often on flimsy charges, and were given prohibitively high bail. In Warwickshire three men were sentenced to death, whilst closer to home, W. P. Roberts, William Carrier, and William Potts were apprehended at Devizes. Frost himself, who offered assistance to his friend Roberts, was also under threat. Speaking for much of respectable opinion in South

Wales, the *Monmouthshire Merlin* and the *Merthyr Guardian* approved this tough policy, and, when serious rioting broke out at Birmingham early in July, the latter recommended that soldiers and policemen should fire not 'over the heads of the people but *at the mob*, and if possible, at those who are evidently *leaders of the mob*'.[15] 'Let them repress their patience', said Zephaniah Williams in response to such aggression, 'if the Chartists must fight, I do believe it will not be an old woman's squabble; and I am persuaded, that in that case the fiercest assailer of the workmen's patience would have his bellyful ere the end.'[16]

For these men of property the punishment of Vincent and Edwards was 'far too lenient'. At the Monmouth assizes on 2 August the Chartists were ably defended by John Arthur Roebuck, the reforming MP for Bath. They were found guilty of attending illegal meetings, and the Englishman received one year's imprisonment and the Welshman nine months. Dickenson and Townsend were each sentenced to only six months, on account, it was said, of their social status and age. The trial was, as intended, a show-piece, with Samuel Homfray and leading county families cheering from the Grand Jury box and newspaper reporters vying for the best positions. Roebuck claimed that the Chartists were no more dangerous than the Whigs at the time of the Reform crisis, but Baron Alderson and the jury, who took fifteen minutes to reach their verdict, were in no mood to listen.

Everyone knew, of course, including the jurymen and some of the reluctant witnesses, that they were now marked men. The London policemen and the soldiers guarding the court-house, and the poisonous letters already in the post, left no room for doubt. So did the crowds chanting 'Vincent for ever' as the prisoners were removed to gaol. For weeks the treatment of these political martyrs was the dominant issue for radicals, journalists, magistrates, and even members of Parliament. Baron Alderson, in a letter to the Under-Secretary of State at the Home Office, stated that the Chartists should 'not be subject to undue indignity', and should be given special privileges in gaol, but the governor of the prison did not fully heed the advice.[17] They were treated, in almost all respects, like convicted felons. The *Western Vindicator* carried graphic accounts of the insults which Vincent had to endure, and on 22 August protests from the prisoners were presented to both Houses of Parliament.

With their hero in gaol, and with the Convention and other

forms of protest declared illegal, it was hardly surprising that the minds of Welsh Chartists turned to the theory and character of revolutionary action. The right to resist a tyrannical and unconstitutional government was a central tenet of Painite radicalism, and the Chartists took as their example the behaviour of the middle class during the Reform crisis. 'Are the magistrates of Newport aware', asked Frost in May 1839, 'that during the agitation for the Reform Bill, many men, high in authority, advised the people to resist the law?'[18] In fact, 'one of the most noisy brawlers for Reform' had been Thomas Phillips. Initially, Chartists like William Edwards and Henry Vincent were at pains to underline the peaceful nature of their movement and were drawn unwillingly into a discussion of physical force. 'The Chartists have not the slightest intention of appealing to arms', said the latter in March, 'EXCEPT IN SELF-DEFENCE'.[19] In spite of considerable provocation in the following months, no serious outbreak of disorder occurred in South Wales.

As the radicals became more pessimistic and alarmed by government policy in the summer of 1839, so the debate on their own defensive preparations increased. At the beginning of June it was suggested that Lord John Russell should provide them with the following number of weapons in case of assault by armed associations, specials, and the police: Newport district 5,000, Pontypool 8,000, Caerleon and vicinity 500, Blackwood and Tredegar districts 10,000, Nantyglo and its vicinity 10,000, and the Merthyr area 20,000.[20] Expressions of defiance, and a determination to repel 'force by force', were now a regular feature of lodge meetings, especially in the region of Pontypool. At the town's Working Men's Association on 22 July the following resolutions were agreed unanimously:

1st. That as the Convention have hitherto strenuously advocated the rights of the unrepresented millions of this country, they are worthy of our support, and we are determined to defend them to the death; we also most earnestly request all who are able, to provide themselves with arms immediately.

2nd. That we view with indignation the cowardly attack of the Government upon the brave men of Birmingham, and we are determined to provide ourselves with the arms of freemen, to defend our wives and labour against the illegal attacks of our oppressors.

3rd. That this meeting is of opinion that we shall never obtain just and equal laws for the industrious wealth-producers of this country, until the People's Charter becomes the law of the land; and we therefore present our united thanks to Messrs Attwood, Fielden, and others, for their exertions in endeavouring to obtain justice for all classes.[21]

Five days earlier, the neighbouring association at Abersychan had also stated its abhorrence of the behaviour of London policemen in Birmingham, advocated exclusive dealing against clergymen and the apathetic middle class, and implored the Convention to seize the initiative now that Parliament had turned down the people's demands.[22]

It was indeed the outright rejection of the National Petition by the House of Commons on 12 July which obliged the Chartists to consider other methods of advancing their case. Some Convention delegates, including Frost, believed strongly that an economic crisis was imminent and that, with careful planning, the people could induce a financial panic that would bring the government to its senses. In July a delegate meeting of Welsh Chartists recommended withdrawing money from banks and changing paper money into gold, and the *Western Vindicator* urged that taxes should not be paid in cash and that radicals should abstain from using exciseable commodities.[23] On the eve of the rising some workmen did refuse to accept paper money, but in industrial South Wales financial measures were unlikely to have a major influence on ministers of the crown. As James Bufften of Pontypool explained, they could only make life difficult for the government.

Two 'ulterior measures' were, nevertheless, almost designed for use in the mining communities. Exclusive dealing was not something new to the district, but in the late spring and summer it was adopted by one meeting after another. Chartist associations at Abersychan, Pontypridd, and Coalbrookvale stiffened their resolve, and identified certain ministers of religion, local government officers, tradesmen, and prosecution witnesses who had shown themselves hostile to the people's cause. At Merthyr Tydfil female Chartists stopped buying goods from those shopkeepers who refused to contribute to the Defence Fund, whilst in the Pontypool area chapel members withdrew their financial support from ministers who threatened radicals with excommunication.[24] How effective all this was is difficult to estimate. There were professional men and liberal tradesmen who later regretted their attendance at anti-Chartist rallies and their open hostility to Henry Vincent, but exclusive dealing was open to abuse and it made little impact on central government.

The other measure which evoked a significant response in South Wales provided a greater threat to the authorities. This was a proposal for a general strike, or 'sacred month', and discussion of it dominated Convention debates after 12 July. The idea had been recommended a decade before by William Benbow, and behind it was the belief that when work ceased the whole fabric of society would fall apart. As we saw earlier, there had been support for such a strike in Monmouthshire in the spring, but Frost and some of the more cautious Chartists on the Glamorgan border had been anxious to postpone it. On 2 July, however, chairing the Convention which had just reopened in Birmingham, the Welsh delegate declared himself in favour of the sacred month, and the message was repeated at a closed meeting of Cardiff Chartists thirteen days later. According to the local police superintendent Frost warned them 'of the certainty of a great commotion shortly taking place, when they must be ready "shoulder to shoulder". They must rise against their present rulers simultaneously and . . . he as their delegate would inform them of the time.'[25]

The tenor of this speech contrasts somewhat with the open declarations of Frost in the Convention. Like other delegates he wished to give the localities a chance to state when and how the industrial action should be arranged, and he later agreed with Hugh Williams that the people of Wales were not ready for a prolonged confrontation with their employers.[26] On 5 August the Convention rescinded their earlier decision, and adopted O'Connor's motion of having a two or three days' holiday in a week's time. For some Chartists this was to be an opportunity for holding meetings and petitioning the Queen, but for others it held the promise of a spontaneous outburst and welcome confrontation with the authorities.

Although there was some opposition from Aberdare, Blaenavon, Newport, and other communities to the idea of a sacred month, there was still in South Wales a considerable degree of support. At the beginning of August Chartists in the Pontypool area declared their determination to try the experiment, and their words found an echo at Blackwood and on the Varteg: 'we say appoint the day, delay may be fatal . . .'.[27] As the day chosen for action approached, employers in these places complained of poor industrial discipline and some sabotage. All over South Wales, on the long week-end of 10–13 August, men stopped work and held demonstrations, which varied from orderly Chartist visits to churches and chapels to illegal torchlight meetings on the hills.

The climax of activity was reached on 12 August, when one of the largest gatherings of the nineteenth century was held at Dukes-town. There were, said one report, enough people present to obtain the Charter by force. Once again five magistrates were in atten-dance, and one of them, Samuel Homfray, was even invited to preside. In fact, Dr Price took the chair and introduced a large number of speakers, several of whom spoke in Welsh. On the broadsheet that advertised the meeting it was stated that the Chart-ists intended petitioning the Queen for the removal of her mini-sters, but there were also other objectives, as William Jones and Frost explained. The former demanded the release of the political prisoners at Monmouth, and the latter was deputed to convey the feelings of the meeting on this to Lord John Russell. There was a firm understanding amongst those present that further action would depend on the Home Secretary's response to this, and to an accompanying request for mercy towards the three condemned Chartists in Warwickshire. The other purpose of the Dukestown assembly was to give Frost a chance to explain the Convention's policy on the sacred month. He argued that if the men left work for a month their employers might well decide to lock them out for another six months. Samuel Homfray, the chief ironmaster in the area, was, in Frost's opinion, a reasonable man, and like Somers Harford should not be confused with their main enemy, the mini-sters of state. According to the reporter of the *Monmouthshire Merlin*, this moderate speech was much cheered, but some of those present were annoyed by the postponement of the sacred month and anx-ious to close with their opponents.[28]

It is evident, with hindsight, that two plans of violent action had already been mooted. In a speech at Newport on 25 April Vincent had talked of seizing the magistrates and Queen's ministers, and some weeks later John Frost repeated the advice at a Glasgow meet-ing attended by Peter Bussey, Robert Lowery, George Ross, Bronterre O'Brien, and other leading Chartists:

The advice I have given to my countrymen in Wales is the same as I will give you now. They are determined to hold by the law, and I have advised them to hold to this opinion, that they who break the law make themselves amenable to it. The members of the Convention have never yet broken the law, nor are they likely to do so; and therefore, if they are attempted to be laid hold of by the Government, we are determined to lay hold upon some of the leading men in the country as hostages for the Convention.[29]

The arrest of Vincent and his three Monmouthshire friends brought a local dimension to such threats: 'A coal-pit is quite as safe a place for a tyrannical persecutor as a gaol for an innocent Chartist.'[30] By the middle of May no one in Newport or Pontypool could have doubted the identity of the intended victims. In the columns of the *Western Vindicator*, and in threatening letters and speeches, Thomas Phillips, Thomas Prothero, Digby Mackworth, Lewis Edwards, William Brewer, the Revd Richard Roberts, and attorney Thomas Phillpotts were singled out as the 'lowest of the low', and given nicknames like 'Old Mare', 'Ass', and 'Ourang-outang'. One idea, discussed in the meetings just prior to the rising, was that these enemies, and some of the employers and leading county families, should be held captive underground until the people got 'what they wanted'.[31] Lists were to be kept of those men who, in an unpleasant emergency, would be killed.

The second plan was for the industrial workmen to take control of the hills, and perhaps of the towns, of South Wales and set up the first Chartist state. This notion of a regional revolt had, as William Jones noted in February 1839, its roots deep in Welsh history, but it had become popular again in the early nineteenth century, especially at the time of the Merthyr rising of 1831. Vincent, in his first speeches in the Principality, did as much as anyone to revive the idea. On his visit to Pontllanfraith, for instance, on 26 March, he said that he was charmed by their 'excellent hills'. 'A few thousand of armed men on the hills could successfully defend them. Wales would make an excellent republic.'[32] Both the Chartists and the authorities were aware of the comparatively small number of troops stationed in the country. Since the insurrection of 1831 soldiers had been slowly removed from the mining districts until, in the summer of 1839, there were only 400 raw recruits at the Brecon barracks and in Newport and Abergavenny. Those men of the 29th Regiment who arrived at Newport in May were cheered by the watching crowds, and a few of them deserted. Vincent, Frost, and Zephaniah Williams often assured the Chartists that some of the military sympathized with their politics, and the remainder were oppressed and would lay down their arms when attacked.[33] It was said that Frost even produced letters from soldiers to convince the doubters, but, as we shall see, those miners who had served in the army were aware of the authority wielded by officers. If these were removed or killed, the outlook for revolution was more favourable in South Wales than anywhere else in Britain.[34]

For a variety of reasons it is difficult to know precisely what was happening in South Wales during the late summer and autumn of 1839. So far as the Chartist movement was concerned there is circumstantial evidence of changes in attitude, personnel, and organization. This period saw some of the last, and most desperate appeals to the middle class, from the Convention, the radical press, and individuals. 'If the middle class were to join the Chartists,' wrote Frost on 29 June, 'the Charter would soon become the law.'[35] Within a few weeks he had come to believe that the middle class were incapable of reforming themselves. The note is one of anger. 'I find a spirit rising within me most difficult to repress. If power were placed in my hands, I should be afraid of myself. I should be afraid that revenge would overpower my understanding.' 'Assure the Council that the cause progresses well with us,' wrote the Newport draper on 13 August to Matthew Fletcher, fellow Convention delegate and militant, 'quite as well as ever they could wish; I think that I had (better) not say more.'[36]

This feeling of an impending conflict owed much to the behaviour of the authorities. Pressure continued to be brought against the radical movement: licences were withheld from publicans who favoured Chartism, warnings issued against those who sold radical publications, and clergymen of all denominations were encouraged to denounce the doctrine of equality and the methods of physical force. At a Pontypool church on 25 August, the text was: 'For I have learnt in whatsoever state I am, therewith to be content' (Phil. 4: 11). As an insurance, the gentlemen of Glamorgan and Monmouthshire announced their determination to improve the police force, and protested against the possible withdrawal of troops. At the beginning of October a company of the 45th Regiment under Capt. Stack replaced the 29th Regiment at Newport, and their reputation as crowd controllers arrived before them.

At the same time the Chartists obtained few concessions with regard to the political prisoners. In late August Frost was in London seeking an interview with the Home Secretary, as he had been required to do by the Dukestown meeting, but Lord John Russell's illness and the subsequent cabinet changes delayed the business. Angry female Chartists called upon people to aid Vincent, 'with *their right arms* if *need be*', but Frost promised that their hero was in good health and struggled to keep alive some hope of better treatment if not release.[37] Towards the end of September the Welsh leader talked of the need for a larger address on behalf of the political prisoners and tried to obtain some amelioration of gaol conditions from the Quarter Sessions, but in the same month he received an answer from Lord Normanby which blunted even Frost's capacity for reasoned protest. When the Revd James Coles and Capel Hanbury Leigh also ignored Frost's pleas the die was cast.[38] 'It will be for you to consider what other means you will take to obtain their discharge', he wrote to the working men of South Wales, 'or to get some alteration made in these inhuman regulations.'[39]

One of the methods which Frost and the editor of the *Western Vindicator* recommended in these weeks was for all Chartists to organize themselves into small independent classes. At the end of August 'the Working Men of the Hills' were told that the people in Scotland and the Midlands were forming 'tithings' so that they could be ready for action at a moment's notice. 'Let us . . . pursue this plan', suggested Frost. 'This would be the way to preserve the peace of the country . . . let it embrace the whole of the populous districts of Wales and the west of England; and believe me that it will produce an effect much greater than you are aware of.' On 5 October the message was repeated. 'Let us have recourse to the ancient institutions of our country. . . . Let every ten men select a leader, let them be careful of the selection. . . . We are organizing in Wales; we shall not want special constables here.'[40] ·

The origins of this plan in South Wales are obscure. When Samuel Etheridge's home was searched two or three of the papers that were found contained descriptions of the Irish rebellion of 1798 and an outline of cellular organizations. The latter, on sections, companies, and brigades, may have been discussed by members of the Newport association at the beginning of 1839, and we know that in the spring people sometimes proceeded to meetings in regular company formations. According to William Davies the system known as 'tithings' actually developed out of the arrangements for collecting money for the Defence Fund.[41] During the following weeks several associations of Chartists were organized in this way, and there is related evidence of a growing separation and information-gap between the 'captains' and the rank and file. Increasingly the latter were being identified by numbers, and their leaders were forming small 'councils'. Important decisions were now being taken secretly and at the highest level of command.

We can assume that the new organization was only partially adopted, for at meetings in Blackwood and Blaina at the beginning of October Frost again emphasized its advantages. He talked of the coming dissolution of Parliament and described a new plan, sanctioned by Feargus O'Connor, to return a Chartist assembly. It was, he said, his intention to stand for the county seat, and he would require 30,000 men to descend on Monmouth at election time, organized in companies of 100 and with section leaders wearing white armbands on their sleeves.[42] An anonymous informer claimed that the Chartists of Merthyr took this request seriously, and divided themselves into 'pickets' of 11 men, the eleventh communicating to the others the orders of the central committee.[43]

It is almost impossible, because of the calculated silence and secrecy of these weeks, to discover whether the reorganization of the radical movement extended to arming. Certainly Frost and O'Connor, with their talk of the right of electors to arm themselves with pikes and guns, hardly discouraged such a development. On 6 September the magistrates for the lower division of Miskin in Glamorgan reported that three-quarters of the mining and manufacturing populations of Dinas and Pontypridd were Chartists, and, at the latter place and at Treforest, a considerable number of weapons had been bought, sold, and tested on targets.[44] Richard Cule, shopkeeper, William David, and Dr Price were, it was widely believed, the key figures in all this. The surgeon was even said to have been guarded by four armed men in the weeks before the rising, and at the end of October he was requested by Captain Howells to remove the cannon in his possession.[45] The Lord Lieutenant of the county kept a wary eye on this situation, but remained sceptical about some of the wilder claims. He knew, as the Scotch Cattle movement demonstrated, that the miners were used to guns and that some of their secret evening meetings traditionally ended with the explosive sound of firing. What he did not know was that militant Chartist leaders like Benjamin Richards and George Shell were already checking their pikes and oiling their muskets. Nor was he aware that weapons were now being made in the workshops of Newport, at a smithy near the Victoria works and in caves in the hills.[46] One persistent oral tradition in South Wales is that weapons were stockpiled in a Chartist cave on Mynydd Llangynidr, and a letter in the Treasury Solicitor's Papers gives some credence to the story. The authorities at Tredegar discovered, after the rising, a cavern on the top of the Trefil where 'they have been making pikes'. By the side of a small hearth were bellows, iron, and coal.[47]

In the context of these preparations and the heightened tension, it was perhaps inevitable that the more determined Chartists seized the initiative. Cautious and moderate radicals left the lodges in the summer and autumn of 1839, complaining of indiscreet language and the pressures placed on them. At Newport two of the oldest members, Samuel Etheridge and the merchant Thomas Percy Wells, severed their connections with the movement, as did Daniel Evans, the tailor. The printer related how he and Charles Jones of the Royal Oak fell out with William Edwards over his blustering style and behaviour, whilst Evans claimed that he 'continued with them until I saw they were going on in a bad way that would lead to violence in the end'.[48] Chartists of Pontypool and Tredegar expressed similar fears, and William Barwell, who stayed on as secretary of a Blackwood association, found himself involved in a physical- versus moral-force argument only a week before the rising and was accused of not being up to the mark.[49]

One by one, the militants began to make their voices heard. At Tredegar, where there was much radical activity after 12 August, John Rees, the ex-soldier, and his friend David Jones, were well to the fore, as was 'captain' Isaac Tippins, the tailor of Nantyglo, who was absent from work for long periods in October.[50] Abersychan miners were regarded as extremely belligerent at this time, and in Pontypool George Shell, Solomon Briton, and friends let it be known that they were prepared to go forward alone. William Jones, their leading representative, was now one of the stars of the South Wales circuit, though he and a friend spent some time in September traversing the west country. The other prominent militant was Dr Price, who had chaired the Dukestown meeting on 12 August and had subsequently done a great deal of missionary work on the Glamorgan–Monmouth border. According to Walter Coffin the surgeon was in Staffordshire and the north two months before the rising, though giving it out that he was in London.[51] It is also worth noting that Morgan Williams of Merthyr, traditionally the most moderate of the Welsh leaders, was in close touch with both Dr Price and Frost at this time, and travelled to London at the end of October.[52]

This is a reminder that the developments in South Wales cannot be understood in isolation. Government ministers, military leaders, and that patriotic informer Alexander Somerville claimed that Dr Taylor, Peter McDouall, R. J. Richardson, Major Beniowski, and other notable Chartist leaders had formed a council or committee during the summer of 1839. John Frost knew some of these men well, and by the early days of August the group had made plans for 'an intended rising'. On 26 August these, and other, Chartist delegates took their seats at the reconvened Convention, but after much acrimony this body dissolved itself. Frost, as its president, made the casting vote. William Ashton of Barnsley, writing many months later, claimed that on 14 September, the very last day of the Convention, the Welsh leader attended a meeting which decided on 3 November as the date for a co-ordinated rising. Peter Bussey of Bradford, William Cardo, and William Burns were party to this decision, as were some of the above council. We do not know the precise nature of their plans, although an informer, writing on 22 September, claimed that a Polish immigrant had been put in charge of organization, and it had been determined to attack the soldiers in their barracks. The Pole was undoubtedly Major Beniowski, who had been involved in the rebellion of 1831 and had recently contributed articles on military science to the *London Democrat*. According to the informer, one of Beniowski's appointed tasks was to take command in the mountains of Wales, and a historian has suggested that the Pole visited the area with Frost in September. It is impossible to verify this, although we know that Beniowski was busy in London for much of the autumn. What is clear, however, is that during the next few weeks these schemes of insurrection were discussed at a number of regional and city conferences, and militants in the West Riding of Yorkshire, and in parts of the north-east, the south-west, and Scotland, committed their districts to an armed struggle.[53]

William Lovett believed that the greatest pressure for some form of violent conflict came from South Wales, though others, notably Zephaniah Williams, suggested that the Principality was selected as the first battle-ground because of the absence of troops.[54] What is clear is that soon after the break-up of the Convention the movement in Wales gave evidence of being very much alive, and busy men like Dr Price and John Frost made considerable efforts to keep their contacts with local leaders. In this autumn the Chartists were continually told that 'London, Bath, Yorkshire, & Lancashire . . . were strong and courageous', but in the Welsh industrial valleys organization was more advanced and the spirit more determined.[55] As we shall see, there were already signs of 'a long-laid plot' to overthrow the established powers in the state.[56] By the end of September there was a strong belief, both within and outside the Principality, that the miners might rise in premature revolt, and it seems possible that a meeting of Yorkshire delegates on the last day of the month promised to give them full support.

After the dissolution of the Convention Frost returned to South Wales. Already, a month previously, he had warned people of reports of spies on the hills, 'whose object is to incite you to acts of revenge'.[57] On 3 October Frost travelled to Blaina, and, if some reports are accurate, his purpose was to quell demands for an imminent rising and the liberation of Vincent. This meeting was, contrary to some historical opinion, only one of a number of meetings held in this period at Blackwood and along the heads of the valleys, and there may have been some confusion between them.[58] However, most people seemed agreed that the Blaina assembly on 3 October, and the secret meeting immediately afterwards in the Royal Oak, were the most significant of the period. After them revolution was probable rather than possible.[59]

Of the meeting of some 500 Chartists at the back of Zephaniah Williams's public house we have a fairly detailed account. It was chaired by a 'working man', and the front ranks were filled by his militant colleagues, loudly demanding quick action to recover their rights. Frost began by expressing relief that no outbreak had occurred, and informed them that the vital decisions would be taken by their commanders and that the people elsewhere in Britain were not yet ready to join them. To act precipitously could be disastrous. This speech did not please all his listeners, and after Frost sat down he was offered a second attempt to convince the audience.

William Jones, whose late arrival was greeted with much cheering, quickly took the temperature of the meeting. He had returned from his 'appointed' visit to the Forest of Dean and brought with him promises of assistance. He hoped for peace but if their enemies used force they must answer in kind, and he was prepared to sacrifice his life. On behalf of Frost and himself, Jones declared that their leaders would stand by them at the end as they stood at the beginning. Frost then rose to his feet again, and issued what was later regarded as a deliberately ambiguous statement. He pleaded with those present to support another peaceful effort to release Vincent, and he called for their support of his candidacy at the next general election. They should, he said, organize themselves into sections and 'be ready at any time to meet me when called upon.' ('We are.') He offered them the prospect of the Charter within a matter of weeks. ('Now, now is the time.') Finally, according to a prosecution witness the Newport Chartist declared that if the Whigs continued to be obstructive, 'I will stand through and will head the ranks to anything that will take place.'[60]

At the secret delegate meetings held that evening in the Royal Oak, and at Dukestown or Sirhowy about the same time, the meaning of Frost's remarks was made plain. The discussion in the Oak lasted for several hours, and was attended by Frost, Zephaniah Williams, David Lewis of Brynmawr, and other prominent Chartists of the area. According to one report, when the meeting ended, at 2 a.m., such was the noise inside and outside the public house that respectable neighbours believed a rising had begun.[61]

Sadly for us, the only participant who revealed what happened in these secret delegate meetings was Dr Price, and he was writing forty years after the event. However, a number of people believed that the surgeon played a major role in the early planning of the Newport rising, and his account tells us much about the atmosphere of these tense affairs and the plight of John Frost:

I remember that I was to lead the people from Merthyr, Brecon, the Aberdare Valleys, Pontypridd, and Dinas. . . . Six weeks before the Chartist riots he [Frost] sent for the delegates to meet him at Twyn-y-star, Blaenau Gwent. I went there as a delegate from the Merthyr and Aberdare district. Frost, who was chairman, said 'I have called you together to ask will you rise at my bidding, for it must be done?' Well, upon that, one of the delegates, an old soldier named David Davies, of Abersychan, who had served for 25 years in the army, and fought in the Battle of Waterloo, got up and said, 'I will tell you, Mr. Frost, the condition upon which my lodge will rise, and there is no other condition, as far as I am concerned. The

Abersychan Lodge is 1,600 strong; 1,200 of them are old soldiers; the remaining 400 have never handled arms, but we can turn them into fighting men in no time. I have been sent here to tell you that we shall not rise until you give us a list of those we are to remove—to kill. I know what the English army is, and I know how to fight them, and the only way to success is to attack and remove those who command them—the officers and those who administer the law. We must be led as the children of Israel were led from Egypt through the Red Sea.' This we understood to be a sea of blood. Every delegate gave a similar reply, and Frost promised that he would not call them until he had given them the list asked for. That meeting lasted until two or three o'clock in the morning.[62]

Dr Price, it must be said, never fully trusted Frost, and at this time, too, some working men had begun to suspect the latter's courage and purpose.[63]

From a reading of the surviving evidence one obtains the clear impression that by mid October a decision, at least in principle, had been taken to prepare people for a rising. Although most of the newspapers hardly acknowledge the fact, seven 'missionaries' had been appointed in the autumn to 'explain the Charter' in the three industrial counties.[64] Some of these men, like David Lewis of Brynmawr, were known militants, and it is possible that their visit to Brecon and Abergavenny a fortnight before the rising had a more sinister intention than was revealed. We know that at this precise moment attempts were being made to persuade soldiers to desert their regiments, and men of the 45th Regiment at Newport were asked by Chartists how they would react to an attack from a people's militia.[65] Meanwhile, on various parts of the coalfield, there were clear signs of the reorganization which Frost and others had demanded. At Merthyr over thirty district meetings were held weekly, under the eye of a controlling committee and from neighbouring mining villages came the first complaints of aggressive recruiting and oath-taking. The tone was belligerent and the mood expectant. According to one farmer, who met William Shellard in a public house near Chepstow on 15 October, the Pontypool Chartist denounced landowners and the Poor Law and looked forward to an immediate alteration.[66] If a repentant Zephaniah Williams is to be believed, at this time plans were being made to establish a people's republic and the news of this was being carried to parts of England and Scotland.

All this excitement helps to explain Frost's frenetic activity in the month of October. Between 3 and 8 October he was on the hills, giving at Blackwood an account of his stewardship as Convention delegate, and talking much of the need for discipline and of his hopes for Vincent and a new People's Parliament. He promised to visit Pontypool and Merthyr, but within days he was in the north of England. He was in Manchester on 14 October, but did not attend, as expected, the dinner for Dr Fletcher at Bury, although a 'Mr. Batley from Wales' was present. So was William Burns who told Robert Lowery that 'some of our leading men had been there . . . under cover of this supper some had met to concoct a rising'.[67] Feargus O'Connor claimed that at this time the Welsh leader received a message calling him back home. By 19 October, when he addressed a letter 'to a magistrate', Frost was once more in Monmouthshire, and three days later he wrote his last letter to the farmers and tradesmen of the county. The theme was the old one of resentment against natural allies, and it also contained a threat to a government that relied on 'soldiery and police'. 'If they yield not, resistance becomes a virtue, and resistance we advise.' Frost had already told Peter Bussey of the Welsh determination to rise and, before the end of the month, Dr John Taylor also learnt the news in London. The Scotsman, who chased revolutions as others chase butterflies, complained of the lack of warning, but sent a promise of support to South Wales. There John Frost was uneasily aware that 'stopping the movement is now out of the question . . .'. Only the Attorney-General, the Marquis of Bute, Sir Josiah Guest, and the editor of the *Monmouthshire Merlin* could still talk of the decline and imminent 'Extinction of Chartism'.[68]

Of all the problems surrounding the history of the Newport rising none is more intractable than the plans discussed by the leaders of South Wales Chartism in the month of October. Virtually nothing was disclosed, even in court, of what took place at secret delegate meetings, and we have to rely on vague contemporary impressions, a 'confession' of Zephaniah Williams, and the memory of Dr Price. It seems, from these sources, that one of the original and most ambitious Chartist schemes involved all parts of the coalfield. According to this, some time between 3 and 5 November men from the heads of the valleys were to march on Abergavenny, those from Merthyr district were to hold Brecon, and the rest of the workmen were to capture Newport. There were soldiers in all three of these towns, but their numbers were small, many of them were new recruits and some had already promised not to oppose the Chartists 'provided it was a general outbreak'. Even so it was thought prudent to infiltrate armed Chartists into these towns before the main assaults occurred. In addition, there were rumours of plans to hold Pontypool, Monmouth, and Cardiff. When all this had been achieved, Chartists elsewhere in Britain would receive a signal, and it was hoped that the government would be unable to contain the subsequent outbreaks and defection of soldiers.[69]

This plan, and probably others like it, occupied the minds of radical leaders in early and mid October. What part John Frost played in these discussions is uncertain, not least because of his absences and because of his later claim that he was pushed into direct action by his colleagues. Dr Price argued that Frost deliberately scuttled their ambitious schemes and even ensured the failure of the march on Newport. According to the surgeon's memoirs, on Saturday night, 26 October, he was summoned to see Frost and asked to support a modified plan of a march on Newport at the following week-end. 'I refused to agree to anything except what had been decided at the Twyn-y-star meeting', recalled Price. '"What", said he [Frost], "do you want us to kill the soldiers—kill a thousand of them in one night?" "Yes," I said, "a hundred thousand if it is necessary." "Dear me", cried he, "I cannot do it, I cannot do it", and he cried like a child and talked of heaven and hell.'[70]

One cannot vouch for the authenticity of this conversation, but at this time Dr Price does begin to withdraw from the preparations for a Chartist outbreak. It seems likely that neither he nor Frost was present at the important delegate meeting on Monday, 28 October, at Dukestown. Zephaniah Williams and William Jones were there, and most coalfield communities were represented. The nature of the discussions was never fully revealed, though one can piece together some of the debate. Certain delegates, including possibly those from the Aberdare district, were more cautious than others, and anxious to discover just how much support they could expect for a popular rising. Others, such as the local militants, wished to push ahead and challenge the authorities. Eventually it was decided to hold some demonstration early in the following week, and to meet again, perhaps at Dukestown, to work out the precise details. In the meantime the delegates were required to hold nightly meetings and to encourage people to arm themselves in self-defence and to be ready for any emergency.[71]

So it was that, on Tuesday night at John Llewellyn's beerhouse, Pontnewydd, John Phillips informed the WMA of the decisions of the Dukestown meeting. Phillips, the Trowbridge butcher, had already been about the hills on their behalf, and reported that a great many workmen were organized and armed. He and John Llewellyn called upon the people of Pontypool to be similarly prepared for the worst, and most members put up their hands to register their approval. At the end of the meeting the class leaders—including William Shellard, who had marched a contingent of men to Llewellyn's beerhouse—were called into a private room. On the following day, at Bristol House in Pontypool, John Davies, the association's secretary, read a letter from Frost which asked them to prepare, to form themselves into groups, and to obtain arms for their defence. A message from Monday's delegate meeting also reminded them of their support for the Convention's ulterior measures, and required them to meet every evening until Sunday.[72]

From several reports during this week there can be little doubt that developments and changes in strategy were closely identified with John Frost. From 28 October, if not before, he was regarded as the leader of the rising, and Zephaniah Williams and others, when addressing meetings later that week, spoke of 'Frost's policy' and 'Frost's promise' to get the Charter in three weeks or a month.[73] Until an important private meeting with Williams and Jones on Thursday the Newport leader kept to himself, though he was the centre of correspondence in South Wales and between the region and the rest of Britain. At Blackwood, his base for much of the week before the rising, he received visitors and letters from Bristol, London, and other places to the north. Such was his authority that he was later accused by the press of misleading his followers with false claims of support and fake correspondence. According to one report Frost was attended for several days at Blackwood by an agent from the north of England or Scotland, who left in confident mood on Friday. It is just possible that this messenger was Charles Jones, the hunted Mid-Walian who was thought by Lovett to have been a vital go-between.[74]

The role of the two other leaders, Zephaniah Williams and William Jones, was defined by Monday's delegate meeting. They were given the task of 'stirring up' the lodges, each lecturing in his native tongue. On Tuesday the former was at his own Royal Oak, expounding the merits of the Charter, the benefits of free trade, and the evils of workhouses, and hinting that many gentlemen actually supported their cause.[75] If everyone stuck together, argued Williams, there would be no bloodshed—a constant theme of the Blaina rationalist. On the following day he delivered another speech at the Royal Oak, and this time called on them to give up their work in order to prepare for the coming conflict. He was, however, when pressed, unable to say whether the people would be 'on the mountain' on Saturday or Sunday night.[76]

On 29 October Sarah Edmunds of the Greyhound, Pontllanfraith, reported that the Blaina leader attended a lodge meeting there, and left his horse with them for a few days. On Wednesday, at the Coach and Horses in Blackwood, Williams and Jones stated their intention of visiting all the lodges in the neighbourhood. At this hostelry they called upon the people to meet every evening, and Jones wanted them to bring torches and candles to a great meeting on the hills. If they resisted the authorities, he said, they could have the Charter within a month. A short time later the two leaders were at the Navigation Inn, Crumlin, and again Williams explained how the Charter could be obtained peacefully if the people were organized and legally armed for self-defence. His colleague then attacked the law which protected property and not people, talked of action on Sunday night, and said that it was their resolve to liberate Henry Vincent and put Lord John Russell in his place. At the end of the speeches Williams called the local leaders together for a secret discussion. The landlord, Richard Williams, believed that 'a new plan' of organization was being considered: 'Zephaniah thought that the Charter would be the law of the land sooner than many expected it.'[77] After a brief farewell the two missionaries journeyed back to Blackwood and sleep.

On Thursday Williams and Jones completed another round of speeches and consultations. In the Llanfabon–Llancaiach area colliers were instructed to attend the Colliers Arms to hear what these Chartists had to say. Williams told them that Frost had promised the Charter in three weeks if they followed his advice. Those who wished to give Frost their support were asked to put up their right hands.[78] It was also decided at this meeting that Thomas Giles, the chairman, should go as their delegate to Blackwood on Friday. At

Pengam, in the house of Benjamin Davies, where a stranger took the chair, Williams and Jones warned people to be ready for whatever their leaders should ask of them, and for the moment their daily work should be a secondary consideration. In the evening both men returned to the Coach and Horses, and some time during the day reported to Frost on their missionary efforts.[79] Frost, who slept this night some distance away at the home of Job Tovey, could now anticipate the likely spirit of the delegate meeting which he had called to Blackwood.

We know just a little of the other Chartist representatives and local leaders who were involved in the discussions and plans of this week. At Blackwood those consulted by the three leaders were William (Bill) Barwell, secretary of a radical association, and John Reynolds 'the preacher', a coal-haulier, and important figures elsewhere were John Phillips, widely regarded as William Jones's right-hand man, and David Lewis of the King Crispin, Brynmawr. Benjamin Richards, William Davies of Blackwood, Thomas Giles, who worked at the Gelligaer colliery, another collier, John James, and possibly John Llewellyn of Pontnewydd, Isaac Thomas, and Frost's son Henry, were the men who carried the messages across the mining communities in the last days before the rising. Working closely with them were prominent militants, like Richard Jones, the Tredegar sawyer, who probably chaired the Dukestown meeting on 28 October, and four 'captains', Shellard, Shell, and the brothers Isaac and Edward Tippins of Nantyglo and Brynmawr. According to *The Times* and ironmaster Samuel Homfray, John Rees (Jack the Fifer), who had fought with the Texans four years previously, and David Jones of Tredegar also played an important part during these last days, as did the Rorke family of Newport and Blackwood, and other local leaders such as Thomas Guttery of Blaina, Lewis Rowland, secretary of the lodge at the Angel, Maesycwmmer, and Charles Waters of Newport.[80]

These radicals had an unenviable job in the last week of October. They were ordered by Frost and his colleagues to prepare their districts for a rising, without being fully aware of what was intended and having been sworn to secrecy. In some districts they followed instructions and held meetings on almost every night. Lists were made of new members, people were organized into small sections under captains, and by Thursday the books and records of the associations had been placed in safe keeping. Scores of people, even hundreds at some of the ironworks and at lodges in the Horse and Jockey, Dukestown, the Royal Oak, Blaina, and the Colliers Arms, Nelson, joined the Chartists during the week, usually paying 5*d.* and receiving a card by return. The pressure on families to obtain a card, already considerable at the beginning of October, became intense after Monday's delegate meeting. Determined characters like Benjamin Richards and Abraham Thomas of Coalbrookvale warned people that everyone had to sign up, and threats of loss of job or worse were held out against those who refused. 'If any man was at home and could not show his card after they returned from Newport . . . they would destroy them like killing toads', recalled Richard Arnold, a puddler who had recently moved from Pontymister to Blaina.[81] Sometimes the wives of stubborn conservatives such as William Lewis, a blocklayer of Sirhowy, and William Howell, a gasworker of Blaina, took cards 'to protect' their families.[82] Rachel Howell, who received a card from Zephaniah Williams when he called at their home, was mortified when her husband burnt it. In some cases exemption could be bought, and William Edmunds, the Argoe blacksmith and preacher, paid 10*s.* for the privilege.

Altogether, a considerable amount of money came into the lodges at the end of October. Apart from the card money there were one or two other sources of income. Some reports suggested that colliers in the upper Rhondda and Blackwood area insisted on being paid wages in sovereigns and silver at this time.[83] Draws and banknotes were frowned upon; after all, as George Shell told William Thomas over a drink on Tuesday, in a few weeks they would not be worth the snap of his fingers.[84] In the middle of this week money was also recovered from innkeepers who held it for the Chartists, and there were plans to use some of the funds of friendly societies. On Wednesday night Lewis Lloyd was visited by the Newport mason, John Gwilliam, who told him, on good authority, that a rising was imminent, and asked him to persuade the leaders of his Oddfellows branch to withdraw their money from the bank.[85] This was done on the following day, and news of it soon reached the mayor of the town.

All the money that was received by the Chartist committees was quickly expended. Some of it was paid out to the delegates and missionaries who travelled across South Wales during this week, and some may have been used to bribe soldiers. Most of the money was spent on the making and buying of arms. The rank-and-file Chartists were urged to get weapons for their defence, and long hours were spent putting together home-made pikes. Many of these were only sharpened poles, or broomsticks with pan-handles fixed on the end, but a number of workmen had more impressive implements. Towards the end of the week, smiths at Pillgwenlly and Beaufort were persuaded to make hundreds of iron pike-heads. As we saw earlier, a make-shift smithy was also set up in Mynydd Llangynidr, and there were several reports of weapons being made at work and of metals being removed from the forges. After the rising bullet-moulds were discovered, and Evan Edwards, clock- and watchmaker of Tredegar, revealed that he had made bullets for the Chartists on condition that he could remain at home with his sick wife.[86] In these last days guns and pikes were openly sold in the lodges and the public houses of the district, and Thomas Bowen (a Nantyglo puddler), Benjamin James (a neighbouring collier), and George Shell were amongst those who placed orders. Meanwhile, at Blackwood, William Davies was given £10 by Richard Pugh, and travelled to Newport to buy rifles for the association.

On reflection it is surprising that all this activity made so little impression on the propertied classes of South Wales. Many appeared quite unaware of the preparations going on all around them. William Needham of the Varteg ironworks first learnt of the affair at 1.30 a.m. on Monday, 4 November, when he was woken with the news that the blast to his furnaces had been stopped.[87] Yet rumours of an outbreak of popular unrest had been circulating in the area for some time. On 29 October policeman Homan told Captain Howells that he had information of a 'simultaneous rise throughout the kingdom this week', and he spoke to magistrate William Thomas and Thomas Booker about the arming which he knew was in progress.[88] Others, remarkably acute after the event, later protested that they had heard during this week of Chartist plans to release Vincent and 'try their strength' on Tuesday, 5 November or possibly on the 4th or 6th, but in truth the leaders of South Wales society were in a state of almost total confusion.

On Saturday, 2 November, Samuel Homfray of Tredegar, who had been supplied with new information by Homan, wrote that 'all the respectable people around', especially the shopkeepers, 'are completely frightened'. Although it was pay-day, the market was comparatively quiet, as were the public houses. His workmen had gone to Dukestown and elsewhere to confer. Griffiths the Tredegar currier reported to Homan that he had just sold a lot of gunpowder, and had received many requests for bullet-moulds, whilst not far away, at Ebbw Vale, the Harfords had sent their money to the bank and were leaving the district. As a postscript, Homfray told his correspondent, Thomas Jones Phillips, magistrates' clerk at Newport, that he had just heard the news that 'tomorrow evening or Monday is to be the day'.[89]

One of the reasons for the anxiety and bewilderment of the authorities was remarkably simple. Until the very last minute the people who were being organized were kept ignorant of the purpose of Sunday's action. By Wednesday most of the committed Chartists knew that one evening soon something would happen and it would be their 'last chance' to obtain the Charter. This was certainly the message which two prominent Newport Chartists, Jenkin Morgan and John Gwilliam, gave to their friends on that day. More than this they did not know, and the secrecy was a cause of a little concern and, ultimately, of anger. We noted earlier that on Monday, 28 October, there was a conflict at the Coach and Horses meeting over a physical-force strategy, and not all the people in the lodges took 'Frost's side' when called upon to do so. Much depended on the communication skills of lodge officers, on the presence or otherwise of the main leaders, and on the character of the men who had recently been persuaded to take Chartist cards. Perhaps the two most fractious lodge meetings occurred at the Angel, Maesycwmmer, and at the Maypole, Crosspenmaen, at the week-end. On Friday night, at the Angel, secretary Lewis Rowland asked some fifty people if they would get weapons and march on Newport. Two new and reluctant 'Chartists', Lewis Lewis, a banksman, and Jacob Thomas, a shopkeeper, wanted things done peacefully, and were angry about the whole enterprise and the lack of information. Rowland replied that they needed weapons to deal with capitalists like Thomas.[90] On the following day, at Henry Charles's Maypole there was a slightly different conflict. Seventy-four-year-old David Stephens, a 'comfortably off' and 'highly respected' local figure, was appointed chairman, and he called on those present to arm and nominate captains. This was rejected, partly perhaps because Stephens would disclose the destination of Sunday's march only to the class leaders, who had not yet been elected. When William Jones passed through the area twenty-four hours later he found Chartist members in a state of considerable disarray.[91]

No one was more secretive or cautious than Zephaniah Williams. While calling upon his supporters to stop work and obtain arms, he did not tell them until the last minute where they were bound and on which day the plan would be put into operation. On Saturday Rachel Howell at least was determined to find out something. 'I asked him what we should do for victuals when they should take the men away,' she stated under examination. 'He told me not to mind that, that he should mind for victuals for women and children. I asked him to let me know where he would find shop—(that is, credit)— for us, until the men should come back.'[92] Throughout the week Zephaniah fended off other awkward questions, and, as the week-end approached, his caution still showed through. On Saturday he told Thomas Bowen that he could not let him and others have their pikes for some workmen might get drunk and out of control.[93]

Despite the doubts of examining magistrates it is clear that people actually participated in the rising without fully knowing what to expect. The colliers of Llanfabon, for instance, were told by one of their leaders on Friday that they would hear on Ystrad Bridge on Sunday evening about the precise details of their route, and others were informed that Frost would be waiting at Blackwood or Risca to reveal the ultimate purpose of the march.[94] Similarly, some Pontypool Chartists, as they walked through the night of 3 November, kept asking Shellard and William Jones for the latest instructions. Small wonder, therefore, that a few working people joined the rising with a degree of scepticism, proved to be less committed than was hoped, and finished the venture wet, half-drunk, and angry.

The crucial decisions about the rising were put to a delegate meeting, held at the Coach and Horses in Blackwood late in the morning and afternoon of Friday, 1 November.[95] There were about twenty-five to thirty people present, and amongst the associations represented were those at Dowlais, Rhymney, Dukestown, Sirhowy, Ebbw Vale, Blaina, Brynmawr, Llanelli, Llanhilleth, Crumlin, Crosspenmaen, Pontypool, and Newport, and those in the immediate vicinity of Blackwood. Merthyr was not represented, nor perhaps the communities in the Rhondda, despite claims to the contrary.[96] According to the landlord of the Coach and Horses,

Dr Price came only to his door at midday and spoke to Frost. Apart from Frost, Williams, and Jones, others present included Barwell, Reynolds, William Davies, Thomas Giles, possibly Waters and Gwilliam of Newport, Morris Owen 'from the hills', an English-man from the Abersychan area, and John Phillips and David Lewis, who both arrived late. There are also claims that a delegate from the north was in attendance for some of the day.[97]

The meeting was chaired by John Reynolds, and opened with a prayer given by an unnamed Englishman, possibly a native of the Forest of Dean who had been dismissed from his job at the British Iron Company. Then followed reports on the level of preparations and arming in the various districts, and William Jones, who took the details down, reckoned they could count on 5,000 armed men. The absence of reliable support on the western front must have caused some concern, though it emphasized the advantages of the modified scheme of a march on Newport. It was decided, after some debate, that musters would be held at Dukestown, Black-wood, the racecourse near Pontypool, and other places, and all were to meet at Risca at midnight on Sunday for further orders. People were to be placed in units of ten, and they were to march in military fashion, carrying weapons. Should they come across their enemies on Sunday night, these should be taken and held as hos-tages for the release of Chartist prisoners. Others on the road, unless they had written exemptions or knew certain passwords, could be recruited into the people's army. It was also decided that no indiscriminate destruction or looting would be tolerated.

Several reports suggest that this meeting on Friday was domi-nated by Frost. He argued strongly that with only his and Zepha-niah Williams's men they could accomplish their object, and after that they could move on to more ambitious schemes. One has the impression—though information is sparse—that most of the Chartists between Pontypool and Crickhowell were to be held in reserve and used at a later date. William Jones, too, although prominent as an organizer, seems to have been given a lesser mili-tary role than his two friends. Unfortunately, accounts of this meet-ing do not tell us precisely what was to happen at Newport, although Job Tovey claimed that his lodger stated that when the Chartists got to Stow hill the noise of their approach would be the signal for local Chartists to seize certain vantage points. The work-house, where the soldiers were billeted and arms stockpiled, was to be a special target. Frost is alleged to have told Friday's meeting that bloodshed was unlikely because the soldiers would be sleeping, and would be too cowardly or sympathetic to face the massed ranks of the Chartists.[98]

There was some discussion at the Coach and Horses over what was likely to happen once the Chartists had taken Newport. It was hoped that this would be the signal for risings elsewhere, and there was much talk of sympathetic action by workmen just across the border. William Jones had already promised them the help of the 'Forest men', and it is worth noting that at least two of the people at Friday's meeting were from that area. In fact, reports sent to the Home Office from magistrates of Kingswood, Wotton-under-Edge, Trowbridge, and other places indicated that miners and weavers on both sides of the Severn estuary were discontented and expectant. As for the rest of Britain, the delegates at the Coach and Horses were assured, by letters and word of mouth, that everything was going well. Some of the leading English and Scottish Chartists already knew, of course, that something was being planned in Wales, and it is likely that a messenger was sent from Blackwood on this Friday to give them the precise details.[99] Some consideration was also given by the men at the Coach and Horses to how their success, or failure, was to be communicated to other areas, and there was a related debate on the probable response of the government. It was decided, according to Zephaniah Williams's confession, to adopt a fortress policy, cutting off the advance of the troops from inside and outside Wales, and relying on fellow Chartists to divert or slow them down. Frost is reported to have said that with the main Newport bridge in their hands and with no mail leaving the town, the world would soon know of their brave venture. In three weeks, he again promised, the Charter would be won. Finally, it is possible that this meeting was the one which authorized the posting up of proclamations in the event of victory on Monday morning. As the delegates took tea and separated, the rising could not be stopped.

The March

ONCE the delegate meeting was over, South Wales was already in the throes of a rising, and the directing voice was unquestionably that of John Frost. He spent that night at the home of Job Tovey, and it is on the evidence of that family, and of William Davies, that much of the following story is based. On Saturday Davies, son of a Blackwood shopkeeper, visited Newport in a search for arms, and whilst there he was given two letters and a parcel by Mrs Frost for her husband. Some time later Henry Frost persuaded Davies and his father to give a lift, on their return, to a Chartist delegate from Yorkshire, a young workman of medium height who kept himself very much to himself. According to Professor Williams, the stranger was 'undoubtedly Charles Jones', but one cannot be certain of his identity. When they arrived at Blackwood the young man was taken to Tovey's house, and there he presented Frost with a letter which, like those from Mrs Frost, was quickly read and destroyed. After late tea the delegate was urged to return via Newport and Monmouth as soon as possible, but before leaving the district he attended a private meeting in a bedroom at the Coach and Horses. There he told Frost, John Reynolds, William Barwell, and one other person of the Chartist preparations elsewhere in Britain, and apparently counselled delay, perhaps for ten days. This sounds probable, for at this very moment, on Peter Bussey's instructions, George White was travelling around the West Riding of Yorkshire, requesting people to postpone the action planned for 3–5 November. Frost, however, asked the young stranger to pass on the message that South Wales was taking a lead which others could follow. About 9 or 10 p.m. the man left Blackwood for the Carpenters' Arms in Newport, and on the following day he was escorted by a post-boy to Monmouth, and then set off for Worcester and Birmingham.[1]

Long before this messenger had left Monmouthshire news of Friday's decisions had reached the various lodges in the area, and preparations for a march on Newport had begun. At the Colliers

Arms in Nelson, for example, people congregated on Saturday to hear the report of delegate Thomas Giles. He informed them that they would 'be off' on Sunday, and would be told their destination at Ystrad Bridge. There was, according to the keeper of this beer-house, a reference to a password being given at Ystrad, and Giles interspersed his speech with horrible threats against backsliders.[2] Not far away, at the Angel in Maesycwmmer, Lewis Rowland also gave the news of a Sunday demonstration, though his call to arms was not received with unanimous acclaim. Up at Blaina, Zepha-niah Williams confirmed that the day of reckoning was imminent, whilst in the Prince of Wales at Newport Charles Waters and a hun-dred friends greeted the news of Friday's delegate meeting with loud cheering.[3] One hostile observer claimed that another band of Newport Chartists, under John Lovell's leadership, met on Friday or Saturday evening and discussed, with some relish, the probable fate of those in authority.[4]

By no means all the Chartists were told of the plan to march on Newport. Many people were simply ordered to meet several times during the remaining 48 hours and to obtain weapons. There were promises that families would be looked after during the men's absence, and strong hints that no soldiers would oppose them. In some lodges the degree of planning was considerable. Lists were made of those willing to join the assault on Newport, captains appointed over the latest recruits, and orders taken for pikes. At William Williams's beerhouse at Argoed on Saturday some 50 men were collected together under the watchful eye of two stewards, and the eleven new members were called by name and told to obey a collier named 'Harry'. As each contributed his 5d., his name was entered in a book. They were told to meet near the chapel early on Sunday morning, when their captain would give them instructions for later in the day. Those people in the neighbourhood who had not joined the association by that time would be the first to have their blood spilt.[5]

On Saturday it was clear that something important was about to happen. Men were not turning up for work, and the markets were poorly attended. Up at Blaina the Abergavenny Brewery Com-pany, still oblivious to the gathering storm, delivered the usual £200 in silver to Zephaniah Williams's beerhouse.[6] The Chartist leader was, in fact, at home for much of the day, and he and Thomas Guttery gave several impromptu speeches to the old and new radicals who crowded into the Royal Oak. Zephaniah promised them that the Charter would soon be the law of the land, and told them to meet armed on the following evening when all would be revealed. According to collier Benjamin James a few people entered a small room in the beerhouse where Thomas Ferriday and others were handling guns.[7]

It was in the interests of those later examined by magistrates to stress the compulsion used during this weekend, but the level of intimidation was considerable. Joseph Coules (Coles) maintained that he did not join the Chartists until Saturday evening when, on his way from the colliery, he met a gang who directed him to the Argoed lodge and obliged him to throw a shilling on the table.[8] George Beach, who was there making a speech in Welsh and English on the need to arm, was, as we shall see, just about the most formidable Chartist on the coalfield. There were others, too, who did not share Zephaniah Williams's propriety in these matters. Thomas Giles, on Saturday evening at Llanfabon, warned his followers that it was useless to hide in pit or level, and it was said that Chartist spies would be left behind to deal with traitors. 'I was afraid to go—& afraid to stay—,' said Richard Davies, collier of Llancaiach, 'so I went.'[9]

Some people, of course, refused to participate. Families locked their doors or feigned illness, and some hid in mines, farm buildings, woods, and caves. Those who anticipated the call of Chartist gangs set off towards chapels or beerhouses several miles away. John Owen, blacksmith, travelled to the Lion beerhouse, Llangynidr, and told friends that if the Chartists won the victory at Brecon (*sic*) he would stab a sheep or fowl and pretend that he had played his part.[10] By midnight on Sunday, Abergavenny, Brecon, and Crickhowell were full of workmen and tradesmen who had decided that discretion was the better part of valour.[11] Richard Williams of the Navigation Inn, Crumlin, hearing the news on Saturday of a 'general rise', immediately set off to join his sons in Breconshire.[12] Others who fled the coalfield included employers, managers, clerks, bankers, farmers, ministers of religion, shopkeepers, and even a few constables. The Harfords of Ebbw Vale, with their domestic servants, set out for Cheltenham and London, whilst the manager of the Tredegar Bank carried in his coach all his cash, valuables, and securities. Samuel Homfray, increasingly isolated at Bedwellty House, bemoaned the timidity of his friends, and hoped that soldiers would arrive in time.[13] Everybody, there-fore, whatever his subsequent verdict on the events, took the threat of a rising seriously at the time.

It was, and is, difficult fully to understand what was happening along the Glamorgan and eastern flanks of the coalfield during the last few days before the march on Newport. Meetings were held most evenings in the lodges at Aberdare, Merthyr, and the Rhondda, but it was claimed that the only local representatives at Friday's delegate meeting were those from Dowlais and Rhymney. It has been suggested by some that the former areas were domi-nated by moral-force men, and that the absence of important Chartist leaders, the confidence of the Guests, and the continued operation of the ironworks confirms this view.[14] The situation was, inevitably, more complex than this, for these districts had been involved in the early discussions of revolutionary action. There are hints in Dr Price's account that some of these people felt slighted by Frost's modified plan of a rising, and Reginald Blewitt believed that the Glamorgan men were simply not informed of the 'last minute' decisions at Blackwood. The new plan belonged 'to the Mon-mouthshire men', though it is probable, as Seymour Tremenheere claimed, that other Chartists were ready to play their part once the attack on Newport had succeeded. At Brecon residents anticipated an offensive against the military by the Merthyr and Dowlais workmen.[15]

A number of people from the Glamorgan iron district did join the Monmouthshire men on Sunday night and one, William Grif-fiths, was killed at the Westgate hotel. Two others, who were arrested on the road near Newport, left Dowlais at 5 p.m. on Sun-day, and one of them, 71-year-old miner John Bowen said that, like his two sons, he had wanted 'to do his bit'.[16] Some time on Sunday evening Guest saw scores of his men setting off towards Rhymney, and late that night they passed through Tredegar. The Dowlais ironmaster, who was impressed by the comparative quiet of neigh-bouring Merthyr town, was warned on this day that a general rising was afoot, and that the miners intended to proceed to Monmouth and release Vincent. Scouts later reported to him that 'the only cer-tain thing was that some [of the marchers] had proceeded to New-port and others to Abergavenny'.[17] Even so, to the lasting delight of Dr Price, the numbers of Aberdare and Merthyr ironworkers who participated in the rising was small.

The same may have been true of the small Rhondda colliery settlements west of Pontypridd, though the story is a confusing one. It seems, as we noted earlier, that the two key leaders in the area, Dr Price and William David, had dissociated themselves from Frost, but there are signs that people here were also stockpiling arms, cheekily intimidating respectable neighbours, and possibly still considering joint action with Monmouthshire colliers and an assault on Cardiff.[18] When information of the decisions of Friday's delegate meeting reached Dinas, Porth, and Pontypridd, William David and a number of other Chartists were in an obvious dilemma. According to collier Daniel Llewellyn, David, who had a shop and several houses in the Dinas locality, told him on Saturday that there was to be 'serious work at Newport' on Monday, 'the great men would be secured, and if the people all co-operated they would get what they wanted'. 'It is better for me to join with them than to turn a lout or a coward', declared David, 'and it will be the safest way for you all to co-operate with the Monmouthshire men . . .'. The collier, in reply, advised the Dinas leader to flee to America, and he 'seemed much affected and agitated and wept till the tears ran down his face'.[19]

Walter Coffin, the chief employer of colliers in the Rhondda, claimed that many of his men took to the woods and hills to avoid being forced to join the march on Newport, but we know that some did travel to Pontypridd, and from there to Llanfabon or Caer-philly. Several newspaper reports suggest that a number of houses and works near the last town were visited by the Chartists.[20] At the time there were real fears, given credence by later events, that the Glamorgan colliers were considering an attack on Cardiff as well as Newport. Owen Morgan, drawing on local memories, tells us that on this Sunday night a considerable number of men set out from Dinas along the Tonyrefail road towards the capital. In anticipation of trouble, the Cardiff authorities swore in special constables, the police were held in readiness, and parties of the 41st Regiment and the militia took up defensive positions.

Much to the satisfaction of magistrate Evan Williams of Pwlly-pant, near Caerphilly, the only districts in Glamorgan where large numbers enthusiastically joined the rising were those of Gelligaer and Llanfabon.[21] As we have seen, Zephaniah Williams and William Jones were well received there in the middle of the week, and their leader, master collier Thomas Giles, attended Friday's delegate meeting. Meetings were held in the district on Thursday, Friday, and Saturday nights, and just after tea-time on Sunday 'strange people' told them about the march on Newport planned for that evening. Soon most of the colliers in the area had been collected by Giles and his brother-in-law Thomas of Llechwan, and were congregated at the Colliers Arms. Richard Davies, a collier who worked at Llancaiach and lived in one of Evan Jones's houses near the Nelson, takes up the story. '"Well Boys", said Giles, "we are here every one now in this house, you must attend to what I tell you seriously—every man that is now here is bound to be at Newport and go down with me tonight—every man that will turn back on his journey will be a dead man before 12 o'clock tomorrow and any man that stops in his house tonight will be one and all dead men before 12 tomorrow—all the pits shall be broken to pieces and closed on the people in the levels—and every man must plunder every house as we go along and search for guns." He had another man with him of the name of Wm. Owen a collier of Llancaiach— he was an old soldier and assisted Giles to march us on—we were marched three abreast. . . .' On the way these Chartists met a large number of men near the Boot, between Ystrad Bridge and the Rhymney tramroad, and there Giles made a speech in Welsh. Morgan Morgan, the keeper of the Colliers Arms, who was allowed an extra hour's grace to say goodbye to his sick and tearful wife, caught them up at Gelligroes.[22]

At Gelligroes hundreds of Chartists were in the road, for this mining village was, with neighbouring Pontllanfraith, a natural communications centre. Most of the people here were from Blackwood and the smaller collier communities that surrounded it. For the previous twenty-four hours these places had been hives of activity. From the accounts of meetings in the area one obtains the impression of almost undue haste and some anxiety, as vital documents were gathered up, lists made and then destroyed, and arms desperately sought. As we saw earlier, there was some anger at Crosspenmaen and Argoed about the pace of developments. At the former place the Chartist lodge met at about 10 p.m. on Saturday, when collier George Beach urged them to arm themselves by the following day. In this district Beach, together with secretary Daniel Jones and Charles Powell, the shoemaker, were probably the 'most forward in the plot', but others had to attend two further meetings on Sunday before they received information on the

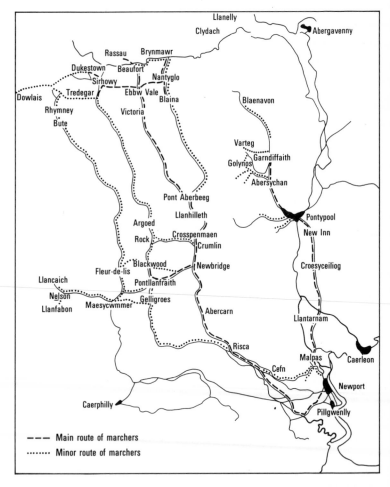

MAP 2. The March on Newport

Chartist intentions.[23] They were told that they would be meeting Frost at Newbridge. A few then commandeered swords, cleavers, and billhooks, but it is likely that the men of this area had fewer weapons than those in the iron-mining towns. Muskets were especially needed, as frightened innkeepers and tradesmen soon discovered.[24]

As the news reached people that something was about to happen, the response, even within families, was a mixture of elation and panic. Some, it is alleged, fled at once, making for upland cottages, barns, and disused coal levels, whilst Thomas Watts, a haulier of Gelligroes, set off late on Sunday morning to inform Samuel Homfray of the intended outbreak.[25] He narrowly escaped being lynched by a mob on the road. Other unwilling marchers were trapped by leading Chartists and by gangs of enthusiasts who called at their homes or at work to remind them of their duty. In Pontllanfraith, for instance, people were still signing on as Chartists and paying money at the Greyhound at midday on Sunday. About the same time Joseph Lewis, a butcher living a few miles to the east, was given a card by Thomas Morgan and David Stephens. He was told by William Gimlett of the Sun beerhouse that, if the Chartists won at Newport, it was best for them to be seen on the road.[26]

A few hours later came the awful decision of whether to attend the agreed points of departure. A few men locked their doors instead, and when friends called or their absence was noted by the captains, it was usually the women of the house who tried to bluff it out. About Argoed there was the sound of women crying and the noise of people running into their houses as the Chartists, some from Tredegar, came down the tramroad. Husbands and sons were dragged from under beds and ordered forward at gun-point. A few of them had long been marked men. John Walters, who had once kept the Castle inn at Argoed, was celebrated for his opposition to the Chartists. When twenty men arrived at 6 p.m. he and his sons refused to answer the call. A large rock was then rammed against the door, sending the bolt and locks flying through the room. 'Walters, you must come out', shouted one of the Chartists, 'your life is no better than ours.' One of them put a gun to his chest and George Beach, sword in hand, handed Walters a shilling and told him that he would not want for anything. In answer to the inevitable question, about their destination, Walters learnt that all would be revealed at Newbridge.[27]

During the late afternoon and early evening there were similar scenes within a two-mile radius of Argoed and by about 6 o'clock there were over 300 Chartists on the road.[28] A third of these gathered at William Williams's beerhouse, where the local associa-tion met. Led by George Beach, and with guards watching possible deserters, they set off towards the Rock and most of them probably turned off towards Crosspenmaen and Crumlin. At the former place David Stephens joined George Beach in his appointed task of impressing the waverers, and so it was a mixed collection of revolu-tionaries which arrived at Newbridge at the appointed hour. They learnt, to their disappointment, that Frost had already left for Cefn.

Apart from the formidable Beach, we know the names of half a dozen other people who cajoled, forced, and led the Chartists from the Blackwood region. At Gelligroes prominent figures were the Batten and Fisher families, and it was at the home of the former that many people met during the evening. Other captains included Thomas Llewellyn and Benjamin Davies of Fleur-de-lis. Llewel-lyn, who had been arrested in the summer for trying to rescue Henry Vincent, was a leading figure on the march, and carried an ugly-looking mandrel over his shoulder. Some time after 7 p.m. Llewellyn and about fifty others set off from the small mining com-munity, and in a short while reached the Angel, Maesycwmmer, where hundreds of colliers were waiting.[29]

The hub of all the activity in the coalmining heartland of Mon-mouthshire was Blackwood itself, and especially the home of Job Tovey, the Coach and Horses to the south of the town, and the Greyhound in nearby Pontllanfraith. According to some reports, when Frost was at Richard Pugh's public house on Saturday even-ing, he expressed the hope that thousands would arrive at Newport and that the gentlemen there would be brought back to work the mines and pay the taxes. The Chartist leader returned to the Toveys' on Saturday night and had breakfast and dinner there on Sunday. Throughout the day people visited the house, including John Reynolds 'the preacher', who had a vital role at this time, and a messenger from Zephaniah Williams. The latter was told that Frost would be collecting his men about 6 p.m. and wished to be at Cefn by 10 p.m. and Newport at 3 a.m. The Newport draper told his closest companions that he expected to take the town with 2,000 men, and would fortify it and perhaps send a few men on to Mon-mouth. His ultimate hope, so often repeated in these days, was that the Charter could be won within three weeks. William Davies, who had great faith in his leader, believed that Frost would not have risked his neck unless he had been reasonably confident of victory.[30]

About the time that tea was being taken in the Toveys' house, Chartists in the neighbourhood were gathering up their weapons and making their farewells. One of these was William Ferriday, who had some fifteen hours to live. The illiterate son of a fairly violent and militant family, William lived opposite the Lamb and Flag beerhouse in Blackwood and worked just over a mile away at Fleur-de-lis. On this day he was unusually quiet and when, about 6.30 p.m., two men called for him, he told his wife that he did not know where he was going or when he would be home. 'I cried aloud', recalled Mary Ferriday, 'and the children as well. Some of them went out after him. He kissed them again in the road and then said Goodbye. . . .'[31]

In the meantime Frost, in his sailor coat and red cravat, William Davies, and others had walked the short distance from the Toveys' to the Coach and Horses, where people had been gathering since 5.30 p.m. There, Reynolds, Barwell, and other leaders were waiting for Frost and, on his arrival, they withdrew to the parlour for a brief discussion. What happened after that is a little confused, because of the unreliable evidence of James Hodge, Israel Firman, and William Harris.[32] It seems that one person in the parlour had come from Newport, or at least had received information that everything was ready there and the soldiers would not offer resistance. This man, who also called at the Greyhound on this evening, had a glazed hat. Professor David Williams believed that if this man existed, which was unlikely, he was an *agent provocateur*, but Harris firmly identified him as Reynolds.[33]

After their talk the leaders came to the front of the public house, whilst George Such, a saddler, the one-legged George Turner (Cole), and others tried to put the crowd into some kind of military order. There is some unconfirmed evidence that one of the marshals was a deserter, a man named Williams who moved across the country on horseback, encouraging Chartist groups to speed onwards towards their easy victory at Newport. Oliver Jones asserts that John Rees the Fifer had also just arrived, though the evidence for this is not conclusive.[34] As for Frost, he waited impatiently in the pouring rain for perhaps half an hour before agreeing to start. It has been suggested that it was the arrival of William Jones which finally moved Frost into action, but Richard Pugh indicates that Jones had probably left the Coach and Horses before his friend arrived.[35] About 7 p.m. the order to march was given and, after some confusion over whether to go up into the town for more recruits, the main body set off southwards. William Davies, who stayed behind, remembered the sight of candles in the dark and the sound of wailing women and children on the wind.[36]

Frost and an advance party of marchers took a minor road over the hill to Pentwyn Mawr, but most people followed John Reynolds towards Pontllanfraith. There they met crowds of people, including Edmund Edmunds, a sympathetic mine agent, who urged the Chartists to move on quickly to Newbridge, where they were expected. Not all, however, took this route; for some members of the associations at the local Greyhound public house and at Gelligroes appear to have moved directly down the valley. At the Greyhound Chartists had been gathering since the early hours of the morning, and had been supplied with free refreshment by the radical landlord. Prominent organizers in the area, such as Jack Barrill, his partner the 25-year-old collier Thomas Davies, and young Moses and William Horner, spent the whole day securing arms, checking recruits, and probably receiving messages from Reynolds and even William Jones. By 7 p.m. over 200 men were outside the Greyhound, and to the sound of Barrill's bugle and in the company of a few Blackwood Chartists they made their way, first to Gelligroes, where crowds and gunfire greeted their arrival. One body of men then set off down the Sirhowy valley to Risca and beyond.[37]

The journeys through the night were hard and wet, and many of those from Argoed and Blackwood who travelled eastwards into the neighbouring valley stopped at the beerhouses of Crumlin and Newbridge. Hundreds of workmen from different localities had expected to meet Frost at Newbridge, but the crowds who arrived early outside a blacksmith's shop in the town were told that he had gone ahead to Cefn. As they marched southwards, now in a more leisurely fashion, some of the Chartists began to search for arms and recruits. At Abercarn they visited the great house of John Llewellyn, agent to Sir Benjamin Hall, and took guns and powder from the home of James Woolford, gamekeeper.

The companies of men marching down the turnpike road, tramroad, and canal-side from Abercarn had gunmen guarding the sides and rear. On the route guides were waiting to give them the latest news and directions. John Reynolds and a colleague appear to have been stationed near Risca 'bridge, and from there they urged men on, cursing those without arms, and telling people to take what they could find from houses in the area.[38] At Risca, Duffield's Old Bridge public house and other drinking-places were packed from about 9 p.m. until 2 a.m., and so were other shelters. As promised, a large pile of weapons had been collected for the marchers, but those who had brought guns with them were worried by the effects of the appalling weather. Some workmen decided to dry out themselves and their weapons at Risca, whilst others pushed forward a short distance to the Welsh Oak, just below Pontymister. There 'a great stop' had been made and by 1 or 2 a.m. there were already some 2,000 people huddled together.

Frost had arrived at the Welsh Oak about midnight, and soon afterwards set off towards Cefn, some two miles nearer Newport. Cefn had been chosen by Friday's delegate conference as the most suitable meeting-place, and in the early hours of Monday morning Thomas Davies, a few other Newport radicals, and an advance party of Pontypool Chartists were moving in that direction. Sadly, we do not know what happened at Cefn, though the traditional historical view is that Frost waited, with increasing annoyance, for William Jones and the main Pontypool contingent.[39] Yet hundreds of Pontypool men were already encamped at the northern entrance to Newport, and by the early hours of Monday morning Frost must surely have known that he had sufficient resources to mount an assault. Perhaps, as some claimed, the Newport man was waiting to discover how the authorities were defending the town and whether a number of soldiers were ready to desert. Did he, in the absence of this information, now decide to take the safer southern route into town, thus confusing those Pontypool and Newport Chartists who were expecting the main assault to be made via Cefn, High Cross Road, and the Stow hill workhouse? Dr Price even suggested, somewhat unfairly, that Frost's nerve had gone. Whatever the reason for his long absence, the Chartists at the Welsh Oak remembered that they waited for what seemed an eternity. Some recorded how they spent the wasted hours: testing their guns and relishing the thought of pulling the workhouse down, or, in a few cases, praying that the whole venture would be called off. In the meantime, messengers on horseback were passing up and down the columns of frozen men, and one of these was, according to James Hodge, the deserter who was soon to guide them into Newport.[40]

About the time that Frost made his way back from Cefn towards the Welsh Oak, companies of Chartists from the heads of the valleys had begun to arrive in the neighbourhood. As we have seen, good communications had been established between Frost and Zephaniah Williams over the week-end, and in the northern iron towns preparations were well in hand for the rising. Large numbers of people had been obliged to buy cards, lodges were kept open throughout Saturday and Sunday, association books were collected, lists drawn up, and captains appointed where not already known. At the Royal Oak in Blaina, Zephaniah Williams's son took charge of much of the administration, and captain William Davies, whose ten men worked together in the same level, was given his instructions. On the march Davies and other officers were required to wear armbands and to address their sections by numbers. They were also made responsible for collecting their men and seeing that they were well armed.[41]

In the lodge meetings towards the end of October Zephaniah and other leaders had urged the Chartists to secure some means of self-defence. Quite a number had rifles and bullets were obtained from people like Griffiths, the currier of Tredegar. Evan Edwards, clockmaker and dealer of the same town, cast balls especially for the Chartists, as did James Godwin, a mason of Brynmawr. The making of pikes was more common, as one would expect in the iron district. John Owen, a blacksmith living by the side of the tramroad in Ebbw Vale, was said to have made over fifty pikeheads, which were deposited at Rassau lodge.[42] Collections of weapons were, in fact, stored in caves and at several addresses in Blaina and Sirhowy. New Chartist recruits were sometimes offered the opportunity of buying these weapons, but most made them from sticks and knives at home.

On Saturday, as the news from the delegate meeting reached up the valleys, a new urgency entered the Chartist preparations. At Brynmawr, for example, new and old Chartists met upstairs in the King Crispin and swore an oath of secrecy on the Bible. Ishmael Evans, chairman for the evening, told them that the English and Welsh Chartists were rising on Sunday and that they should not be afraid. They were to be divided into tens, with a captain over every hundred men, and Frost was their commander-in-chief. He was to be obeyed, and when they met him they would receive further instructions. David Lewis, the 37-year-old shoemaker who had been at Blackwood on Friday, then warned them that they could not lose this fight. If they had to kill anyone it should be the army officers and those in authority. Those Chartists used to firing at targets might be called on to perform this disagreeable task. Lewis himself had arms, and there would be cartloads of pikes waiting for them at Sirhowy. He looked forward to the time when the distinctions between rich and poor would be swept away. Only the sea, he said, would stop them.[43]

On the same day Zephaniah Williams was delivering less forceful speeches to the people who crowded into his Royal Oak. He told them that the Charter would soon be the law of the land and that the soldiers in Wales could not halt their progress. He asked them to meet again early on Sunday evening when they would be given more details of Frost's intentions, as well as the pikes which they had ordered. Meanwhile his captains, such as the tailor Isaac Tippins, were combing the neighbourhood for people without cards and weapons. A few miles across the mountains, at Ebbw and Tredegar, there were similar scenes: gangs of workmen, who had recently demanded wages in cash from their employers and the closure of the works, were terrifying the faint-hearted and the people of property. Samuel Homfray, in his fortified residence, remained aloof from the strife, but as he listened to the gloomy reports of policeman Homan and as he watched his men streaming up towards Dukestown for a meeting, he knew that something extraordinary was about to happen.

On Sunday morning the people of the iron district made their way towards those beerhouses used as Chartist headquarters. By 11 a.m. some 200 men had gathered at the Royal Oak, and were told by Zephaniah Williams to prepare for the greatest meeting ever on the mountain. He warned that those who stayed away would be the cause of bloodshed. Early in the afternoon, as two stewards guarded the door of his beerhouse, Zephaniah gave his followers more information, and William Jones may have also addressed them. According to several reports, about 5 p.m. a tall thin man, who had come from Blackwood, conferred with the Blaina Chartists about the time when the latter would meet on the mountain. He inveighed against turncoats and urged the men to bring food and weapons. Zephaniah, who translated his speech into Welsh, assured some confused listeners that more would be revealed in about an hour's time. One hostile witness claimed that the owner of the Royal Oak also talked vaguely about a people's march to London, and promises of help from sympathetic gentlemen. It seems almost certain that Zephaniah was trying, in the face of some opposition, to curb the violent spirits in the audience. He was against over-zealous impressment, confident that all cowards would be noted and that their lives would become 'a misery to them'. Similarly, the Blaina leader wanted those on the march to keep the law and to refrain from bloodshed. If, as seemed unlikely, the soldiers fired at them, they were to do 'their best'.[44]

At 6 p.m., or soon afterwards, the crowd at the Royal Oak set off on their two-mile walk to the appointed meeting-place on Mynydd Carn-y-cefn between Nantyglo and Ebbw Vale. They took with them candles and lanterns to guide them through the night. On arrival Zephaniah placed himself under a large umbrella on a mound by the roadside. From time to time a horn was sounded and guns tested, and the Chartist leader kept boredom at bay with a couple of short speeches. In one of them he dissociated himself from David Lewis of Brynmawr, who had predicted that people would return from Newport up to their shoes in blood. Once again, Zephaniah urged them to be orderly and united, promising that the soldiers would be no match for them.

As he waited impatiently for up to two hours, the crowd on the mountain grew to perhaps 4,000 strong. People arrived on their own or in contingents, and some were dragged along by gangs of miners. One of the early arrivals was Abraham Thomas of Coalbrookvale, who had joined the Chartists five or six weeks before and was one of William Davies's group of ten. He left home at 7 p.m. despite his wife's pleading. In her anguish his wife put the youngest child in her shawl and ran after Abraham through the rain to the Royal Oak, only to be told by Zephaniah's wife that her husband had gone straight to the mountain. They were never to see each other again.[45]

William Howell, a gasworker noted for his hostility towards the Chartists, and George Lloyd, a labourer of Blaina, were another type of recruit. The wife of the former claimed that she and her husband were about to go to chapel that evening when, near the Royal Oak, three or four men 'wanted to drag him from me. There was something in my hands; I could not tell what; I was near out of my senses. They parted me from him; I was near falling. One man in particular, pushed me against the wall, and I was hurt. I went home then; I could go no further. I did not see my husband again till the Tuesday evening.'[46] About the same time George Lloyd was returning home from the Bush in Nantyglo when he fell in with a gang who put a pike to his breast, and persuaded him to join them as they ran and hooted from one block of houses to the next. Lloyd then spent over two hours on the mountain, with an increasingly restless mass of Chartists.[47]

These people were waiting for, amongst others, the companies of men that had been ordered to meet on the hill at Rassau and in the Star Field, Dukestown. Many of the workmen from Brynmawr and Beaufort were taken, willingly and unwillingly, to Rassau, but hundreds of neighbouring Clydach ironworkers had already left the area 'in droves . . . feeling alarmed'. From teatime onwards people had begun to call at the Brynmawr homes of David Lewis and Ishmael Evans, and some of these later collected weapons and ammunition from James Godwin. As they journeyed through the night they fired off their guns and impressed men on the road. Those who considered escaping quickly realized that it was 'all the same in every corner of the world'. John Powell, for instance, was dragged from his home at Beaufort to the usual Chartist meeting-place at Rassau. There, in a room full of men and pikes, Llewellyn Davies was choosing captains and John Thomas, a 48-year-old tailor, was handing out tickets. When all was ready the crowd outside moved off in companies to join Zephaniah Williams.[48]

We are able to follow the activities of one of the best-remembered Chartist gangs in this area. Up at Rassau David Howell and William David, who worked for the Harfords, John Jones, William Williams, and perhaps fifty more were knocking on doors, putting spears through beds, and giving occupants five minutes to dress. When another John Jones protested that he was an old army pensioner he was told he was the very man they wanted. About 8 p.m. they stopped outside Carmel chapel, by the Beaufort ironworks, and half a dozen of the gang interrupted the service. David Howell and his friends required the congregation to follow the Chartists, but some of them managed to hide. A coal-miner, Thomas Waters, ran home, put his money into his pockets, and fled to a house in Breconshire and the comfort of a blazing fire.[49]

One suspects that during this business of impressment a number of old scores were settled. At 11 p.m., when most Chartists in the area were already marching with Zephaniah Williams to Newport, David Howell's gang broke into Lloyd's Beaufort Arms. The owner of the place had always refused to allow Chartist newspapers to be read in the tap-room. Having pushed their pikes through all the downstairs windows, the gang demanded drinks and the presence of the landlord and his son. Neither could be found but, before they left, the Chartists put a spear through Lloyd's dog. Perhaps, as Zephaniah indicated hours before, these were the men who had been left behind to deal with the people's enemies. As they moved through the night with their guns firing, they were also suspected of having designs on Brecon and Abergavenny. Certainly a number of recently recruited Chartists, such as Charles Lloyd and Owen Williams of the Brynmawr lodge, reached the Monmouthshire town on Sunday, though they claimed to be seeking only the protection of the soldiers stationed there.

Further west, at Tredegar and Sirhowy, the preparations for the march on Newport were already under way early on Sunday afternoon. At the Red Lion and other houses in Colliers' Row, Tredegar, William Evans, his brother-in-law Thomas Morgan, John Morgan, and other prominent radicals were making plans and pikes. Evans was a little downhearted, and others were perplexed that they knew so little about the rising.[50] By the early evening large crowds had gathered in the town and we are told by two historians that Jack Rees, with his blue coat and military manner, took his Tredegar contingent down the Sirhowy valley to meet John Frost at Blackwood.[51] Perhaps Rees did set off early, but many of the Chartists from Tredegar who travelled in that direction did not leave before 7 p.m. Henry Hughes, who emigrated to America in 1851, recalled many years later: 'I remember that on a Sunday night I was on my father's back coming from church. It was a dark night with mist and rain and we were meeting troop after troop of Chartists with pikes and rifles on their shoulders and one troop after another would be asking my father if he had met troops ahead. . . . My father did not go to sleep that night expecting that they might come to our home. . . . On that Monday morning there was not a young man or an old man to be seen in the place, only girls and women and they were in great fears and tears.'[52] At 8 p.m. large numbers of men, with pikes on their shoulders were seen going towards Sirhowy bridge, and eventually this company made its way through Ebbw Vale to Newport.

Benjamin Richards, one of Tredegar's most flamboyant and active Chartists, may have been in the crowd. Richards lived at the Colliers' Arms, near the Baptist chapel in Park Row, and it was here over the weekend that people collected their cards. On Sunday his house had been turned into a pike-making foundry. Richards, his cousin Lewis Rees, and several other shoemakers were busy heating iron and fixing it on to wooden poles. By 7 p.m. there were scores of people in the vicinity, and soon Richards, who was head of a lodge at the Star in Dukestown, led the crowd in that direction. On his own admission they met, at Sirhowy bridge, a lot of people coming down from Dukestown.[53]

Twyn-y-star had long been a favourite meeting-place for the Chartists from the heads of the valleys, and on this Sunday evening hundreds were there, waiting in the driving rain. Rees Meredith, soon to be killed at the Westgate, checked the various groups as they arrived, and called over the names of the captains present. These included David Jones the Tinker of Tredegar, in his velvet jacket and spotted neckerchief, William Morgan, and a man with a wooden leg.[54] Perhaps as historians have suggested, they were wary of moving too soon because of the absence of companies from Dowlais and Rhymney, but at 8 p.m. the order to march was given and they hardly stopped until they arrived at the Welsh Oak.

As the men from Dukestown raced down through Ebbw Vale some 2,000 people were awaiting them in a field near the Harfords' Pen-y-cae ironworks. Their arrival was signalled by loud cheers and gunfire. About this time one of the managers from the neighbouring Victoria works came upon this assembly, and, although 'extremely frightened', had the good sense to gallop away at speed. According to one report, the number of local Chartists who made their way to the Pen-y-cae field was comparatively small, and it was strangers to the area who were most active in searching for additional support.[55] Abraham Thomas of the company shop, George Hutchins, a roll-turner, and several other 'turncoats' were dragged from behind locked doors by men with high collars covering their faces. Tradesmen in Ebbw Vale were required to sell these Chartists food and tobacco, and the keepers of beerhouses were also busy. About 7 or 8 p.m. Thomas Morgan of Tredegar and twenty others, armed with guns and pitchforks, pushed their way into the Lamb and demanded beer. Some of them, reported William Adams, seemed happy to stay there until the morning, but within half an hour they were off. An hour or so later another gang arrived at the Lamb, with the landlord of the Wyvern Inn, Sirhowy, and his wife in tow. He fell down and cried, and his spouse declared that if he were being taken to Newport she was going as well. In an effort to avoid similar embarrassment, Thomas Williams, his father and grandfather, and two neighbours, had locked themselves in the parlour of this Ebbw Vale beerhouse but a leader with a ribbon on his left arm checked the blindness of Evan Williams, and took his son Thomas instead. After a short while the gang, as often happened, grew tired of their wailing recruit and, on the instructions of 'No. 6', he was left face downwards on the ground near a forge.[56]

Between 8 p.m. and midnight the triangle of land between Cefn mountain top, Pen-y-cae, and the Victoria ironworks to the south was full of a heavy mass of sodden people. After a long spell on the mountain Zephaniah Williams and many of his followers had joined the crowds near the Harfords' residence. When the blast to the furnaces there was shut off the Blaina leader expressed his satisfaction, but to questions about the purpose of the march he remained elusive. Only Frost could tell them, and the sooner they reached him the better. For that reason, said Zephaniah, steam trams could be appropriated. Yet, as different companies set off about 9 p.m. progress was fairly slow and tortuous. An observer, who arrived on the scene hours later, as more Chartists were leaving the area, gives us this picture: 'I could see them going along the tram-road towards Newport not *en masse* but in straggling groups armed, some with pikes, others with fire-arms, of all descriptions, &c. They appeared to be under no controul, and acting only by impulse, each for himself.'[57]

The pace of these marchers varied considerably. David Williams of Ebbw Vale remembered that as he passed the Victoria works the clock was striking 10 p.m., an hour later he was at Pont Aberbeeg, and within a further hour his company were at the Foundry, Llanhilleth.[58] It then took these Chartists another six hours to reach Risca. The main reason for the delay was the appalling weather and the welcome sight of the public houses in the Brynithel area. James Samuel of the Coach and Horses claimed that at least three distinct parties came to his home, the first led by a tall man in a smock frock, the second by a very big man, and the third led by a nervous triumvirate of Zephaniah Williams, a middle-aged man carrying a mandrel and tin horn, and a young man in a plaid coat.[59] Williams, who, with his colleague Thomas Davies, spent much time pulling men out of the bars, had a pint of beer himself and obtained the hire of a horse-drawn tram and servant.

When Zephaniah left the Coach and Horses at 2 a.m. he was in low spirits and complained of being late. As he rode in the tram he passed groups of men moving slowly but noisily through the gloom. Some had already obtained food, drink, and weapons along the way, and others were soon to do the same at Newbridge and Abercarn. At a public house in Newbridge Mary Thomas attended to several parties during the night, and about 3 a.m. David Jones the Tinker arrived, gun in hand, and told her that the bread and cheese he was eating could be the last he should ever want.[60] Zephaniah Williams, meanwhile, was travelling on to Tŷ'n-y-Cwm, near the Welsh Oak. On arrival he called at the home of farmer Thomas Saunders, where hundreds of men had sought shelter from the rain. After a warm in front of Saunders's fire, Zephaniah sent them all on their way. It was now about 6.30 a.m.[61]

Some time earlier Frost had returned to the Welsh Oak from Cefn, and it is possible that the two leaders held a brief council of war. Frost had brought with him information from Cefn, and a messenger now arrived belatedly from Newport. By this time a number of Newport and Pontypool Chartists were at the Welsh Oak, and it appears that at least some of these people wrongly expected him to call a retreat. On the contrary, Frost had decided to carry out his proud boast at Friday's delegate conference that he and Zephaniah Williams alone could take the town, and it would be done through one turnpike entrance and not three. Frost was embarrassingly aware that several thousand of their people had been waiting for five hours along the road from Risca bridge to the Welsh Oak. Some, like Isaac Phillips, had spent the time combing the area for weapons and calling people by name out of their houses. In the early hours of the morning, for example, Phillips and thirty other men burst into the home of Richard Arnold, demanded guns, but took Arnold and some candles instead.[62] Arnold went under guard to the Welsh Oak. There guns and other weapons were repeatedly checked, and before the people moved off Frost called on those with firearms to come forward and test them. Zephaniah Williams and some of his men were placed at the rear,

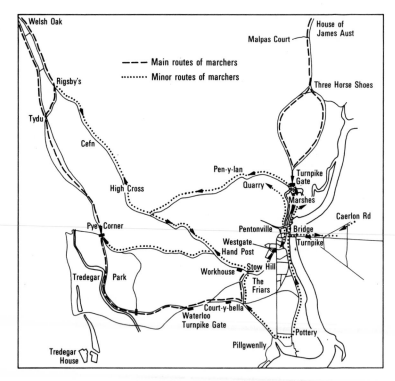

MAP 3. The Attack on Newport

and when Richard Davies of Llancaiach and others tried to escape, guns were trained on them.

Thus, at about 7 a.m., great chains of people made their way along the three miles from the Welsh Oak to Pye Corner. This route into Newport was not the one originally planned, and any intention of meeting up with Pontypool men at Cefn before a direct assault on the workhouse appears to have been abandoned. John Lewis of Tydu saw at least 2,000 take the lower road into Newport past his house, and when he remonstrated with some of them a leader took out a pistol and asked him why he used such language. In their opinion this was the way people had secured their rights in America and France.[63] By 8 a.m. most of these Chartists had arrived at Pye Corner, at the entrance to Sir Charles Morgan's Tredegar Park. Once inside the Park they moved along the tram-road, and were ordered to stop for about half an hour. By this time the men with pikes and bludgeons were in ranks behind the three hundred or so people carrying muskets. After another round of combined gunfire, they all moved on again, until required to stop a mile ahead by the Waterloo turnpike and Court-y-bella weighing-machine. This halt was a short one, and whilst 5,000 people caught their breath, some of the leaders held a conference.[64]

Whose the directing voices were at this point is not fully clear. Great efforts were made at the examinations and trial to place the main responsibility for organizing the marchers on arrested men like Frost, Williams, and Edmund Edmunds, but only the first of these played a prominent role in the Park, and he was dejected by the lateness of the proceedings. Those present on the day remembered other figures who pressed the people forward more vigorously and 'ranked them tidy'. Thomas Giles was close to Frost, as was Thomas Llewellyn and perhaps Wright Beatty and John Reynolds, and there were other unnamed captains wielding swords and long spears. A man with a wooden leg, now on horseback, was well to the front, as was a man in a long blanket smock. These men, and possibly John Lovell, the Newport gardener, his colleague, the tall and thin Charles Waters, and the deserter mentioned earlier, were joined in Waterloo public house by John Rees and David Jones of Tredegar. When they emerged, Rees in particular helped to put the cheering crowds into a better marching formation, with six men abreast and a gun at the end of each line. The final assault had begun.[65]

For most of these people one question remained unanswered. What had happened to the Chartists of Pontypool and the mining communities to the north of that town? The story has never been properly told, and perhaps it never will be. Contemporary investigators and historians have been tempted to fill the gaps in information with their own imaginative theories. It was said, for example, that the Blaenavon and Varteg ironworkers repaid employers' paternalism by keeping aloof from the rising.[66] Mr E. J. Davies tells us that the Blaenavon contingent assembled in silent misery on the Varteg road and then went home.[67] It is possible, however, that some of these men went up to Brynmawr and Nantyglo, and others may have been told that their appointed task was a secondary one, of moving on nearby Abergavenny and Monmouth if Frost were successful at Newport. Perhaps some actually travelled there, for the authorities in those towns were convinced that not all the hundreds of strangers in the streets were refugees. As for the men of the Varteg these were, as we shall see, not inactive.

Many of the Chartists around Pontypool spent the weekend in the manner of their friends to the west. According to their delegate at a secret meeting early in October, Abersychan was a militant locality with a high proportion of old soldiers amongst their membership, and the preparations for the rising confirmed his opinion. William Wood, manager of the British Iron Company Works, was told on Saturday that the men had been 'regularly organized to the use of arms'. Very early on Sunday morning people began to collect at David Richards's beerhouse, and William Jones arrived to give instructions and assure the men that everything would be well. In line with some of the speeches at Friday's delegate conference he called on the audience to force the cowardly, and to take prominent people and policemen as hostages. He may have mentioned Capel Hanbury Leigh, Reginald Blewitt, and Constable Jordan by name. Arms were not a problem, for over a thousand pikes were stacked at the race course just south of Pontypool, and other pikes and guns were stored in a number of places.[68] Two of these were Parry the farrier's at the top of Trosnant, and the Bristol beerhouse, which had been left in the charge of William Shellard. Shellard, like several other notable Chartists in this area, did not go to Newport, but was said to be waiting for further instructions from Frost after the anticipated victory at Newport.

As the time for the rising drew close it was apparent that at least two plans of action were in the minds of Pontypool Chartists. The first, which had been agreed at Friday's meeting, was for contingents from Abersychan, Pontnewydd, and elsewhere to meet at the racecourse in the afternoon and evening of Sunday. By 6 p.m. large crowds were already passing through Pontypool on their way to the meeting-place. Some like George Shell, the young cabinet-maker who left his lodgings about two hours before, needed no second bidding, but others had to be pushed along. John Thomas (Jack the Sailor) was especially active in this business, and amongst the main targets were company clerks and shopkeepers.[69] Those who were found were taken to John Llewellyn's beerhouse at Pontnewydd or to the Bristol in the town. By 8 p.m. there were large numbers outside the latter place, and Shellard ordered them to march to the racecourse, where William Jones would join them. At the gate of the course were thirty armed men, and inside commanders Powell and Davies kept a watchful eye on the unruly and the fearful.

One of the complaints, which has been passed down the generations, was of the undue delay to which the men at the racecourse were subjected. An advance party set off comparatively early in the direction of Newport, but the main body waited until the arrival of William Jones. About 10 p.m. he appeared, dressed in a bottle-green coat and corduroys and riding a horse. The mob, some 2,000 strong, were soon organized in the manner recommended by Friday's conference, with guns and pikes to the front. On the road they followed Jones, John Phillips the butcher, and another anonymous friend of the Pontypool leader, and during the march the crowd made a number of unscheduled stops for rest and refreshment. Contrary to some impressions, Jones urged the men forward.

As they, like the advance party, passed through New Inn, Croesyceiliog, Llantarnam, and Malpas, a number of travellers were captured, notably the brewer Barnabas Brough and his friend, Thomas Watkins. By the early hours of Monday morning well over a thousand men were encamped near the Newport turnpike. Some were in disguise, and all of them responded to the numbers which were read out by their captains. According to Brough, the crowd expected to enter the town from the north as soon as they received news of the western assault by Frost and Williams. In the meantime, hundreds of Chartists were still leaving Pontypool. We

know, from several sources, that these spent hours at public houses
in Croesyceiliog, so that when they eventually reached the Marshes
gate at the northern reaches of Newport it was about 6.00 a.m.
There they were joined by a party of Chartists from Newport itself,
and a few of them ventured into the town and the arms of special
constables. In the meantime the small advance company of Pontypool Chartists had arrived at the Cefn, and William Jones, a very
early arrival at the Marshes, had probably already returned to his
home district.[70]

In the Pontypool area the story of the rising was, as perhaps Jones
had always intended, significantly different from that elsewhere.
Whilst the main body was moving southwards towards Malpas,
small and large groups of Chartists were still active in the mining
communities between Pontypool and Blaenavon. About 9 p.m.
they succeeded in stopping the furnaces at the Pentwyn ironworks,
and within an hour a crowd of 300–400, led by Thomas Lewis,
Edmund Richards and others, did the same at the British Iron
works in Abersychan. Richards, who carried a large shovel, told the
furnace-keeper to obey them or have something through his guts.
Col. Thomas Mitchell, whose father worked for the company,
remembered the affair many years later. A neighbour rushed in to
tell his father that the Chartists were coming.

All immediately came out to the front of the house whence could be distinctly seen by the light of the blast furnaces, large bodies of men moving
about the works, whose shouting, blowing of horns, and discharging of
fire arms could now be distinctly heard. . . . The first act of the rioters was
to cause the blast engines to be stopped, thus cutting off the blast from the
furnaces, the immediate effect of which was to throw the whole place into
utter darkness. . . . A large number of the workmen's cottages and agents'
houses were situated on the side of the hill and for these it was evident the
rioters were making.[71]

The homes of James Price, furnace-manager, and others were
raided for recruits and weapons. Lewis Morris, a machine-man,
reported that at 11.20 p.m. the mob burst into his home and told
him to dress, but relented because of his age and took his two sons
instead. Thomas Ball told him that it was 'now or never', and when
Morris complained that a blanket smock had just disappeared he
was promised that the thief would be killed.

The ferocity of the gangs in this area reminds one of the Scotch

Cattle. Women, who invariably answered the door to the Chartist workmen, were warned that a spear would penetrate the first liar. At midnight, in the house of John Jones of Abersychan, his wife Mary pleaded with Thomas Keys and other Chartists for her husband's life. He had hidden himself under the bed, and was being kicked about the body as he dressed. Amy Meredith, whose 11-year-old son was also with the gang, told a man carrying a gun to fetch Jones out and finish him off. Jones and a lodger were taken as far as Pontnewydd. The sense of urgency was understandable; these Chartists were still hoping that people could be sent to Newport in time, and a few of them eventually joined the late arrivals at Malpas.

Soon the Golynos furnaces and other works in the area had been brought to a standstill, and in the early hours of the morning at least 400 people moved northwards on the Varteg. The attitude was belligerent and vengeful. When Thomas Westbourne, a cinder-haulier at the furnaces told one of them that he was not a radical, a gun was pointed at him and he was informed that anyway he belonged to the Chartists now. James Moore, who also carried a gun, David Williams, Charles Bucknall, and four or five others rushed into the engine-house and ordered a frightened Edmund Jones to stop the engine. All parts of the ironworks were then visited by the mob, before they turned south towards Garndiffaith and Pontypool. At Garndiffaith, which between the hours of 2 and 5 a.m. was full of workmen, more houses were broken into and occupants seized. In this task the two Britons, Solomon and John, together with Thomas Davies, were said to have been the guiding influences, and their work was not without a touch of farce. Moses Cooke, one of the victims, recalled that the gang outside his door about 3.30 a.m. was singing 'come along lads. Roll up . . .', whilst George Coles, another miner, when taken to the bottom of the Garn, challenged William Jones to a fight in the mud.[72]

The fact that groups of people were still arriving in Pontypool at daybreak, when Frost and Zephaniah Williams were already close to Newport, indicates that there was a strategy here which historians have largely ignored. 'What their plans are I do not know', wrote William Wood from Abersychan on Sunday. 'Some say they are going to Monmouth to liberate Vincent and Edwards, others that they are going to Newport to seize the magistrates who have been most active in arresting them; and others that they are going to attack Mr. Leigh's house.'[73] Some of those taken by the Chartists in the early hours of Monday knew only that they were going to Pontypool. In the town two of the schemes which were considered were those of seizing the police station and the arms within it, and of doing likewise to Pontypool Park, the home of the Lord Lieutenant. For weeks people had talked about putting Hanbury Leigh down a coalpit and keeping him there until he signed the release of the political prisoners at Monmouth. More recently there had been suggestions that Reginald Blewitt and Thomas Prothero would also make good hostages, and hints, too, that on the day after the Newport rising hundreds would invade Monmouth and possibly hold Abergavenny, Brecon, and Usk as well.

Were these references to the original plan outlined by Dr Price, and were some of the Pontypool Chartists saddened that their role had been diminished? William Jones had always promised his followers more, rather more quickly, than had Zephaniah Williams and Frost. According to a reformed Pontypool Chartist, Jones told them that on Monday, after the triumph at Newport, posters would be displayed in the county announcing a new 'Executive government of England', with Frost as its 'President' or 'Protector', and that within a week the Charter would be the law of the land. Professor David Williams dismisses this evidence, but it is interesting that Zephaniah also refers to posters already printed, and a strange letter was sent some days later 'to his Mightiness' John Frost, 'Lord Protector of South Wales'.[74]

It is instructive at this point to consider the reactions of the authorities in the area during the week-end. Capel Leigh, who heard the news of an intended outbreak on Sunday morning, sent messengers to Abergavenny and Monmouth to warn them of a possible attack; and in the afternoon he travelled to Newport, returning home with a personal bodyguard of four soldiers and information that 'a formidable rising' was expected at Pontypool. He was later mocked for this act of self-defence but perhaps his concern was justified, especially as the town had no military presence and there were so many firearms stored at Pontypool Park. In fact, thirty resident pensioners and a considerable number of special constables were given some of these rifles on Sunday. Eighty specials were placed on duty at the Park and another fifty at the police station, and lines of communication were kept open between them. At the station, for part of the day at least, were two officers hated by the Chartists, Superintendent Roberts and his assistant Jordan, and these men, together with specials John Hair and David Jones, ventured out during the night to check on the crowds' movements. Under cover of darkness they made forays to Abersychan, and were fortunate enough about 3 a.m. to capture a man carrying a long pike. On several occasions mobs appeared to threaten their positions, and, as daylight broke through, several hundred Chartists marched on the station only to withdraw at the very last moment. They had decided to hang fire until orders were received from Newport.

Throughout this terrible night the authorities at Pontypool and Abergavenny were bombarded with requests for help from their friends in the interior of the coalfield. That old campaigner, the Revd William Powell, chairman of the Abergavenny Petty Sessions, held on to what cavalry he possessed, and urged the military at Brecon to come to their aid. At 7.30 p.m. his 12th Lancers were placed at the Angel and Greyhound hotels, and half an hour later the need for special constables was cried through the town. During these hours the absence of soldiers in South Wales was never more apparent, as employers and tradesmen fled 'in terror' from places like Abersychan. William Needham of the Varteg ironworks went to bed oblivious of the events around him, but surgeon John Laurence and other local notables received anonymous messages warning them to leave the district. The streets and inns of Abergavenny were the nearest sanctuary. In the meantime, at Pontypool, as the morning broke, large crowds were roaming about, anticipating a great victory at Newport. According to the correspondent of the *Monmouthshire Merlin*, some of the women of the town set off in a southerly direction, wishing to check the truth of the early reports of soldiers killed and hoping to join in the plunder.[75]

One mystery then, and since, was the behaviour of their leader William Jones. Old people from the area recalled years later that the watchmaker was chiefly responsible for the comparatively late arrival of many Pontypool Chartists at Newport.[76] Early on Sunday morning James Emery and John Dyer brought a horse to Jones at Abersychan 'for the purpose of getting the Chartists together, to come back to this place . . .'.[77] Later in the day Jones was seen at a number of places, including Tredegar and, in the middle of the afternoon, on the road from there to Blackwood. Some time earlier he was said to have been at the Royal Oak, Blaina, and Richard Pugh of Blackwood insisted that Jones had a brandy at his Coach and Horses between 5 and 6 p.m.[78] Just after 7 p.m. he came with two other men to the Navigation Inn at Crumlin and was surprised by the lack of armed preparations. He reported that Zephaniah Williams and his men would be down soon, and promised that their flag would be flying on Newport church by 10 a.m. on Monday.[79] Within half an hour he was away, and a couple of hours later arrived at the racecourse where the main Pontypool contingent was waiting.

It is now impossible to discover the motives behind Jones's circular tour. Oliver Jones and other writers, influenced no doubt by the subsequent animosity that grew up between the Pontypool watchmaker and Zephaniah Williams, were inclined to believe that the former now wished to pull out of the rising.[80] In support of this they rely heavily on the evidence of William Watkins, who, although dubious about the Chartist leader's identity, claimed that he had to be forced to do his duty at Croesyceiliog by rank-and-file Chartists.[81] Perhaps Jones was unhappy about the nature of the rising, but there could have been other reasons for his travels on this day besides plain cowardice. It is worth recalling the last-minute instructions that were sent from Frost to Zephaniah Williams on Sunday afternoon, and it is highly probable that Jones had to obtain similar information and pass it on to his people around Pontypool and beyond. There is little evidence that on his tour Jones encouraged people to hold back; if anything the reverse was true. Could he have been, as Dr Price was, a little wary of Frost's will and Zephaniah's cautious nature? It is even possible that Jones, still the actor, preferred a more ambitious scheme which gave his Pontypool Chartists a special role, and offered the immediate prospect of the release of Vincent at Monmouth. According to one witness, the watchmaker late on Monday morning talked vaguely about Dr Price coming to their assistance with his seven pieces of cannon.[82]

As we have seen, Jones left the racecourse at Pontypool about 11 p.m. on Sunday with a large body of Chartists, and probably reached Malpas somewhat earlier than most of his followers. The evidence is confusing and even contradictory at this point, but it is likely that the leader returned, either all the way to Pontypool or to Croesyceiliog, in the early hours. James Hodge heard about 8 a.m.

that Jones was at High Cross, not far from Cefn, but the weight of evidence suggests that at this time he was near Croesyceiliog with another company of Chartists.[83] Several tradesmen were taken on the way and, when this crowd reached Malpas, they entered the estate of Thomas Prothero and forced his coachman and a gardener to accompany them. On the last miles of their journey the Chartists were cheering the first rumours of an easy victory at Newport, but when William Jones met James Aust, a well-known Chartist of the town, at his home near Malpas Court he probably learnt that the assault had not yet been mounted.

During the night some of the hundreds of people occupying and surrounding the Malpas turnpike had made their way up to Cefn, and others, giving the appropriate password, had passed by the Chartist guards into Newport. Most, however, remained at Malpas, sometimes for hours, and it is difficult to explain this policy. Had Frost, after consultation with the first arrivals at Cefn, decided to launch the attack on Newport with only his and Zephaniah's men, and were the Pontypool Chartists given the secondary task of descending into the town only if needed? It is worth noting that rumours of a premature victory were circulating at Malpas in the early hours of the morning, and that some of the crowd,when asked about their purpose, said that they were waiting for the Blackwood men before moving onto the next stage of the rising. Certainly there was a lack of urgency amongst the 2,000–3,000 people at the turnpike, at least until William Jones heard from James Aust and other local leaders the true story of the delays below. Then, some time after 9 a.m., the order was given to march up the lane that led from Penylan to High Cross and Cefn. Having passed the stone quarry the Pontypool Chartists were just negotiating the steep hill when they caught sight of people running in their direction. According to one version of the story it was now about 10 a.m. and William Jones, having asked a collier the reason for the panic, shouted 'Damn me, then we are undone.' Contrary to some impressions William Jones and his closest supporters continued up as far as High Cross and skirted the western perimeter of the town, trying to rally other Chartists and talking of a second assault, but Jones's calls went unheeded and by midday he was alone.[84]

The Rising

WITHIN Newport both the Chartists and the authorities had anticipated the arrival of the men from the mining towns. Over the week-
end there had been Chartist meetings at the Royal Oak, Mill Street,
near Frost's home, at the Prince of Wales beerhouse down
Commercial Road, and at several other places. A delegate from the
town was at the Blackwood conference on Friday, and even before
then news had reached Newport of preparations in the hills. On
Thursday the mayor was warned that radicals from the coalfield
had been down to confer with those at Newport, and others were
soon to follow in search of arms.[1] This seaport was, as we have seen,
the depot for much of the iron and coal produced in the county, and
the men of Pillgwenlly, the dockland district, had close ties with the
miners.

No one personified these connections better than Morgan
James. His home was in Pillgwenlly and it was there that he enrolled
as a Chartist. Some time later he was obliged to seek work at the
Fleur-de-lis colliery near Blackwood, but he returned home at
weekends. Returning to Newport on this particular weekend he met
Jenkin Morgan, a 40-year-old milkman and father of three from
Pillgwenlly, who was renowned as a radical and had taken a day off
work to attend Vincent's trial a few months before. According to
James, he was advised by this passionate Chartist not to leave the
town as serious work was afoot. Since Wednesday Jenkin Morgan
had told his friends that he expected bloodshed at Pillgwenlly and
Newport. He spoke of a simultaneous rising across the kingdom,
and mentioned a plan to take over the workhouse and its arsenal, as
well as the home of Lewis Edwards close by. The soldiers were to be
surprised and disarmed. Groups of Chartists were also to apprehend the family of Parson Roberts and to secure the gunpowder
warehouse of Aaron Crossfield situated in Corn Street, near the
Westgate hotel. According to Jenkins the town would be invaded
by hundreds of people through the Malpas, Stow, and Court-y-
bella turnpikes, and when Frost came down Stow hill in the early

hours of Monday morning the noise of cheering and exploding crackers would be the signal for the Chartists in and around the town to go about their appointed tasks.[2]

Whether this information was entirely accurate or not, it is quite evident that Newport Chartists were ready for action on Sunday night. Captains had been appointed, people had been urged to join the cause, and since the middle of the previous week pikes had been made and the search for firearms had begun. Jenkin Morgan and a man called Davis, who lived near the Pottery above Pillgwenlly, were especially active in the business of arming Chartists, and much of the work of making pike-heads was carried out locally at Evans's foundry and at William Stephens the blacksmith's shop. On the eve of the rising, weapons and gunpowder were handed out at a number of places, including the Royal Oak and the homes of Jenkin Morgan, and Jonathan Palmer, a radical stonemason of Pillgwenlly.

If we can believe the evidence of informers it seems that in the working-class areas of Newport, as in the mining communities, impressment and oath-taking were common. Down by the Pottery, for instance, 'captain' Palmer asked men and women on Sunday to kiss the Bible and swear to the following: 'You must be afeard, and you must not be bribed with money; you must fight for the Chartists, so help you God.'[3] The captains then required the Chartists to disperse to strategic points in the town. Some of the men in the Royal Oak made their way towards Pye Corner, whilst Jenkin Morgan's gang marched to the Usk bridge and stopped along the Caerleon road. A group of men were also seen near Aaron Crossfield's gunpowder warehouse. Meanwhile, the people from the Pottery district were setting off in two opposite directions. One group, led by Palmer, moved along the Sirhowy tramroad and up the Friars to Stow turnpike, where they were hoping to meet other Chartists in the vicinity of the workhouse, whilst a second group, in which young Patrick Hickey was prominent, walked up the canal side to the northern turnpike at Malpas.

By the early morning several hundred Newport workmen could be seen on the Marshes and at an old quarry to the north of the town. Like the Pontypool men arriving at the turnpike gate, these people were waiting for instructions and anticipating victory for Frost's men entering by the west. Some of the town Chartists, like James Aust of Malpas, had the special task of making contact with the incoming forces, and these messengers were on the main thoroughfares out of Newport at a very early hour.[4] Charles Groves, the 18-year-old secretary of the Young Men's Association, and the young sawyer, Thomas Davies, were actually arrested on the road before the main body of Chartists arrived. Davies, who was stopped at 4 or 5 a.m. by a special constable, had on him a cutlass, a pick, a hammer, two pocket knives, a pistol, balls, caps, and powder. He claimed that he was carrying this arsenal to protect himself, and that he was going towards Cefn in search of work.[5]

These arrests by special constables and policemen in the early hours of Monday morning indicate that the authorities at Newport expected trouble. Thomas Phillips, mayor and personal enemy of Frost, had been receiving information since Thursday that feeling was running high amongst the miners. On Saturday, after consulting with the secretary of the Oddfellows, he warned Captain Stack, in charge of the seventy infantrymen at the workhouse, to be ready for a surprise attack, and ordered Police Superintendent Hopkins to summon 150 special constables to be on duty that evening.[6] On Sunday, with the arrival of Capel Hanbury Leigh, John Llewellyn of Abercarn, and some terrified refugees from the mining towns, the tension became unbearable. Almost every hour news came through of Chartist preparations in the hills, and the families of Thomas Jones Phillips, magistrates' clerk, and of a number of special constables gathered up their belongings and fled into the country.

In the late afternoon and early evening the authorities in the town knew for certain that a rising was in progress, and that before too long they would be under siege. Warnings were received that the workhouse, with its 200 stand of arms, was under threat, as were the homes of Lewis Edwards and the mayor. Phillips himself sent urgent requests for help to Bristol and London, and informed Abergavenny, Monmouth, and Cardiff of the dangers which might soon threaten them. Early in the evening the mayor had a final briefing with his fellow magistrates, Thomas Walker of the Kings Head was sent on horseback to chart the rebels' advance, and the small police force was ordered to summon all the 500 specials who had been sworn in over six months before. About 9 p.m. Phillips left his home for a tour of the Westgate, King's Head, and Parrot inns, where some of these constables had already gathered. He decided that most of them should move with him to the Westgate, and there they were placed under the control of Thomas Hawkins, soon to be Phillips's successor as mayor of the town.

The specials, and policemen Hopkins, Moses Scard, and William Lewis were on duty for much, if not all, of the night. The former were divided into companies, and given clear instructions. One company was sent to protect the home of Lewis Edwards, the magistrate who was now at the workhouse with the men of the 45th Regiment. Others were directed to the workhouse itself and to the strategically important bridge over the Usk. Some specials, relieved every two hours, were also required to keep open the lines of communication between the Westgate, where the mayor and fellow magistrate William Brewer were stationed, the barracks, and the police headquarters at Stow hill and the Parrot.

The most dangerous tasks facing the specials during the night were reconnoitring and apprehending Chartists on the road. Thomas Walker and Richard Webb, two of perhaps twenty scouts, came upon a small party of men at Rigsby's above Cefn and the licensee of the Parrot was fortunate to escape with a six-inch wound in his thigh. Stephen Rogers and his constables patrolled the road between High Cross and the Stow turnpike, whilst others were sent up to the Marshes. Altogether, they apprehended about two dozen men and boys, though some of these were very quickly freed, either voluntarily or because of the presence of an angry mob.[7] These 'suspicious characters' comprised both natives of the town and miners from some distance, and several of them were well armed. After questioning at the Westgate, some were released, a few kept in the hotel, and others escorted to the workhouse. Captain Stack, who received them, was told during the night that he should, as far as possible, keep the soldiers out of sight and fire only if attacked.

After day-break Henry Williams, ironmonger and special constable, and several others reported to the mayor that 4,000–5,000 Chartists were on the outskirts of the town. Phillips, who had concentrated most of his forces at the Westgate, was now alarmed for their safety, and about 8 a.m. he sent a request for military aid to the workhouse. Within a very short time Lt. Gray, Sergeants Daily and Armstrong, and twenty-eight privates arrived and stood guard at the front of the hotel. On the orders of the mayor they were then placed in the yard behind, but, as the sound of the mob came nearer, the young, inexperienced, and predominantly Irish soldiers were called inside to a large end room in the east wing.

They were joined by some of the sixty or more specials at the hotel who had not returned home for breakfast. Other specials remained in the hotel yard and in the passage to the front door. The door was guarded by two constables, who were instructed to allow only their comrades entry.

One of the reasons for the last-minute preparations at the West-gate hotel was the fear that the Chartists, when they left the weighing-machine at Court-y-bella, no longer had the barracks as their primary target. Until the early hours of Monday morning most people on both sides had expected the main western assault on Newport to be made via Cefn, High Cross, and the Union poor-house on the top of Stow hill. When, however, the miners and col-liers reached the area around Tydu most of them followed Frost's circuitous route through Tredegar Park. The reason for this is not clear, though, in the light of the exceptional delays, the new approach offered the possibility of avoiding a direct and daylight confrontation with the soldiers. At the exit of the Park the idea of mounting a two-pronged attack on the barracks and the Westgate appears to have been considered, but the Chartist leader almost certainly preferred to concentrate his forces on the hotel. For Frost the decision was not difficult; the mayor and some of his friends had chosen the hotel both as their place of refuge and as a prison for Chartists taken during the night, and, at that moment, it was defended by the hated special constables.[9]

How soon the Chartists were aware that Thomas Phillips had obtained military assistance is a fine question, and one which occupied the lawyers endlessly at the trials. The marchers left Court-y-bella at about 8.45 a.m., perhaps a quarter of an hour after the soldiers arrived at the Westgate three-quarters of a mile away. The thirty-two men of the 45th Regiment were un-doubtedly seen going rapidly down Stow hill, but the two boys who confessed to giving information on their movements to Frost and Jack the Fifer at the machine were unconvincing witnesses.[10] Their evidence on the direction of the mob after Court-y-bella was also suspect; most of the Chartists went north-wards up to the Friars and Stow turnpike. There they made a short halt, and their leaders resisted some rank-and-file demands to attack both the workhouse, which was openly defended by soldiers only yards away, and Lewis Edwards's residence. Then, in good order, most of the Chartists walked down the hill, cheering and occasionally firing their weapons, and putting fear into the hearts of respectable onlookers.[11]

Although Frost and Jack the Fifer were prominent figures on opposite sides of the long snake-like procession, other marchers now caught people's attention. Some witnesses claimed that Thomas Llewellyn and Richard Rorke were well to the fore, as was Charles Waters, secretary of Newport's radical association.[12] Another local Chartist, the gardener John Lovell, was especially vociferous and belligerent, calling on passers-by and the men building the Catholic chapel to join their crusade.[13] One suspects that these local guides, and more anonymous persons like a short man with a sword and the tall man with a wooden leg, were as important in these last minutes as Frost and Rees.[14]

According to people who lived near the scene, when the front ranks of the Chartists came to the bottom of Stow hill, an attempt was made to enter the courtyard of the Westgate from the rear. Although the soldiers were well hidden behind shuttered windows, it seems likely that someone would have signalled their presence. People had seen the men of the 45th Regiment form up in Commercial Road and then retreat into the courtyard.[15] However, for the moment the Chartists, who were vainly trying to push open the barred gate, seemed more concerned with the specials and the ammunition they knew to be almost within reach. After a few words of abuse most of these workmen returned to the file of marchers, and walked confidently into Commercial Road. It was now about 9.20 a.m.

As the Chartists came around the corner of the hotel shop-keepers peered out of premises recently closed by magistrates' decree and women pulled inquisitive children out of harm's way. The mob gave three loud cheers, a sound which filled the special constables with considerable apprehension. The front ranks of the Chartists were in regular order, with five abreast and armed men at the end of each or every other line. Although several observers were unable to distinguish any leaders, one man appears to have guided the first group past the front of the Westgate to the large doors of the courtyard.[16] At this point the Chartists were within feet of the soldiers and prisoners located in the east wing of the building. Having found the courtyard entrance barred, the front ranks turned round and all the other lines of the mob now in Commercial Road faced to the right. The focus of their attention

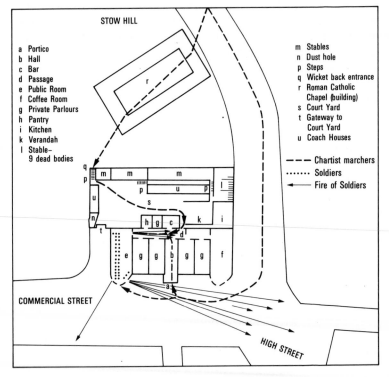

MAP 4. Ground Plan of the Westgate Hotel

was the main door of the hotel, and the gun- and pikemen were well placed for an attack.

John Frost and Charles Waters were seen by some people near the hotel, but perhaps the men who were most noticed at this time were Jack the Fifer, waving his hat and a pike or sword, John Lovell, carrying a rifle, the tall man with a wooden leg, and another gun-man who may well have been the deserter. After a brief word between some of these men, two, three, or even more of them went up the steps to the open front door. What happened then is con-fused, partly because the witnesses in court were being used to prove a particular point or were seeking a share of personal glory. It appears that one of the Chartists with a rifle, perhaps the deserter, called on the authorities to surrender either the prisoners inside, or, less likely, the specials and magistrates. Whether an answer was given to this request is uncertain, but within seconds there was a scramble for weapons in the doorway.[17]

Each side claimed that the other was the aggressive party, though the traditional view is that the Chartist spokesman fired the first shot. A feasible alternative is that the spark which lit the fuse was accidental. Thomas Bevan Oliver, a special constable stationed at the door, claimed that he knocked the door against one of the Chartist guns, which went off.[18] With Lovell prompting, the ranks rushed forward, their loaded guns and pikes at the ready, and a few shots were fired in the lobby. There were twenty or more specials in the hall, and at the first advance of the Chartists through the door-way they retreated rapidly, some upstairs but most into the court-yard behind and even homewards. Police Superintendent Hopkins, one of the targets of the crowd, was in the bosom of his family within minutes.

It is difficult to establish the extent of firing from the Chartists. Some hostile observers suggested that as many as eighty or more shots went crashing into the hotel, and the man who had earlier led the front ranks to the courtyard gates, the tall man with the wooden leg, and Wright Beatty, a local coal-trimmer, were singled out as keen marksmen.[19] Apart from a few shots at the east and west wings of the building, most of the early firing appears to have been in the direction of the fleeing special constables, though the danger of hitting fellow Chartists was soon apparent. In their anxiety to obtain an entry, men at the front beat on the shutters and smashed in other windows with their pikes and mandrels. Soon the hotel was

7. The battle of the Westgate, 1839

full of people, and in the smoke and confusion the Chartists released some of their anger on the nearest property to hand.[20]

The pace of events caught everyone by surprise. John O'Dwyer, one of the specials near the door, was separated from his colleagues and trampled underfoot, and two other constables, ironmonger Henry Williams and draper Edward Morgan, received deep stab and gunshot wounds. A number of Chartist intruders were also, as we shall see, severely injured and dying. Mayor Phillips, who had a copy of the Riot Act in his pocket, had hoped to avoid a clash between the Chartists and the soldiers, but the situation was now out of control. When the order was given for the military to load with ball, it seems that the leading insurgents had already entered the passage from the hall, and were searching for the prisoners and their enemies. In removing the bottom shutters from the three projecting windows of the long public room, the mayor and sergeant Daily were hit by snipers, and other shots ricocheted from the ceiling.[21] The young soldiers then filed past the windows, firing in sequence on the crowd and inflicting heavy casualties. The official version is that this enfilading fire lasted for only a few minutes, but others spoke of prolonged target practice on a stunned crowd.[22] As people slumped to the ground, someone shouted 'Fall off', and the Chartists retreated, as best they could, to the nearest cover.[23]

Their last hope was that those inside the hotel could capture it from the soldiers and specials. Those stationed in the long room had been obliged to lock its doors against the Chartist invaders. Once the firing outside had stopped, the men of the 45th Regiment warned the specials to keep clear, opened the door to the passage and for ten minutes or so filled it with lead. One intruder was killed instantly, but in spite of this the Chartists used the smoke to make a number of courageous attacks on the soldiers' position. Thomas Watkins, one of the specials at the hotel, described the result: '*there was a scene, dreadful beyond expression—the groans of the dying—the shrieks of the wounded, the pallid, ghostly countenances and the bloodshot eyes of the dead, in addition to the shattered windows, and passages ankle-deep in gore . . .*'.[24] The battle of the Westgate had lasted for some 25 minutes and about the final act of the victorious was to order shopkeeper Isaac Venn to close the front door, which had been held open by the arm of a dead Chartist.

Out in the street the picture was one of complete desolation. Scores of weapons lay where they had been dropped, as desperate

Chartists ran for shelter. Unable to retreat up the hill still thronged with people, those in the sights of the soldiers' guns fled into side-streets and the shops and houses close by. Any untoward move-ment in front of the hotel was liable to provoke more firing from the 45th Regiment, and those who had been shot and trampled under-foot remained where they fell in the street. It was said of one man that he lay dying under the portico of the mayor's house for up to one and a half hours, pleading for help and receiving none.[25] Until the authorities in the Westgate decreed it otherwise, time stood still.

No one can now establish the number of people wounded on that morning, but fifty was a moderate estimate. Some were taken limping and bleeding heavily into the homes of Chartist sym-pathizers near the hotel, and others were carried piggy-back or on engines and coaches up to their own villages.[26] Contrary to some impressions, local radicals were amongst those injured by the soldiers. John Lovell, severely wounded in the thigh, was dragged to the house of Jenkins, the shoemaker, in Market Street. He was visited in the next few days by many well-wishers, but when Jack the Sailor from Pontypool called a surgeon to him the inevitable happened, and both of them were taken into custody.[27] Other New-port Chartists who were shot were James Rawlings, a pikeman, and Davies, the potter of Pillgwenlly, who lost an arm. Amputations were common over the next forty-eight hours, and from Tredegar Samuel Homfray reported that six men had returned injured, some seriously. John Morgan, who was one of these, eventually received proper medical care, and was persuaded to give evidence against several of his friends.[28] Other notable victims were Ben-jamin Davies, the Chartist organizer from Fleur-de-lis, who was wounded in the arm, Matthew Williams, the Argoed quarryman, who was hit in the leg by his own men and later turned Queen's evidence, and William Jones. This 24-year-old miner of Sirhowy, fleeing from the soldiers' guns, was shot through the back, but managed to escape by tram and canal boat to Trallong in his native Breconshire.[29]

The number and names of all the people who died in the battle will never be known, partly because the authorities were secretive about the matter. Certain Chartists, echoing early reports, insisted that several of the soldiers in the Westgate were killed and quickly buried, but the evidence still available indicates that only two of the military were seriously injured.[30] Sergeant James Daily, who collapsed with six slugs in his head, came nearest to justifying Jack the Fifer's boast that they had 'got a few'.[31] At least three people tried to kill the mayor, and two of these were themselves shot, including young George Shell, who had to be fired at several times before lying still. Even then he took three hours to die.[32] A number of special constables were also attacked and wounded, though none lost his life. In fact Henry Williams and the mayor, who suffered most physical injury, did fairly well out of the conflict, the former receiving a pension for life and the latter a knighthood.

On the Chartists' side the local newspapers were probably nearest the truth when they gave the figure of some twenty-two deaths. One correspondent stated that he had actually seen the bodies of seventeen men, and Samuel Homfray reckoned that at least thirty Chartists were dead.[33] If we discount some of the wilder claims such as the two men killed above Llanhilleth for refusing to join the mob and the six Chartists found dead in Caerleon, it is still probable that over half a dozen dying men, carried home by families and friends, have to be added to the official totals.[34] Two or three bodies were found around Newport itself, and one Chartist expired at Pillgwenlly. David Morgan, from Tredegar, died in Friars Fields, and was later identified by his grieving widow. Altogether, maintained Newport policeman Moses Scard, he had seen sixteen bodies in the town.[35] At the Westgate, the authorities took possession of nine bodies, five from within the hotel and four from outside. Daniel Evans, whose tailor's shop was almost opposite, described how some of these people died: one was felled by the soldiers' fire at the west corner of the hotel, another collapsed on the front steps, a third was shot in a doorway, and the last fell backwards out of a window and crawled some distance on his hands and knees.[36]

Ten of these bodies were placed in the hotel stables on 4 November, and guarded day and night. Two of the victims were soon identified in the press, a deserter named Williams of the 29th Regiment, whose body was laden with ball cartridges, and William Griffiths ('Will Aberdare'), who carried the card of his WMA and a note that he was 'No. 5 of H Division'.[37] Soon afterwards, George Shell was also identified, as was miner Abraham Thomas of Coalbrookvale, who was called by his wife 'a very wild man'.[38] Families who suspected that their missing relatives were amongst those in the Westgate stables made their way rapidly to Newport, sensing perhaps the intentions of the magistrates. Within three days a perfunctory inquest had been held on the ten bodies, and on Thursday, under cover of darkness, they were buried in unmarked graves at the north side of St Mary's chapel in St Woolos churchyard. The church register records simply that 'ten men, names unknown' who were shot by the 45th Regiment were buried 'at once' there.[39]

From public and private sources we can name some of the people in these and other graves who lost their lives in the rising.[40] Apart from George Shell the only other Pontypool victim appears to have been John Davies (Davis), a carpenter and Chartist secretary, and one of the few Blackwood casualties was William Ferriday. Days after the burials his wife Mary arrived at Newport and pleaded with the magistrates for permission to see her husband's body. She had seen his coat but wanted the final confirmation.[41] Along the heads of the valleys there were many other grieving widows. James Brown, of the Cwm Celyn and Blaina works, said that two 'of our greatest ruffians are dead' in the Westgate stables, as was a third who used to act as gamekeeper for his brother.[42] At least four of the dead on 4 November came from the Tredegar area, though only David Morgan and William Evans, a married man employed by Samuel Homfray, can be easily identified. Another half a dozen victims were named by contemporaries, and these included Rees Meredith, who organized the marchers at Dukestown, David Davies of the Brynmawr district, William Williams (Wilson) of Cwmtillery and John Codd, whose wife was from Pembrokeshire, but one would like more supporting evidence before being absolutely convinced of the veracity of such lists.[43] What is definite is that on this morning in November 1839 the British authorities inflicted greater casualties on the civilian population than at any other time in the nineteenth and twentieth centuries.

The Chartists who escaped the muskets' fire fled to the outskirts of the town or found what shelter they could along the wet and muddy streets. Charles Waters, and another armed Chartist, were seen running across the fields at Gold Tops, with soldiers from the workhouse in hot pursuit.[44] Some of those in the rear of the column down Stow hill went into the fields below the church after the firing, and a few fortunate souls were pulled into friendly homes and given food and shelter. Not all, however, instantly took to their heels, but waited around corners, angry at the scene they had just witnessed and willing, like the wounded Jack the Fifer, to consider a second attack. At the top of Stow hill there was some regrouping, and at one point during the morning William Jones was seen encouraging men there and elsewhere to return to the town centre.[45] He was more aware than anyone else of the hundreds still waiting on the Pontypool and Caerleon roads for orders and news of the battle. In the event, the only other confrontation took place near the workhouse, after eighteen anxious soldiers had left there to assist their beleaguered colleagues in the Westgate. A group of Chartists moved in the direction of Lewis Edwards's home, only to be turned back by Ensign Stack and nine soldiers lined across the road. When the military threatened to fire, the workmen retreated rapidly.[46]

If, as it appeared later, Jack the Fifer was content with the injuries which they had inflicted on the authorities in the Westgate hotel, others were less than pleased with the morning's work. The town was still not in their hands, and hopes of Chartist assaults on Monmouth and other places were fading fast. Within an hour of the battle at the hotel, hundreds were setting off homewards, jettisoning their weapons and informing those still arriving on the outskirts of the town that all was lost. David Davies, a collier from Ebbw Vale, was told in Tredegar Park that 'tis time to run'. Chartists moving quickly up the tramroads and catching lifts on engines shouted that 'we have had enough to do to save our own lives', and warned that more soldiers would soon be in the town.[47]

By midday and early afternoon people were passing the same refreshment houses in Risca, Abercarn, and Newbridge which they had visited twelve hours before. Some of the local property-owners, fearing news of a Chartist victory, felt it wise to offer the returning marchers a hearty welcome. For their part the workmen expressed anger as they came upon the persons and homes of those who had not joined the march or who had fled before the confrontation with the soldiers.[48] A few hours later they were back with their families. According to Charlotte Guest those arriving in the darkness at Tredegar were defeated and dispirited, but this was not true of all of them. Benjamin Richards admitted that things had gone badly at Newport, but two friends, the sawyers James and Richard Jones, told those who came out to meet them that the conflict was not over. What was needed were more arms.[49]

A more common appraisal by the returning miners was the need for better leaders. As the authorities and the press quickly set about ridiculing the Chartist leadership after the rising, evidence of such a view has to be sifted carefully, yet there can be no doubt that many men were disillusioned. In general, the rank and file had been ignorant of the real purpose of the march on Newport, but almost all of them had been given the promise of an easy victory. The strategy of the assault, and the urgency and fears associated with it, had not been fully explained to them, nor had the methods of defeating determined soldiers. Henry Lewis of Rogerstone Castle, who met some retreating workmen on the road near the town, claimed that they regretted their action and the deceit of their leaders. They had been told, he reported, that the military would lay down their arms and deliver up a chest of weapons and ammunition.[50]

Zephaniah Williams, who had repeatedly assured his followers that they had nothing to fear from the authorities at Newport, was amongst the last to enter the town and was heard to shout 'cowards' at the men running from the bullets. He was, so it is alleged, responded to in kind.[51] John Frost wandered from the battle like a stunned animal, and was seen to be crying as he made his way back through Tredegar Park.[52] William Owen, the old soldier of Llancaiach, could not be found on the last stage of the march, whilst his colleague Thomas Giles, and David Jones of Tredegar, ran as quickly as anyone once the soldiers opened fire.[53] Like William Jones of Pontypool, the last two were most criticized by those whom they had pressed down to Newport. A few captains, including possibly John Reynolds who secured a horse at Risca, seem to have disappeared before the end of the march, and one or two Chartist officers never joined at all. At Blackwood there was the discouraging example of William Davies, the shopkeeper's son, who stayed at home until 12 noon on Monday and was barracked by the women for his cowardice.[54] Davies, Job Tovey, and other marked men left their homes rather than face the returning Chartists.

There were also, of course, communities which, sometimes as a result of their leaders' directions or inactivity, gave only limited support to the rising. Now recriminations were the order of the day, so the newspapers would have us believe. During the winter of 1839, and three years later at the time of the General Strike, there was apparently a strong feeling amongst the Monmouthshire miners that their Glamorgan colleagues hardly deserved support after their own performance on 4 November.[55] The sense of frustration was understandable, for Edward Dowling, Thomas Watkins, and many cautious observers agreed with Dr Price's assessment that 'if the Chartists had only been properly commanded and directed they could have carried everything before them'.[56]

It was, amongst other things, an awareness of this unpleasant fact which kept the population so alert for several days at Newport. 'I am glad and thankful this morning to let you know we are all alive,' wrote an inhabitant on 6 November.'I did not expect we should have been alive here now. We did not dare go out, nor try to make our escape, for the whole town was expected to come down.'[57] Some of the first reports of Monday morning's conflict wrongly indicated that the town was in the hands of the Chartists, and this information was well received in parts of Manchester, Newcastle, London, and Paris.[58] William Brewer, acting on behalf of the wounded mayor, sent at midday a despairing message to the Bristol authorities, saying that a counter-attack was anticipated and the defences could not hold.[59] Moses Scard, fearing the worst, had changed out of his police uniform, whilst a number of specials refused to apprehend Chartists in the town.[60] No one believed that the battle was yet over, and scores of the respectable families, especially the women and children, fled into the countryside.

Reginald Blewitt, MP for the boroughs, travelled to Newport on Monday, and found, to his surprise and relief, that the Westgate hotel was still intact. Almost immediately on his arrival he issued placards forbidding popular assemblies, closing beer- and public houses, and offering a reward for the apprehension of John Frost. He also sent a report on the rising to the Secretary of State at the Home Department, and demanded a special commission to try the rebels.[61] However, hopes of early assistance were soon dispelled, for the mayor of Bristol and Major Smith, commanding officer of that district, turned down the first request for military help, and it was only at midday on Tuesday that a company of the 10th Hussars entered Newport.

Their arrival was well timed for, on that day, news reached the town that 10,000 men were assembling at Aberbeeg for another evening assault. The inhabitants, who had already been warned of the dangers of arson and an attack on their gasworks, placed candles in their windows and for twelve hours relived the horrors of Sunday night. Once again the infantry was ordered into the Westgate, scouting parties sent along the Risca and Pontypool roads, and a curfew imposed on shops and drinking-establishments. Messengers reported that workmen were gathered some five miles distant, but nothing else happened, a pattern which was to be repeated several times in the next three weeks.[62] On Wednesday a degree of normality returned to the world of Newport work and commerce, and the examination of Frost, Waters, and other Chartist prisoners began in earnest.[63] A week later the only evidence of the recent battle were the bullet marks on the hotel and the unmistakeable presence of hundreds of soldiers.

Pontypool during these days shared many of the fears and experiences of the seaport town. On Monday, when the official news of the Chartist defeat reached the former place, the pleasure of the propertied classes was incomplete. Pontypool, without a military station, was about the most obvious target for workmen seeking revenge. On Monday and Tuesday groups of ironworkers and colliers in the area issued challenges to the authorities, and on the second of these days came the additional threat of several thousand men marching on the town from the direction of Crumlin. As with the proposed assault on Newport, nothing materialized, but for several days there was a sort of uneasy truce. The station-house was guarded day and night by armed volunteers, and rather feeble efforts were made to arrest known Chartist leaders. Only the appearance of a new company of soldiers on 12 November brought a return of confidence, and for a while they controlled the movement of people and traffic in the manner of conquerors. To all intents, the first towns threatened by the Chartist rebels were now safe.[64]

For some places in South Wales the battle of the Westgate marked not the end but the beginning of alarm. As we saw earlier, it was claimed that the Chartists had originally planned either a simultaneous attack, or more probably a staged assault over several days, on the main towns near the coalfield. Within hours of the conflict, reports spread that men were going over to Usk, Monmouth, and Brecon, and that parties on the hills were considering attacks on other centres of population. The county town of Monmouthshire had become since the summer almost immune to rumours of Chartist plans for its gaol, but urgent messages from Charles Lloyd Harford and Thomas Phillips on Sunday night sent the mayor into action. About 4 a.m. thirty men of the 12th Lancers were ordered to patrol the town and five hours later the respectable inhabitants were called to the jury-room to hear the latest news. Special constables were sworn in, pensioners given their appointed tasks, and a request for additional soldiers sent to Bristol.

During the day a number of colliers entered Monmouth, and a few of them were taken, briefly, into custody. On Tuesday news of the deaths of Chartists in Newport was confirmed, but the delight at this news was balanced by a later report that an attack on Monmouth gaol was imminent. This was to be mounted by Welsh and English Chartists, and the arrival of the prisoner Frost in the town on Wednesday increased the likelihood of a dramatic rescue. Patrols and scouts toured the area during the hours of darkness and, although a change of mood became apparent later in the week, constables guarded the gaol until, as promised by the Home Secretary, men of the 45th Regiment arrived.[65]

Abergavenny, which was nearer the coalfield and on a direct line from the heads of the valleys to Monmouth, also had reason to be anxious at this time. Throughout Sunday, company agents, tradesmen, bank officials, and over 400 miners poured into the town, some bringing their belongings with them and all recounting terrible tales of what they had left behind. The 12th Lancers, under Lieutenant Tottenham, were placed, as we have seen, at two hotels, and by the late evening the Revd William Powell had armed shopkeepers and sworn in more than 300 special constables. A party of the latter were asked to patrol the Usk bridge during the night. For some fifty hours, during which the soldiers and their horses were constantly on duty, the sense of being under seige hardly abated, and the vicar ignored all outside requests for military assistance. On Tuesday, when there were confirmed accounts of gangs of Chartists in the vicinity of Abergavenny, William Powell even countermanded an official order to send Lancers to Usk. At the end of the week, when his services were no longer needed, he travelled to London and explained his behaviour to Lord Normanby.[66]

The headquarters of troops in South Wales had been, since the end of the Napoleonic Wars, the town of Brecon, and at the time of the rising 300 young men were stationed there. The Chartists had discussed how to neutralize them, and the men of Merthyr and Dowlais, the nearest industrial complex, were probably chosen for this purpose. On Monday a 'great number of refractory workmen from neighbouring works' arrived in Brecon, and in the evening magistrates discussed their response. In fact, the authorities there had already been alerted to the danger, partly, it seems, by those who had escaped in their hundreds from the coalfield. As in Monmouth, Usk, Crickhowell, and Caerleon a public meeting was quickly called, large numbers of specials organized, and posts manned at the entrances to the town. Late on Monday night a large detachment of the 12th Foot set off from the barracks to answer desperate pleas for help from Tredegar and Nantyglo. Early on Tuesday news was at last received of the battle of Newport, and the well-protected inhabitants of Brecon breathed more easily. By Thursday most of the refugees from the coalfield had left the town, and the first of the Chartist prisoners had been escorted to Brecon gaol by the returning soldiers.[67]

It is significant that the growing confidence in these established Breconshire and Monmouthshire towns was not wholly reflected on the Glamorgan side of the coalfield. People who had not been directly involved in the Newport rising often felt they had most to fear in its aftermath. Observers as different in character as Henry Scale and Seymour Tremenheere believed that had the soldiers been defeated on 4 November, the Glamorgan ironworkers and colliers would have gone about their revolutionary role with a will.[68] Some of these had hopes of moving on Brecon and Cardiff, but the setback on 4 November led to consideration of a second march on Newport and a concerted attack on Monmouth gaol.[69] At the time of the rising some of the men of Aberdare, Merthyr, Dowlais, and the Rhymney valley were still at work or walking homewards through the rain, but after breakfast on Monday the mood changed. Many took the day off work, and were to be seen in the streets and public houses discussing their immediate strategy. A few may have set out on the road to Brecon at this time, whilst others sought news and contacts in the mining communities to the east. The Merthyr magistrates met, as they had done in the rising of 1831, in the Castle Inn and over the next two days swore in 500 specials, obtained the assistance of 60 armed pensioners, and sent an express to Cardiff seeking help from the Glamorgan Militia. On the evening of Monday information was received that a large Chartist meeting was to be held within a matter of hours, and the Guests, usually such calm industrialists, began to fear the worst. According to *The Times* correspondent, plans were now afoot to capture the iron town. At 4 a.m. on Monday the Guests' five children and their three nurses were sent away in a coach, under cover of darkness.

Tuesday proved to be a day of considerable excitement, and a turning-point in the history of the rising. About 8 a.m. a few hundred Chartists gathered on the hillside near the Big Pond in Dowlais, but were apparently disappointed by the absence of colleagues from the nearest Monmouthshire valleys. A group of men were instructed to proceed to the Bute ironworks and stop the blast-furnaces there, and it was decided to hold another meeting later in the day. The magistrates issued a proclamation banning the proposed assembly, but at 6 p.m. a large number of people met at Penrheolgerrig on the Aberdare side of town. According to Josiah Guest, who attended the meeting, the first speaker called on those present to 'strike while the iron is hot', but he was outvoted. The workmen preferred to obtain their rights by peaceful means, and agreed to return to work on the following day. In the opinion of the local newspaper and several observers, these resolutions marked a welcome reappraisal of the power of the authorities and saved the country from a second 'explosion'.[70]

Not everyone, it must be said, accepted the decisions of the meeting, and public anxiety in Merthyr remained close to the surface, at least until after a second Chartist scare, on 9 November.[71] In the meantime, however, it was their southern neighbours at the collieries above Pontypridd who were causing most alarm. Few of the men of Dinas and Porth had joined the march on Newport, but on Monday William David and his Chartist friends ensured that all the men were brought out of the levels. By mid-morning several hundred people had collected, apparently awaiting the return of a horseman who had been sent to bring them news from Newport. Although the departures of Dr Price, and later of William David, deprived these Rhondda Chartists of some leadership, the local magistrates were convinced that they were well armed and quite determined to support the cause. For most of this week the pits and levels were quiet, and respectable citizens were abused by men with beer in their stomachs.

It was later suggested that the workmen of the newly emerging industrial districts north of Cardiff had originally been given the task of laying siege to the capital city, and in the two days after the rising there was persistent talk of preparations for such an assault. There were reports of colliers from Dinas leaving the area, and of noisy excitement in the streets of Caerphilly and Pontypridd. In the middle of the week the mayor of Cardiff was informed, on oath, that the Chartists from these towns and villages were joining hundreds from Blackwood, and would be in the city within hours. Their purpose was, he was told, plunder, and their main target was the new union workhouse.[72]

Cardiff had been aware of the rising since Sunday, when two or three messages were received, notably one from Thomas Phillips warning the authorities that an outbreak was imminent and that it was imperative to secure all firearms in the city. The mayor, Charles Williams, quickly got together his fellow magistrates and Captain Howells, adjutant of the Royal Glamorgan Militia, and it was decided to ask gun-sellers to deposit their weapons in the station house. A guard of sixteen 'dependable people' was placed on the armoury during Sunday night, and, on the following day, the defensive preparations were extended. The staff of the Militia and a small recruiting party of the 41st Regiment were asked to help, as were the pensioners of the city, whilst those people already enrolled as specials were warned to be within easy reach. Scouting parties were sent out on the roads, and over the next three days they and casual visitors returned with reports of possible Chartist attacks. The greatest alarm was felt on Tuesday evening, when it was confidently expected that Chartists from Pontypridd, Caerphilly, and Merthyr were on their way southwards. On this occasion buglers were placed on the roads out of the city, and two six-pound cannon, which guarded one entrance, were manned by pensioners and twelve sailors from the American ship *Warsaw*, then at the docks.[73]

Captain Howells always believed that an attack was unlikely after the victory at Newport, but the inhabitants and magistrates of Cardiff were sufficiently anxious to demand and obtain a permanent military presence.[74] It was a point of view shared by a number of neighbouring authorities, including those in the lower Rhondda and at Swansea. In these rapidly growing industrial areas there was a new awareness of their own vulnerability. Within hours of the march on Newport, Chartist deputations made great efforts to win support from, for example, the men of the Neath Abbey ironworks and the Swansea copper works, but achieved only limited success. According to James Melvin, who lived in Oxford Street, Swansea, the leading Chartist of the town met Thomas Evans of Aberdare and two other coalfield Chartists on the night of 4 November. They told him of the march on Newport and Monmouth, and talked further of destroying workhouses in South Wales, and then of walking, with west country miners, to London.[75] Although the results of this discussion were disappointing, the tension of this week stimulated fresh demands for greater police and military protection from many parts of Glamorgan.

In the heart of the Monmouthshire mining districts the sense of fear remained strong for days. At Bedwellty House, the home of the Tredegar ironmaster, Homan the policeman and 30 war veterans took charge of Homfray's small arsenal, but outside this fortress 'the least report frightens all in the place & every one [is] ready to stand off'.[76] Agents, doctors, and tradesmen played hide-and-seek, and every alarm brought another exodus from the mining towns and villages. In the early part of the week most of the ironworks and collieries closed down, as did many of the shops and markets.[77] At Monday lunchtime, and again in the evening, there was talk of further marches on Newport and Monmouth, and on Tuesday the people of Nantyglo anticipated a visit from Merthyr workmen, whilst lower down the valleys the colliers gathered in large numbers. The purpose of these meetings was never discovered, for the secrecy in these days was total.[78]

At Nantyglo three magistrates, twenty special constables, and a detachment of the 12th Foot from Crickhowell arrived in the early hours of Tuesday, and helped in the arrest of the Brynmawr Chartists, David Lewis and Ishmael Evans, but in many communities the authorities were quite unable to act. In the immediate aftermath of the Newport affair, the workmen, and especially the colliers of Tredegar, Sirhowy, Ebbw Vale, and Blackwood, were said to have been 'uneasy' and still awaiting the return of their leaders. Chartist evidence was destroyed, lodges regrouped, William Jones was seen in the area, and the streets were full of people discussing the next step. We know that several mass meetings were held along the heads of the valleys, though the decisions taken at them remain a mystery. Some reports talk of a dejected spirit amongst those who had been at Newport, but it is interesting that workmen who had reason to fear Chartist anger kept quiet or left their communities, sometimes for ever.[79]

Great efforts were made in the press to accelerate the return to normality, but privately there was some criticism of the inactivity of the authorities on the hills and of the lack of military support where it was most needed.[80] Towards the weekend the situation improved, though at Beaufort and on the fringes of the coalfield, at Merthyr and Pontypool, there was renewed concern and fears of another rising. As a precaution, Col. Considine, now in charge of military defences in South Wales, ordered a hundred soldiers to march to Cardiff and Pontypool. In fact, it was not until Thursday, 14 November, that all the ironworks and collieries in the area were in full operation, and even then several hundred workmen were reported missing.[81]

The third week of November brought with it more accounts of a restless industrial population, and now there was the additional threat of an attempt to rescue the Chartists being taken into custody. The propertied and the government were extremely nervous about every twitch on the coalfield, and Capt. Howells at Cardiff and Col. Considine at Newport had a difficult time meeting their demands. The Chartist leaders were still in touch with each other, and on certain nights people gathered in large numbers to debate both political and economic grievances.[82] The two occasions which most worried the authorities were Monday, 18 November, when at least six communities from Aberdare to the Varteg anticipated Chartist meetings developing into a rising, and Wednesday, 27 November, when news was received in Newport of attacks planned on different towns in the county.[83]

Merthyr happens to be the best reported example of a town which lived through these experiences. In this area there was physical opposition to the apprehension of any persons implicated in the rising, and at Hirwaun there was a short strike in the third week of November and talk of arming. Most annoying of all to the authorities was the organized resistance to all discussions of an improved police force and the appointment of a stipendiary magistrate. At a given signal the people were brought out of the works to pack public meetings or to harrass magistrates at Petty Sessions. By 23 November the fraught nerves of Merthyr tradesmen had snapped, and on that day a very strong memorial was presented, requesting a large military presence. Within two days a company of the 45th Regiment from Cardiff had arrived and was given temporary accommodation in the Dowlais stables, a replica of the events of 1831.[84]

It is wrong, therefore, to see the conflict between the Chartists and the authorities as one which occupied just one morning in November. The silent warfare at Merthyr, which was to continue throughout the winter, could be compared to that at Beaufort, Pontypool and other places. The men of property, whilst demanding strong action from Westminster, struggled desperately to recover patterns of respect and channels of information. In the lower Rhondda relations between the working class and their social superiors broke down for at least a fortnight. With the return of Walter Coffin, the chief employer in the area, on 23 November, the authorities were at last able to mount an effective response to Chartist intimidation. Agents were encouraged to obtain any information which could prove useful, spies were set on suspected Chartist leaders and arms dealers, searches made of their homes, and warrants and rewards issued for the arrest of those who had organized the marchers. The Rhondda magistrates, meeting at Pontypridd, also began to consider schemes for better police and military protection.[85]

The irony of all this was not lost on the Chartists. One of the least known and most vulnerable areas of Britain was being taken into the possession of the ruling classes. In the frantic days after the rising there were two strident demands on the government: for a special commission to punish the rebels, and for military assistance to prevent anything like it happening again. On 4 November there had been 300 soldiers stationed at Brecon, about seventy at Newport, and small numbers of the 12th Lancers at Abergavenny and Monmouth. Within a day, however, orders were given for eight companies of the 45th Regiment to move from Winchester to Bristol, *en route* for Newport. Artillery was also sent rapidly from London, and Col. Considine of the 29th Regiment was appointed to take charge of Monmouthshire and the adjacent mining districts. By the end of the week he had almost a thousand men at his command. Most of these were stationed at Newport, in the workhouse and at the Pillgwenlly mill kindly lent by Samuel Homfray, and others were sent to Pontypool, Monmouth, and Cardiff. At an early date it was decided to use Cardiff as a second depot for the 45th Regiment, with men billeted first in private accommodation and then in the old workhouse, but this did not meet with unanimous approval in the county. Eventually some of these soldiers were moved to Merthyr and Swansea, thus supplementing the local pensioners and property owners who were armed and organized for weeks after the Newport insurrection.[86]

The impact of all this was considerable. Despite Samuel Homfray's caustic comments, most of the industrial communities were now within comfortable reach of Considine's men. The arrival of the soldiers increased feelings of security, allowed magistrates and constables to apprehend known Chartists, and ensured a smoother running of the industrial machine. It certainly added to the frustrations of angry workmen. Not only towns but also magistrates' meetings, court proceedings, and county gaols were given formidable military protection. Sometimes even the news of the advance of soldiers was sufficient to disperse Chartist assemblies. No one, exclaimed Thomas Phillips, could now doubt the determination of the military.[87]

Towards the end of the month the confidence of the authorities was well expressed at a number of thanksgiving services and congratulatory meetings. In Newport the respectable flocked to dinners and presentations, and the injured mayor was given a silver plate valued at £200. At these gatherings the industrial and urban gentry of South Wales defended themselves against the accusations of ignorance and complacency in their handling of the rising. They stood firm on the rights of property, demanded tough action from the government, and launched a blistering condemnation of the over-paid and secretive workmen of the hills. With the help of God, the mayor, and the small company of the 45th Regiment they had 'done their duty', and saved not only South Wales but also Britain and the civilized world. 'If the insurrection here had succeeded for a day, or even for half a day—nay, even for two hours—', said Thomas Prothero at a meeting on 21 November, 'the signal would have gone forth, and we should have heard of similar insurrections. . . .'[88] It was now time, through the majesty of British law, to send a very different message from this neglected part of Victoria's empire.

Punishment

In view of the trauma of the days after the rising it was not surprising that the search for those involved took some time to get under way. The authorities were determined, however, that the interests of public safety and justice required full retribution. At Newport, where matters were most advanced, a number of men had been taken into custody on the night of the rising, and others, like the two Tredegar miners Richard Benfield and John Rees, were captured during the assult on the Westgate. These, and several wounded Chartists, were placed in the union workhouse under military guard. In the next few days, as the presence of soldiers and policemen in the town increased, a small number of local radicals were also arrested. John Frost was apprehended on the evening of 4 November, hiding with Charles Waters in the home of John Partridge. Both men were armed with half a dozen pistols and a considerable amount of powder and ball cartridges. Thomas Jones Phillips, town clerk, took them and Partridge, into custody, and they were joined in a short while by James Aust of Malpas and John Lovell. By the end of the week over twenty people had been lodged at the workhouse, though it was acknowledged that some of the leading town radicals had simply disappeared.[1]

Elsewhere the arrests were fewer and more difficult to secure. This was especially true of the heart of the coalfield, where James Brown of Blaina and Samuel Homfray of Tredegar complained of the absence of resident magistrates and the intimidation of the mining population. Scouts reported to Homfray that the leading figures in the rising had vanished, and policemen Joseph Hall, Homan, and Henry Crowe could pick up only small fry like Thomas Bray. Most of those examined were bound over to keep the peace. Eventually, several wounded Chartists fell into the authorities' net, as well as a number of important characters like the Ebbw Vale miner William Williams and the collier Thomas Davies. At Brynmawr there was an early success, for on 5 November a company of constables and soldiers at the King Crispin discovered

David Lewis hiding in a chest. Lewis and his fellow radical Ishmael Evans were taken, together with Chartist documents and a flag, to the gaol at Brecon, where they were soon joined by five others. This success was loudly applauded, and literally brought hundreds of people on to the streets, but in general there was considerable criticism of the will and direction of the authorities 'on the hills'.[2]

The magistrates in South Wales claimed that people never fully grasped the problems of obtaining information on known Chartists. It took days to get the necessary warrants to search the pubs and houses which were the headquarters of the movement. At Ebbw Vale, Newbridge, Aberdare, and several other places, vital documents were destroyed before the constables arrived. Extensive searches were made of the Royal Oak at Newport, of John Llewellyn's beerhouse at Pontnewydd, and of the homes of Frost, Etheridge, Aust, Benjamin Richards, and others, with disappointing results. When, at last, the house of Thomas Giles was raided, several guns were found and a bullet mould, yet other incriminating evidence and the Nelson leader himself had gone.[3] In the west the Chartists seem to have been especially cautious and astute; John Williams, a prominent radical of Aberdare, William Price, William David, and a Newbridge weaver called Francis left their homes just before the march on Newport began, much to the annoyance of Glamorgan magistrates.[4] Other popular leaders never returned from Newport. A number went into hiding at Blackwood and the iron towns to the north, whilst many joined the trek to Cardiff, Swansea, and Carmarthen in the west or to Brecon, Gloucester, and Bristol. Within a matter of days Job Tovey, for example, found work in the pits at Westerleigh, and Richard Pugh and his friends went to live with relatives across the border. It was estimated that several hundred people left the coalfield at this time, never to return.[5]

Some of the 'captains' and organizers of the rising skilfully evaded capture. Amongst the list were John Barrill, John Reynolds, Richard Jones, chairman of one of the recent meetings held at Dukestown, most of the Rhondda 'captains', and John Rees and David Jones of Tredegar. The last two were keenly sought by Samuel Homfray, and the immediate offer of a £100 reward for their capture is a good indication of their importance. Just how they escaped remains a mystery. Jack the Fifer, after failing to rally his forces at Newport, made for Cardiff, where he sold his gun, and during the following weeks there were several reports of Rees and Jones earning a little money in the public houses of the west country. It was rumoured that they hoped to catch a boat to Ireland, and this is probably what happened. Despite persistent stories of their capture, Rees eventually reached America, and his friend dodged the authorities for many years.[6] A small number of Welsh Chartists, including William David and David Jenkins of Llanhilleth, joined Rees in America, whilst the Pontypridd leader, Dr Price, made his typically devious way, via Cardiff, Liverpool, and London, to Paris. William Jones, John Llewellyn, and Zephaniah Williams also made bold bids for freedom. After lying low in the Blackwood area, Jones was taken in a field near the Navigation Inn at Crumlin. He challenged William Evans, agent of coalowner Martin Morrison, and three other pursuers with a pistol, but was overpowered. The Pontnewydd radical was caught by Glamorgan policemen just as he was about to leave Swansea on the Carmarthen coach. Zephaniah was even more unfortunate.[7] For almost three weeks he used his family connections to hide in the Caerphilly district, and later to obtain a berth on the *Vintage* at Cardiff.[8] On 21 November, as the ship was being prepared for a voyage to Oporto, Police Superintendent Stockdale and four constables boarded her, and arrested the dejected Williams. He was taken, under close guard, to Newport, where crowds had gathered to catch a glimpse of the latest prisoner.

It is easy to appreciate the delight which accompanied each triumph of the authorities. The capture, and even more the committal, of a Chartist represented a small class victory, achieved on the most difficult terrain. Walter Coffin, whose return from Ireland on 23 November gave new impetus to the search for rebels, told his Lord Lieutenant that it was hard to exaggerate the protection given to Chartists and 'the reluctance' with which 'the least information is given'.[9] Morgan Thomas, who worked some coal near Nantgaru, would not give evidence on oath because he lived in the midst of working people and had already been threatened by Dr Price. Another person from the district, who was willing to offer information against the Chartists, had his home surrounded by an angry mob.[10] When Coffin and other magistrates visited the works, seeking evidence against those involved in the rising, they were regarded with the utmost suspicion. As often happened, company agents like Adams and Godfrey of Ebbw Vale provided the best information, supplemented on occasions by private communications from nervous workmen.

All over the coalfield the arrest of Chartists was attended with difficulties. At Merthyr wanted men could not be found, and most of those apprehended had to be released for lack of evidence against them. Even more alarming for the magistrates was the fact that news of imminent arrests in the area produced a stoppage of work and open intimidation. Constables and specials were, in some places, very wary of taking known Chartists without clear legal authority and the physical protection of soldiers close at hand. When those implicated in the rising were captured, people sometimes offered to provide alibis and tried to buy the silence of possible prosecution witnesses. Thus as soon as William Williams, the Ebbw Vale collier, was apprehended by Constables Price and Thomas for breaking into the home of publican Lloyd at Beaufort, his wife ran to their friends. One of them, David Davies, then set off on the road to Abergavenny and, on catching up the party, bravely interceded on Williams's behalf.[11]

The degree of intimidation and violence in these weeks is hard to assess, for so much of it was unspoken and hidden from history. James Brown, of the Cwm Celyn and Blaina ironworks, conveys the impression that fear was everywhere. In his valley those persons suspected of making statements were assaulted and a few of them had to be given police protection. For his own part, Brown, like most energetic pursuers of Chartists, received dire warnings and threatening letters. He confided to Thomas Jones Phillips that his 'house inside has the appearance of a little barracks'. He always armed himself when he went out, and stayed at home after dark.[12] In the mining districts around Blackwood and Pontypool it was a similar story, and those judged to be informers received Scotch-Cattle-type letters and other unpleasant reminders. The governing authorities issued denunciations of such intimidation, but on the quiet they moved key witnesses out of the valleys and into accommodation where they would be safe from interference. James Hodge, a Woodfield collier, and half a dozen other witnesses, were kept in a house just a few miles outside Newport.[13] Even these men were sometimes assaulted, and so, too, were Moses Scard of Newport, William Homan of Tredegar, John Thomas of Blackwood, and other official and unofficial constables.

The search for men implicated in the rising was extremely

thorough. Information, often inaccurate, and offers of help poured in from many parts of Britain and Ireland. Some people chose to convey their information in anonymous letters, whilst others dropped a quiet word about an injured Chartist or a stranger in the community. Thus on 2 December Jonas Williams, a Brecon police officer, heard that a wounded man was recuperating at the home of Lewis Hugh at Trallong. When he arrived at the spot he found William Jones, and the terrified miner immediately named two other colleagues, Rees Jones and William Leyson.[14] Employers and managers also performed a useful function, giving magistrates the names of men who had not returned to work or, as in the case of Robert Smith of Margam, passing on details of new arrivals seeking employment.[15] At the same time Homfray, Coffin, Brown, and others had 'spies . . . out in all directions', and employers Thomas Prothero of Newport and Alderman Thompson of Merthyr kept the authorities informed of the disclosures of 'reliable' workmen.[16]

Some Chartists virtually walked into the hands of the government. Solomon Briton, the self-assured radical from Abersychan, was apprehended when he visited the union workhouse at Newport with two friends looking for a man shot by the soldiers. Similarly, a couple of men were taken, without a warrant, for showing an excessive interest in the Westgate hotel, and a tired Samuel Roberts of Blackwood, when he returned home, simply gave himself up. Some Chartists were caught because of a chance meeting with a special constable, or as a result of loose talking in a public house. Handbills, and rewards advertised in the newspapers, made people in South Wales and the adjoining English counties familiar with the identity of these characters. The financial incentives for a successful arrest and conviction were considerable; from the £100 offered by Crawshay Bailey and James Brown for the capture of Zephaniah Williams to the £20 promised in respect of the Newport stonemasons, William Jewel and Jonathan Palmer. Altogether a sum of £1,000 was made available for successful bounty hunters.

The latter were a small group of dedicated professionals. Daniel Evans and John Gayton of Newport, William Phillips, Henry Crowe, and Richard Lewis of Tredegar, and David Jones of Pontypool were selected for the job of tracking down Chartists and bringing them across country. They worked closely with, and sometimes under, the direction of policemen Scard, Roberts, Homan, Thomas, and Stockdale. It was Moses Scard of Newport, for example, who on 17 November captured Thomas Llewellyn and a friend hiding in a house near the Fleur-de-lis colliery.[17] The most energetic 'thief-taker' was undoubtedly Thomas Watts, a 32-year-old tenant-farmer of Gelligroes who hauled goods between Newport, Blackwood, and Tredegar. On Sunday, 3 November, he ran to Samuel Homfray with news of the rising, and shortly afterwards offered his services to the magistrates at Newport. He was sworn in as a special constable, and entrusted with warrants against a large number of people wanted for examination. He claimed to have apprehended twenty-three people, mainly in the vicinity of Blackwood, and some of these he took from underground.[18] 'It is mainly to his zeal & activity', wrote Thomas Phillips, ex-mayor of Newport to the Treasury Solicitor in March 1840, 'that you owed the presence at the Assizes of every witness that you required save one.'[19] Between 4 November and the end of February Watts worked full time for the authorities, receiving and passing on well over £1,000 in expenses. His financial rewards, however, were soon outweighed by the social cost, for he was forced to leave his home and his relations received threatening letters. When his business collapsed, Watts begged his government masters to give him a job or a new start overseas, but in the summer of 1841 he entered Monmouth gaol as a debtor, a ruined and bitter man.[20]

As a result of the efforts of people like Thomas Watts the number of arrests rose sharply. By late November there were over thirty men imprisoned at Newport, about half that number at Pontypool, and a similar group in the gaols of Brecon, Usk, and Swansea. Perhaps three or four times this total were actually taken into custody in November and December. Many of them, especially in the iron towns, were released fairly quickly, often without explanation or apology, and several Chartists were bound over to appear when called upon. Even at Newport well over half of those apprehended were discharged within a matter of days. The accommodation of the rebels posed a major problem, for police stations and gaols could not hold them all. A few were placed under guard in private lodgings, and in Newport most of those arrested were sent to the union workhouse, where the soldiers had their barracks. So the poorhouse on Stow hill, once the target of the Chartists, now became a prison camp and hospital for the casualties of the rising. There the prisoners were kept under the watchful eyes of the workhouse master and that ever attentive magistrate Lewis Edwards, before being taken to the Westgate hotel for examination and eventual committal or release.

The examinations of the Chartists occupied much of November, and were conducted at Merthyr, Newbridge, Blackwood, Tredegar, Blaina, Crickhowell, and several other centres. Some of these were informal affairs, carried out in public houses by employer-magistrates like the Harfords of Ebbw Vale, Walter Coffin, and William Needham. By contrast, the examinations at Pontypool and Newport were showpieces. When, for example, on 11 November depositions were taken against thirteen prisoners from the Pontypool area, business halted and large crowds besieged the court house. At Newport the drama was perhaps less intense but certainly more sustained. The Westgate hotel was chosen, with a marked lack of taste, as the venue for the examinations, and for some twenty-three or twenty-four days at least 125 prisoners and over a hundred other people passed before the assembled magistrates.[21] In the beginning Reginald Blewitt, MP, acted as chairman of the Special Sessions, but for much of the time the leading figure was the Revd James Coles, and he was energetically assisted by William Brewer, Lewis Edwards, Octavius Morgan, and Benjamin Hall. On occasions, too, George Hall, the new mayor Thomas Hawkins, Samuel Homfray, and others lent a hand. Much of the questioning of witnesses was carried out by Thomas Prothero, one of Frost's great rivals, and the administrative burden fell mainly on Thomas Jones Phillips, clerk to the magistrates.

The Chartists in the invariably crowded court thus faced some of their old enemies, and this confirmed the general impression that the examinations were part of a national campaign to discredit and destroy a great movement. At times the proceedings were conducted with open hostility on both sides. In attendance were local men and women of property, together with dignitaries from further afield who wished to see a Chartist rebel in the flesh. The rest of the respectable population were also able to follow the events in court, because the examinations were reported in astonishing detail in the press. The nation seemed instinctively aware that this was one of the great criminal investigations of the nineteenth century.

On 9 November the Treasury Solicitor arrived in Newport to oversee the examinations. Having displayed great thoroughness at the recent Warwickshire assizes, he had a brief from a beleaguered

Whig government to play down the seditious nature of Welsh Chartism and to select only a small number of radicals for trial. The Attorney-General was alarmed by the enthusiasm of the Newport authorities, and the carefree manner in which they committed people for high treason. 'I own I should have great satisfaction to proceeding capitally against Frost', acknowledged Normanby on 7 November, but the first instinct of his legal advisers was to charge the rebels with attempted murder. Within hours of his arrival, however, Solicitor Maule had understood the serious nature of the rising, and the shocking revelations of the mayor were given added weight by each new disclosure at the Westgate examinations.[22] His revised task thus became one of identifying vital witnesses and likely candidates for a major government prosecution. A treason-trial was extremely rare, and Maule, like many of his colleagues, spent hours in dusty books of legal history. In his endeavours he was aided by a local solicitor, William Harford Phelps, and Thomas Jones Phillips, and he received free advice, too, from Thomas Phillips and Thomas Prothero. Phelps, whose records still survive, was responsible for the collection of evidence and for much of the paper work on the prosecution side.[23] He, in turn, relied heavily on his assistant, attorney J. H. Evans, and on other agents up the valleys.

At Pontypool one of these men, David Jones, performed the same kind of role that he had done in earlier prosecutions against Vincent and others. Throughout this year Special Constable Jones had kept notes on Chartist meetings, and he knew the leading radicals in the area well. On the night of the rising he was engaged as a scout by the Pontypool authorities, and within days was seeking information for them and interviewing witnesses. With Edmund Edwards, clerk to the magistrates, he forwarded statements on the affair to Newport and London. Thomas Llewellyn, solicitor, was employed by Phelps to act in a similar capacity in the mining villages around Blackwood. On 2 and 3 December, for instance, Llewellyn examined nearly twenty witnesses in connection with William Davies, who had recently been apprehended near Canterbury. He found, to his consternation, an atmosphere of fear and a 'strong anxiety to suppress the truth'. Only one person, William Harris, claimed that William Davies was involved in the march on Newport, and he caused Llewellyn, and later the Crown, much embarrassment. 'I packed him off last night with Scard', wrote the solicitor on 3 December to Phelps, '& as he is rather a bad character himself and a slippery fellow, he ought not to be allowed to return here until after the Assizes.'[24]

One of Phelps's main colleagues and rivals at Newport was Thomas Jones Phillips. He had already played an important part in the prosecution of Chartists at the last assizes, and in the late autumn had been asked to report on radical meetings in various parts of the coalfield. On Sunday, 3 November, Phillips journeyed up to Tredegar at the request of a worried Samuel Homfray, and on his return was dismayed to find that his family had fled the town. Within hours, however, he had the special satisfaction of taking Frost and Waters at Partridge's home. Thereafter, by his own account, he was engaged for 105 days and nights in the business of state, and hardly saw his family. He visited Tredegar, Blaina, Nantyglo, and elsewhere to collect evidence, and attended the bench of magistrates at Newport whenever possible. Altogether he transcribed the depositions of over 300 witnesses.[25]

Thomas Jones Phillips's main role was as a liaison officer between central and local government. Late in November he promised the former that he would try to prevent the magistrates from holding unnecessarily long examinations. He made several trips to London to report on developments and helped in preparing the Crown's prosecution. His unique position caused Phelps some annoyance. The latter believed that his own work was insufficiently appreciated and, as the town clerk increasingly won the trust of all parties, so the rivalry between them grew. In the six months after the rising Jones Phillips was largely responsible for sorting out the government expenses and for conducting the political prosecutions at the next assizes, whilst Phelps, now at Bath, sank into a despairing lethargy and bankruptcy.[26]

It is difficult to know precisely who was behind the strategy of examinations and committals at Newport, but its character is absolutely clear. At the very beginning a local decision was taken to apprehend everyone in the vicinity suspected of being involved in the rising or who had no home or occupation in the town. Thomas Gibson, a fustian-cutter from Manchester, who was carrying a begging letter, was one of those arrested, and, like several others, was sent to Usk House of Correction for being a vagrant. Poor John Morris, who just refused to give an account of himself when taken on suspicion, was sentenced to a month's imprisonment. A large number of people, including the Crookes of Abersychan and

Joseph Walter of Blaina, protested that, when taken into custody at Newport, they were on their way to and from relatives in the west country. Their stories were checked, and information sought from employers about their character and job situation. A few admitted that they had been forced down to Newport by Chartist militants, but in the majority of cases no evidence was brought against them, and they were discharged. At the examination of Joshua Davies, a one-legged tailor, it was several days before the magistrates heard from a respectable source in Coalbrookvale that their prisoner had not been near the seaport town on 4 November. Davies was one of the few who was set free with something of an apology, and without 'a stain' on his character.[27]

Apart from giving instructions to detain those people passing through Newport in the days after the rising, the magistrates also sanctioned the arrest of known Chartists and those associated with them. Warrants were issued against Samuel Etheridge, Edward Frost (John's uncle), John Wilton, and many others. Policeman Edward Hopkins and Henry Chappell were sent across the Bristol Channel to find some of these men, but a number were captured in Newport itself. What annoyed some of these radicals was the illegal nature of their arrests; thus Isaac Coleman was taken near the Westgate by Moses Scard because the latter had heard that he was a Chartist, whilst Robert Alexander was dragged across the town although no warrant had been issued against him. It was enough, for schoolteacher Stephen Rees of Blackwood, Henry Hazel, a young man of Newport, and John Jones, a servant at the Royal Oak, to be known as a radical or to be a relative, servant, or neighbour of a wanted man. Both Rees and Jones were given warnings about their past behaviour, and the latter character, who would not or could not provide information on Chartists who used his master's public house, was attacked by William Brewer for having 'contradicted himself grossly', and then discharged.[28] Despite strenuous efforts, the magistrates were unable to sustain serious charges of high treason and conspiracy against most of these people. As he gave freedom to men from the mining villages the Revd James Coles asked them to remind their 'fellow workmen, you were brought down here to be slaughtered'.[29] Most of the prisoners at the Westgate kept a straight face when the chairman gave them the inevitable lecture on the error of their ways. 'Although you do not suppose that your proceedings are known,'

Coles declared when the case against one of the Batten family of Gelligroes collapsed, 'I can tell you that they are. . . .' In future Batten senior would have to tread carefully.[30]

When keepers of beer- and public houses appeared before the bench this message had a particular sharpness. One of the first demands after the rising was for action to be taken against those drinking-places where the rebellion had been planned and where traitors had been harboured.[31] At least a dozen beersellers found themselves in custody. Amongst them were the aged David Lloyd of the Argoed, and Robert Richards, who kept a beerhouse between Newbridge and Abercarn in which the Chartists gathered on Sunday, 3 November. Ebenezer Williams of the Prince of Wales, and Charles Jones of the Royal Oak, Newport, were, in the eyes of the authorities, also deeply involved in the plot, but, after representations from his friends, Jones was discharged without firm evidence brought against him. Like his fellow publicans, he was upbraided by chairman Coles for permitting radicals to meet in his house, and warned of the possibility of losing his licence. Still, the lessons were not always one-sided; Stephen Rogers, who arrested Ebenezer Williams, was later violently assaulted by one of the servants at the Prince of Wales.[32]

The tone of the proceedings at the Westgate hotel was set by the Revd James Coles of Michaelston-y-fedw. He presided over most of the investigations and was loudly applauded for his exceptional zeal. In his attitude, especially towards Welsh-speaking prisoners, he was autocratic and condescending. He warned John Hughes, a witness in the case of Thomas Llewellyn, that he himself might be taken into custody simply for smiling and giving indirect answers. By contrast, John Richards, who gave a detailed and truthful account of the activities of prisoner James Aust, was detained by Coles for knowing too much, and a person who whispered to Solomon Briton in court was also immediately taken into custody. One senses that the reverend chairman, and some of his friends, enjoyed the power which they possessed over those who appeared before them. Late in November, they dealt with Evan Edwards of Tredegar, who confessed to having made bullets for the Chartists. Edwards, whose wife was ill, claimed that he had been obliged to help the miners, and his father, a Wesleyan minister, supported his plea. Coles replied that 'the magistrates are desirous to deal as leniently as possible' with such a prisoner, yet a few hours later they changed their minds and committed Edwards to Monmouth gaol on a charge of high treason.[33]

Over the weeks of examinations, William Foster Geach and other attornies clashed repeatedly with Coles, and sometimes with Phelps and Prothero, about the fairness of the proceedings. During the case of Henry Frost there was a heated exchange, when Geach complained that no warrant had been issued for the apprehension of his client and that the witnesses were being used to implicate other prisoners than the boy at the bar.[34] On one occasion the chairman of the magistrates was attacked by W. P. Roberts, a Bath solicitor and friend of John Frost. Roberts had been arrested, with two of Frost's daughters, at Blackwood by Moses Scard. There was no warrant for this action in South Wales but he was held in custody for forty-eight hours. As this solicitor was acting on behalf of Frost at this time, he was annoyed when no charge was brought against him. Coles, who persistently refused to give an explanation for Roberts's detention, said simply that he was now a free man, which drew the retort: 'Your courtesy is amazing.'[35]

In court, and occasionally in correspondence, the Chartists who faced Coles complained of their treatment at the hands of the authorities. Most of the prisoners had been deprived of the money found in their possession, and were quite unable to retain counsel or bring witnesses to support their side of the story. Benjamin Richards, in an intercepted letter to his wife, indicated that only three or four of his friends could afford legal assistance, and Jenkin Morgan, who did receive advice, thereby reduced his family to penury.[36] The most fortunate prisoner was Zephaniah Williams, who by 11 December had recovered the £100 taken from him by the police. At the opposite pole was George Turner (Cole), who had been arrested chiefly because he had only one leg. 'I am very sorry as anything should happen for poor people to be pulled about the country,' he protested in court, 'for I am innocent.' As a poor man he was unable to bring witnesses from Blackwood to support him, and he spent weeks in gaol before being found not guilty.[37]

Turner was especially annoyed about the evidence brought against him by special constables and the police. Like George George of Sirhowy and Thomas Llewellyn of Fleur-de-lis, he accused Moses Scard of swearing false oaths, and at the Special Commission the Newport policeman finally agreed that he was uncertain about Turner's identity. Scard produced so many 'confessions' and spoke against so many people, that he confused even himself in court. It was partly on his evidence that Solomon Briton was committed for treason, and the Abersychan radical, together with Zephaniah Williams, Benjamin Richards, and several others, declared that nine-tenths of the statements against them were 'all lies'. During the examinations the prisoners launched a bitter attack on key witnesses such as Scard, Daniel Evans, and William Watkins, though Frost, Waters, and Zephaniah Williams soon decided that a quiet contempt was just as effective. The Blaina leader seemed particularly depressed by the whole business; tired from lack of sleep, he appeared almost indifferent to every new disclosure.[38]

At this stage the Chartists believed that the cards were stacked heavily against them. Defence lawyers, acting for a small number of the prisoners, found it difficult to weaken the determination of Newport magistrates and solicitors. Access to clients was more limited than some of them had expected, requests for bail were generally ignored, and copies of depositions and lists of witnesses were often late in arriving. Geach, John Howard, and the other attornies lacked the necessary contacts and time to obtain all the defence witnesses, and those who did arrive in court were closely scrutinized and challenged by the prosecution.[39]

On the other hand, scores of crown witnesses were obtained, and sometimes held and used in the most secretive and arbitrary way. Thus Esther Pugh, wife of the wanted keeper of the Coach and Horses at Blackwood, was suddenly taken from her home by an officer and kept in isolation at Newport for several days. From the experience of the wives of Job Tovey and William Ferriday, and other relatives of dead and wounded men, one has the impression that the prosecution went about the business of acquiring evidence in a very clinical manner.[40] Lewis Edwards and Thomas Prothero realized that isolated confinement at the workhouse and the threat of a traitor's death were sometimes enough to loosen tongues. When people were ready to be useful crown witnesses they were brought before the bench whatever the case in progress. On one occasion, when James Hodge began incriminating Frost during the examination of Jenkin Morgan, Geach's temper finally snapped. He argued, with some reason, that the prosecution side were not obeying the letter of the law.[41] It was also pointed out that Hodge, the boys Rees and Coles, and a few other crown witnesses, had unusually close relationships with Prothero, Phelps, and Phillips. One or two had received donations and jobs from them since the rising. Of course, once people decided to speak out against the Chartists they probably needed a degree of independence and a new home, but Frost and the radical press found much to criticize in the whole examination procedure.

It is easier for historians than it was for the Chartists and their lawyers to appreciate the problems of the prosecution at this time. In committals for the most serious crime against the state it was necessary to obtain two witnesses to 'overt acts' of high treason, and even when, as sometimes happened, the charge was reduced to conspiracy and riot, this could not be supported without considerable skill and persuasion. In some instances the authorities advertised rewards for information against important prisoners, but Edward Tippins and a few other 'captains' escaped for lack of evidence. This itself was partly the result of the secret nature of the rising and partly a testimony to the reluctance of people to talk. Leading prosecution witnesses, notably in the case of Zephaniah Williams, received threatening letters and soon came to realize the personal and financial costs of their action.[42] Some were given police protection and others were hidden from the community for a couple of months. A number of witnesses decided that the pressures were too great, and changed statements or, as in the case of William Davies, simply disappeared.

The prosecution had therefore to be extremely flexible in their approach to the criminal investigations. Almost every day a new line of enquiry was opened and a vital witness proved to be unsatisfactory.[43] Phelps, writing on 6 December about the possible prosecution of William Davies, made the general observation that 'it will be necessary to be provided with ample nay excessive evidence to guard against witnesses who have been examined breaking down which is not at all unlikely to be the case . . .'.[44] Thomas Phillips, the ex-mayor who knew the district better than any imported crown agent, suggested that it was in the prosecution's interest to produce their completed list of witnesses at the last possible moment, a piece of advice which ultimately helped to save the lives of the 'traitors'.[45]

Altogether, several hundred witnesses were examined by the authorities. This fact, and the appearance of working men, and certain conspirators, on the Crown's side was celebrated in the national and local press.[46] Even Feargus O'Connor and some of his fellow radicals used the examinations to warn of the dangers of going 'over the top'.[47] Editorials in the *Northern Star* pointed out that the marshals of revolution were often the first to disappear and inform. Historians have rather confirmed the lesson by suggesting that Chartists were queuing up to provide information against their friends, but the impression is not totally accurate. An analysis of the 236 crown witnesses listed at the time of the Special Commission shows that well over a third were shopkeepers, employers, professional people, and policemen, many of whom resided in the Newport area. About a third were publicans, beerhouse-keepers, women, and labourers of various kinds, and a sixth were returned as colliers and ironworkers.[48] One suspects, despite the feigned shock of certain reporters, that the Chartist prisoners were not too surprised to see some of the last occupational groups in the dock. They included John Walters, coalcutter of Argoed, and William Howell of Blaina, both of whom were noted enemies of the radical movement, and William Edmunds, the Argoed blacksmith and dissenting preacher who had refused, like several other crown witnesses, to join the march on Newport. Howell, incidentally, of whom the prosecutor had high hopes, was unable to identify Zephaniah Williams in court.[49] Other witnesses, like Joseph Brown of Blaina, were also suspected of being employers' agents and informers. Brown had been obliged to take a Chartist card on 30 October, and four days later told an ironmaster that the rising had begun.[50]

Some of these witnesses, including men from Blaina and Coalbrookvale, had been Chartists at the time of the rising, but Daniel Evans, the Newport tailor, James Emery, the Pontypool cabinetmaker, George Essex, a surgeon's assistant from Trevethin parish, John Maggs, shoemaker and labourer of Pontnewydd, and other vital crown witnesses had been disillusioned with the radical movement well before November 1839. Daniel Evans, who spoke against several of the prominent rebels had been removed, at the instigation of John Lovell, from a Chartist club at Newport, whilst other Chartists who appeared in court, like James Hodge, of Woodfield near Blackwood, Matthew Williams, the Argoed quarryman, Israel Firman of Gelligroes, and Morgan James of Newport and Bedwellty parish, were recent settlers in their communities or were widely regarded as fair-weather radicals and unreliable militants. Hodge attended his Chartist club only twice in 1839, and was called a 'spy' even before the rising, whilst Morgan James admitted that he had been to only one meeting. Not surprisingly, Zephaniah Williams, John Frost, and John Llewellyn were upset by the startling, if sometimes confused, revelations of these fellow radicals.

During the month of November the strategy behind the criminal investigation of the rising changed significantly. Initially, as in other parts of Britain, the magistrates sanctioned the arrest of large numbers of radicals, so many, in fact, that clerk Thomas Jones Phillips could hardly take the strain.[51] In an effort to build up a coherent picture of what was essentially a secret plot, almost everybody named by prisoners, informers, and witnesses was rounded up. Israel Firman, the 91—year-old herbalist and scissors-grinder, pulled a long list of wanted men out of his conjurer's hat.[52] It was one of the misfortunes of the Chartist rising that this old Antiguan, who made something of a living out of turning King's evidence, had settled down at Gelligroes a few months earlier. John Fisher of the village, William and John Batten, Henry Harris of Pontllanfraith, Henry Charles of the Welsh Oak, and Edmund Edmunds of the Greyhound were just some of his victims. So was John Williams, the secretary of the Chartist lodge in Firman's district. Like most of the people named by the quack doctor, Williams was imprisoned but ultimately freed with the usual warning to give up his extra-mural activities.

By the last week of November most of the leaders of the rising, and many more besides, had been taken into custody, and it was felt, at least at the Home Office, that enough was enough. With the date for the Special Commission rapidly approaching, it was important to bring the examinations to a conclusion.[53] Thomas Jones Philips, who believed 'that punishment might be carried too far', was given the task of persuading enthusiastic magistrates to hold back on further prosecutions.[54] In late November the rate of discharges rose significantly. 'The magistrates do not want to commit more men than they can help,' said the Revd James Coles to miner Thomas Bray, 'and as your master, Mr. Homfray, has spoken in your favour, go home and work like an honest man, and attend no more of those meetings, which have led so many poor men into trouble.'[55]

Increasingly the prosecution directed their attention towards certain important witnesses and towards those men in custody who could be persuaded to speak against their friends on promises of reduced sentences and freedom. It was well known at the Newport workhouse that Lewis Edwards and Thomas Prothero were prepared to consider deals. Morgan James, accused of helping Wright Beatty to escape, agreed to give evidence against Thomas Aurelius, and James Wall and Charles Groves of the same town did likewise. Of those who turned Queen's evidence perhaps the most notorious was Thomas Saunders, a 'respectable looking' draper's assistant who left his home at Abersychan on the day of the rising and kept a close watch on Zephaniah Williams and the Blaina Chartists. It was widely believed, even by his ex-employers, that Saunders would swear to anything for an appropriate reward.[56] When John Gibby of Pillgwenlly was committed for high treason, he protested through his tears: 'I am sorry to say it, but the biggest rogue is turned Queen's evidence.'[57] Facing him in court were a Chartist colleague, Edward Brickley, and a thief, David Herring, who was currently an inmate of the House of Correction. Everyone, it seemed, was being given a chance to speak.

The real breakthrough, so far as the authorities were concerned, came with the arrest of those who were able to supply inside information on the secret objectives of the Chartist leaders. The examinations of Morgan James, James Hodge, John Harford, and especially of William Davies, Job Tovey, and Richard Pugh of the Coach and Horses, Blackwood, convinced many, including the Treasury Solicitor, that they had stumbled on a genuine attempt at revolution. The decision of William Davies to turn Queen's evidence was regarded as the turning-point in the whole investigation, for he had been privy to the last-minute discussions of the Chartist delegates. Thomas Phillips, the ex-mayor, believed that the young Blackwood radical would make an excellent witness, but sadly he jumped bail, and Tovey, though informative, was felt to be unreliable under cross-examination.[58] Pugh was called on behalf of the Crown at the subsequent trials, but he proved to be a careful witness with a preference for the truth. Ultimately, as we shall see, the prosecution had to rely on the testimony of some fairly dubious characters to support the charge of high treason.

The Newport examinations closed on 6 December, and on the following day the magistrates reported that 125 prisoners had appeared before them. Of these well over half had been discharged, and a dozen had been given short gaol sentences or bailed to appear if called for trial. At least twenty-nine persons had been committed to the county gaol at Monmouth, twenty-one of these on a charge of treason.[59] Despite several protests, the sixteen Chartists committed for trial in Breconshire were excluded from the lists of the Special Commission, but the committals at Pontypool, and elsewhere on the coalfield, joined those from Newport. Eventually some sixty prisoners awaited the government prosecutors, and the ex-mayor, now Sir Thomas Phillips, declared that the 'evidence against the delinquents is so strong that it is hardly possible to anticipate that they will escape, although everything that can be done by intimidation, bribery, fraud, and perjury will be brought to bear on the occasion'.[60]

The Special Commission opened at Monmouth on 10 December. From the start the idea of having a Commission had produced mixed feelings in South Wales. On behalf of the Chartist prisoners, William Foster Geach, solicitor and stepson of John Frost, protested that it would reveal disturbing information about the state of the country and would only inflame passions. It was felt by many radicals that such a trial, held before a Monmouthshire jury and covered by a hostile press, was unlikely to be a fair one. The minimum concession demanded from the government was a postponement, which would allow the prisoners time to obtain money and counsel.[61] In London, and in the country at large, people had begun to collect money for these Chartists, and Feargus O'Connor, who attended the Commission, donated a week's profits of the *Northern Star* to the Defence Fund. O'Connor, like the defence lawyers, was determined at this time to exhaust all the legal forms of protest, and discouraged people from behaving in a way which would prejudice the lives of the men in Monmouth gaol.

For their part, Reginald Blewitt, Samuel Homfray, and most of the wealthy men of property in South Wales wanted a quick trial and a vigorous exercise of the law.[62] Such, claimed the Newport magistrates and Major Charles Marriott, had been the most effective weapon against the dreaded Scotch Cattle, and any hesitation at this stage could prove ultimately dangerous.[63] They were delighted when, within ten days of the rising, the government decided to establish a Special Commission. The news that Mr Justice John Williams was to conduct the proceedings was a bonus; he had presided over the infamous trial of the Dorchester labourers five years earlier. The other two judges supporting him were the Lord Chief Justice himself, Sir Nicholas Tindal, and Sir James

Parke, appointments befitting the first trials for high treason since 1820.

When the judges arrived at Monmouth on 10 December, in the company of the Lord Lieutenant and High Sheriff, they quickly discovered that the town had been taken over by soldiers and interested visitors, only a few of whom had been able to obtain tickets for the courtroom drama. At 11 a.m. the judges and leading men of the county attended divine service, and heard a sermon preached by the Revd John Irvine on the text: 'While they promise them liberty, they themselves are the servants of corruption' (2 Pet. 2: 19). Three hours later, twenty-three persons were chosen to serve on the Grand Jury, and amongst them were Sir Benjamin Hall, Reginald Blewitt, Joseph Bailey, Samuel Homfray, and Octavius Morgan of Tredegar Park. In his charge to the Grand Jury, Tindal elucidated the law of treason and the special nature of the crime. He hoped that in this instance it would be shown that the many had been led by the evil few, but he warned that when the minds of such a large section of the community were affected by seditious ideas greater religious education was essential, especially for the young.

At 3 p.m. on the following day the Grand Jury announced their verdict. A True Bill for high treason was found against fourteen people, two of whom, John Rees and David Jones, had not yet been apprehended, and a True Bill for burglary was found against four others.[64] John Lovell, on his crutches, the exhausted Frost and Williams, and the other men chained together at the bar represented a pathetic picture, an impression confirmed by their lack of legal representation. So far only two or three of the prisoners had obtained the services of Geach and John Owen, 'the Poor Man's attorney' of the town. After a brief exchange with these, the Lord Chief Justice adjourned the Commission to 31 December.

The interval of three weeks was marked by another display of tension in South Wales, both real and imagined. To the annoyance of magistrates and employers some Chartist lodges continued to function and several open-air and secret meetings were held across the coalfield. There were even reports of arming and a popular trade in ammunition. On the eve of the Special Commission the number of soldiers at Merthyr was increased, and the guard on Monmouth gaol doubled. Fears abounded of an attempt to rescue Frost and his friends and it was widely rumoured that the Chartists would stop the trials or indulge in violence and arson.[65] A number of policemen and soldiers were assaulted at this time, and four men of the 45th Regiment at Newport deserted.[66] Magistrates Thomas Phillips and others associated with the prosecution received warning letters. Some of the latter were truly astonishing missives, promising religious vengeance on those responsible for punishing the rebels: 'Ye serpents and generations of vipers, why seek ye the life of Frost? You may succeed but what think ye of the mighty millions? If ye can escape the bullet, who can escape the match?'[67]

No one was subjected to more intimidation than the witnesses whose names were given to prisoners on 17 December. James James, a Blaina miner, and others who had given evidence against Zephaniah Williams, had been physically attacked earlier in the month, and, despite the posting up of handbills warning people of the consequences of tampering with witnesses, other assaults followed.[68] Late in December Phelps revealed that a plan had been uncovered to abduct witnesses, and as a precaution, most of them were transported, under guard, to Monmouth.[69] About this time the Chartists also directed their attention to the newly-elected jury of farmers and tradesmen, cajoling some and threatening others. However, great efforts had been already made by Thomas Phillips and Maule to secure men of proven worth and 'right feeling'. 'It is in the character & opinions of the jury at last that all must depend,' wrote the ex-Mayor on 14 December, '& too much attention cannot be paid to the composition of the jury.' Like the Crown witnesses, the twelve men of the petty jury were minutely scrutinized and given police and military protection. Each of them had the right political background, although one of them, at least, had some difficulty in understanding the English language.[70]

The atmosphere of these days can be fully understood only in the wider British context, for O'Connor and his *Northern Star* decided to focus the movement's vision on the Special Commission: 'the cause of Frost is the cause of the whole nation; in saving him the people do but save themselves'.[71] Chartists in various parts of England and Scotland passed resolutions declaring that the trials must not be allowed to continue or that risings should accompany the news of Frost's conviction and death. At the beginning of December delegates from Wales, Birmingham, and other regions attended meetings at Wotton-under-Edge where some of these proposals were endorsed. Angry delegate meetings were indeed a feature of the Chartist movement in this period, and a small number of the elected Chartists attended a national convention in London on 19 December. A few of these leading militants tried, both in London and in Monmouth, to embroil O'Connor in revolutionary plotting, and there were thinly-disguised requests from Welsh Chartists for the Irishman to join them in another rising 'on the hills'.[72]

As the year drew to a close it was obvious, as a sick Col. Considine observed, that everyone in South Wales was on edge.[73] On the night of 20 December, for example, the firing of cannon and guns at the Ruperra celebrations marking the birthday of the Morgans' heir sent the inhabitants of Newport and Pontypool into a blind panic. Meanwhile, at Merthyr, magistrate Anthony Hill confirmed on 18 December that some form of national rising had been planned, but that the Welsh were waiting upon decisions elsewhere, which perhaps would be relayed to them at a Christmas meeting.[74] Over the next few days there were half a dozen important meetings along the heads of the valleys, and talk of secret consultations and drilling underground. The authorities, fearing a junction of Chartist forces in Britain and the rescue of the political prisoners in Monmouth gaol, sanctioned the movement of more troops to South Wales.[75] However, despite the arrival of a few lesser-known English radicals, the language of the Christmas dinners and debates was restrained, and the caution of O'Connor and his friends appears to have found an echo in the Welsh localities.[76] One reason for this was undoubtedly the unprecedented precautions of Samuel Homfray and other employer-magistrates; scouts were everywhere, special constables sworn in and all the proceedings of the Chartists were closely watched by policemen and soldiers. 'Nothing can exceed the grave consultations of the Justices,' wrote one cynic; 'yet all is very quiet.'[77] The only note of genuine alarm was sounded on 26 December when the residents of Monmouth, a town now filling again with strangers, believed that an assault was about to be launched by the Chartists of both countries. In the event the only march on the county town was five days later, when scores of working men arrived to witness the fate of their erstwhile political leaders.

The Commission resumed its work on 31 December. Five days previously the Chartists had secured two of the ablest advocates in Britain to defend John Frost, and these men, Sir Frederick Pollock and Fitzroy Kelly, were assisted by William Geach. All of them were naturally unfamiliar with the law of high treason, as were the

leading prosecutors, Attorney-General Sir John Campbell and
Solicitor-General Sir Thomas Wilde. To emphasize the exceptional nature of the proceedings, the judges were preceded to the
courtroom by London policemen, javelin-men, and trumpeters,
and the twelve men at the bar were handcuffed and chained
together. After the long indictment had been read, Frost, Williams,
Jones, and the rest all pleaded 'Not Guilty', and the jury and spec-
tators settled down to hear the first case.

This involved John Frost, and it was widely assumed that his fate
would largely determine that of his friends. In the long eight-day
trial, one of the most famous in legal history, Frost's counsel displayed virtuoso skill. From the outset Pollock and Kelly chose their
ground carefully, being conscious that they faced a hostile jury and
could call only a few witnesses on behalf of their client. Their early
victories were essentially technical ones. On the first day they
objected successfully to the large jury-panel being named alpha-
betically, and to the Crown's challenges of certain men on the list.
On the second day Pollock immediately added another complaint
about the delivery of the list of witnesses, but this was held over
whilst a rather mystified Attorney-General made the opening
speech for the prosecution.[78]

After describing the planning behind the rising, and the events
that followed, Sir John Campbell directed the jury's attention to
the objectives of the Chartists:

Arriving at Newport, they were to attack the troops that were there; they
were to get possession of the town, to break down the bridge which is there
erected across the river Usk . . . they were to stop the mail; and this was to
be a signal by which the success of the scheme was to be announced; the
mail bag from Newport not arriving at Birmingham in an hour and a half,
it would be known by those who were in concert with them . . . that this
scheme had succeeded. There was to be a general rising. . . . I hear
nothing of any private revenge; I hear nothing of any private grievance;
this was not a meeting for discussion; it was not a meeting for petitioning
the Queen or either House of Parliament; it was not a meeting arising out
of any dispute between masters and servants . . . it was not any sudden
outbreak from want of employment, or from want of food . . . the witnesses
whom I [shall] call before you speak the truth—that there was this public
object, by armed force to change the law and constitution of the country.[79]

Anticipating the defence case, the Attorney-General declared that
the Chartists' lack of success and their change in plans did not

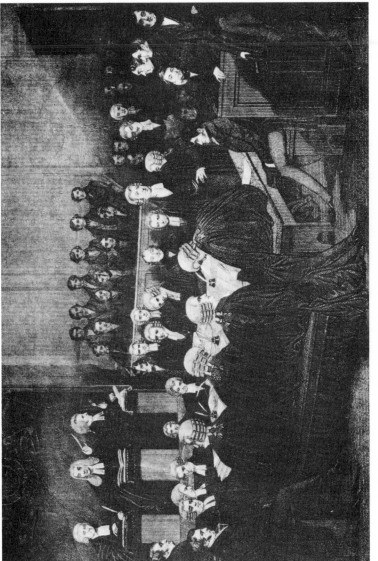

8. The trial of Frost, Williams, and Jones, 1839–40

detract from the original intention to levy war against the Queen, and he further argued that the use of informers was quite legitimate in a courtroom where spies and government agents were happily missing.

As soon as the first of the crown witnesses was called, Pollock returned to his objection about the delivery of lists to the Chartist prisoners. It was shown that Maule, the Treasury Solicitor, had given these men copies of the indictment and a list of jurors on 12 December, but, contrary to statute, he had not delivered the list of witnesses until 17 December, and someone else had later forwarded an extended list. As we have seen, Sir Thomas Phillips and others had been anxious to withhold these names until the very last moment. The three judges decided on 1 January 1840 to pass Pollock's objection to their colleagues in the Court of Exchequer for deliberation, and allowed the trial to continue. Almost immediately Pollock made another objection to Samuel Simmons, the first witness, namely that his residence had been wrongly described, and this protest was repeated when James Hodge, Sergeant James Daily, George Lloyd, and Morgan James appeared to give evidence. There were several other defence objections as well, perhaps the most important being that John Frost, like Lord George Gordon sixty years before, was not responsible for what was done and said by the rebels in his absence. The judges, aware that they were dealing with a secret plot, decided that such evidence should be admitted and the jury left to decide its value.

The number and character of the witnesses at this trial tell us much about the problems faced by both sides. Only a sixth of the people on the Crown's published list were actually called, though it is indisputable that the evidence provided previously by William Davies and Job Tovey helped to form the prosecution's case. The defence counsel was less fortunate, and during the trial used only sixteen people on behalf of Frost. Pollock and Kelly claimed, rather naïvely, that the onus of proof in this investigation rested with the prosecution, and that the Chartist leader was reluctant to call witnesses who might therefore be implicated in the rising. Those who spoke on Frost's behalf paid tribute to his peaceful nature, his work as a magistrate, and his concern for the imprisoned Vincent. He was, it was said, the most unnatural and unprepared revolutionary in history.

Over the eight days of Frost's trial the arguments and counter-arguments attracted enormous public interest, and one can see just how much the presentation of the advocates has influenced historians.[80] There were two main debates, the first of which concerned the actual nature of the rising. The defence claimed that it was merely an exhibition of numbers, a show of strength designed to persuade the Newport magistrates to grant a pardon for Vincent and the other political prisoners in Monmouth gaol. The Chartist marchers, generally unarmed and restrained, had tried, it was said, to avoid conflict with the soldiers, and fled as soon as they were fired upon. Frost and Zephaniah Williams were apparently appalled by the killings, for their purpose in leading the rising was to divert its course away from a direct assault on the authorities. According to Pollock no plans had been made to ensure that news of the conflict at Newport would be conveyed to other centres of Chartism. For their part, the prosecution repeated the telling point that this was unlike any other demonstration, both in character and timing. 'Arrests, restraints, seizing of arms, making prisoners. What else', asked Sir Thomas Wilde, 'could you have to mark the character of an insurrection?'[81] Only the Chartists' late arrival at Newport, and the astonishing bravery of the soldiers, had saved Britain from the most daring and obvious case of treason in recent times.

The second issue, which was debated throughout the trial, were the precise objectives of the Chartist leaders. As several star witnesses had absconded, and as it was decided not to call Job Tovey, the Crown's case rested on the evidence of four men, Matthew Williams, William Harris, John Harford, and James Hodge. The first of these described how a messenger from Frost had spoken of the need to capture Newport and stop its services. Williams, an Argoed quarryman who had a short criminal record and who had lain wounded in the workhouse since the rising, lived close to Frost's messenger but was unable to identify him firmly. William Harris, from Blackwood, was an even more unsatisfactory witness, and eventually the Crown admitted as much. Harford, the Bedwellty collier who had carried a sword on the night of 3 November, was a more sober and solid character. Despite tough cross-examination, he stuck to his story that on the march Frost told the miners to obtain powder from a storehouse and blow up the bridge over the Usk, so halting traffic and the mail. James Hodge confirmed this, adding that Frost had informed him that delegates at Birmingham were waiting for news from South Wales. Although both Hodge and Harford clearly hoped to profit from such disclosures there was, as we have seen in earlier chapters, independent evidence which supports some of their claims.[82]

Over the days of Frost's trial the defence lawyers hacked away at the statements of these and other witnesses. They were successful in undermining the credibility of, for example, the boys Rees and Coles, and in exposing the inconsistencies in the accounts of Sir Thomas Phillips and Captain Gray. In fact, before the end of the trial the Crown had withdrawn some evidence, and conceded other points of detail. Chief Justice Tindal, in his open summing up, drew attention to these concessions, and in doing so infuriated the Attorney-General and those contemporaries anxious for a conviction. For Tindal, however, as for many others in the courtroom, all these matters were subordinate to the central question of 'object, design, intention'.[83] Despite their achievements, Pollock and Kelly had been unable to offer a convincing alternative explanation of why the rising took place. The jury took only half an hour to reach a unanimous decision, and at 6.20 p.m. on 8 January foreman John Daniel of Abergavenny returned a verdict of guilty, with a recommendation for mercy.[84]

Over the next seven days the remainder of the prisoners were dealt with. Zephaniah Williams's case was the longest, his counsel making some prodigiously extended statements. Like William Jones, who followed him into the court, the Blaina radical spoke eloquently in his own defence, but both made no impression on the jury. On 15 January Waters, Lovell, Benfield, John Rees, and Jenkin Morgan changed their pleas to guilty, on the promise of a reduced sentence. This pleased few people in the county; some, like Lord Granville Somerset, who had been foreman of the Grand Jury, and Octavius Morgan, were extremely annoyed with this compromise, whilst the prisoners, when they received sentences of transportation on the following day, believed that they, too, had been cheated. There was further dissension when James Aust, George Turner, Edmund Edmunds, and Solomon Briton appeared in court, for the Attorney-General, obviously tired and lacking vital evidence, decided not to press charges, and immediately received a barrage of criticism from the propertied classes.[85]

Thursday, 16 January 1840, was a special day in the history of modern South Wales. Early in the morning the courtroom was crowded to hear the sentences and, ignoring several objections by

Geach on behalf of the prisoners, judgement was given by Chief Justice Tindal, dressed appropriately in a black cap. The three Chartist leaders were warned that the jury's recommendations for mercy were unlikely to be successful and so they should prepare themselves for the cruel death of all traitors. For Waters and his four friends the prospects were better, though Tindal declared that, as they had played a prominent part in the rising, they could expect transportation for life. John Rees, in an unusual display of emotion at the bar, staggered forward and began to sob. As for the other Chartists on the calendar, thirteen of them, including Benjamin Richards, John Gibby, and Lewis Rowland, were given gaol sentences of up to one year in length, and the remainder entered into recognizances to keep the peace or were acquitted. These men appeared grateful for their comparative good fortune but William Jones, as he stepped into the prison van, shouted 'Three Cheers for the Charter' to the crowd outside.[86] He was at once rebuked by Frost; acquainted as he was with the law, the Newport draper realized that the matter was not yet settled.

So began one of the most dramatic episodes in the story of the rising. The three Chartist leaders were placed, at their own request, in one condemned cell and there they were shielded from the frenzied activity going on around them. The executions were delayed until the judges decided on the technical point referred to them by the Special Commission. The deliberations at the Court of Exchequer took three days, 25–8 January. The objection over the list of witnesses was sustained by nine votes to five, but it was also decided that Frost's counsel had raised the matter too late in the proceedings. Significantly, two of the three judges who had been at Newport voted against this second resolution, convincing some contemporaries, including the Tory Lord Granville Somerset, that judicial murder was now out of the question.[87] On 29 January the Cabinet met and, taking the lead from Lord Melbourne, requested the Home Secretary to write to Monmouth, fixing the executions for Thursday, 6 February. An executioner and a headsman soon arrived in the town, and the scaffold made ready. Governor Ford, whose insensitive conduct at the county gaol was never forgotten by Frost, asked the prisoners whether they had any last requests about the disposal of their bodies.

In the country at large the campaign to save the Welsh Chartists was in full swing. It was a curious mixture of organized threats and pleading. 'If Frost is unfairly dealt with,' ran a typical comment in the radical press, 'no Crown in Europe will be worth one year's purchase. . . .' Militants like Dr McDouall in Chester prison and Major Beniowski at a London convention criticized the lack of solidarity shown over the previous weeks but promised widespread action on the day of the executions. Already, in fact, the trial of Frost and the news of the sentences on 16 January had sparked off a number of violent protests. These varied from the angry demonstrations of hungry Manchester youths to the more serious plotting and conflicts with the law at Bethnal Green, Sheffield, Dewsbury, and Bradford. There was also, in South Wales and London, a small wave of arson, threatening letters, and assaults on Thomas Prothero, John Daniel, Moses Scard, and others connected with the prosecution at Monmouth.[88] Although O'Connor and the *Northern Star* came out strongly against such action, and warned of the power and information in the hands of the state, the message from the grass roots was clear: the death of the Chartist prisoners would be followed by a popular convulsion which would ruin the celebrations to mark the Queen's marriage and might well bring down a shaky government.[89]

The scale of radical activity in these weeks was exceptional. 'Since the late lamentable affair at Newport,' wrote R. J. Richardson, 'and since the arrest of Frost and his companions, the whole of the country, from John O'Groats to the Land's End has been agitated. . . .'[90] Mass meetings were held in London and in almost all the largest towns of England and Scotland, and the rescue effort was co-ordinated by the *Northern Star*, a series of delegate meetings and a national convention. It was decided, in spite of some cynicism, to send petitions to London and a loyal address to the Queen, and these were signed by thousands of people in a matter of two or three days. O'Connor called upon the trades to lend a hand, and suggested a one-day demonstration to focus attention on the plight of the condemned men at Monmouth. In Wales, at Merthyr, Newport, and other places, men and women thanked their leader for his efforts and sent in their pounds and messages of support.[91]

It says much for the divided nature of South Wales society that on 16 January a rival campaign was launched. Lord Granville Somerset, Octavius Morgan, Samuel Homfray, and even prominent liberals evinced surprise at the conduct of the trials, disapproved of the Lord Chief Justice's summing-up, and were angry at the compromises arranged by the Attorney-General. It was suggested, in a string of furious letters as well as in *The Times* and the local press, that the great efforts of the police and magistrates of Monmouthshire had been set at nought. The Grand Jury, in a memorial to the Home Secretary at this time, spoke of the feelings of outrage and insecurity in the county. The implication was clear: a reprieve for any of the condemned men would be disastrous, and the Mayor of Cardiff even asked the government to arrange three separate hangings at Newport, Blackwood, and Pontypool.[92]

For a time at least the Cabinet took a similarly tough line, ministers being anxious to dispel the image of a weak and hesitant government.[93] Just how the Prime Minister and his colleagues came to change their minds is still something of a mystery. The speed of the change suggests that the vital element was outside intervention rather than a considered policy decision. Many people in Wales believed that the young Queen's influence had been crucial, but her journal reveals that both she and Lord Melbourne believed that execution was the right policy. The turning-point was undoubtedly the protests of Sir Frederick Pollock and the interview of the Lord Chief Justice with Normanby on 31 January.[94] Tindal's recommendation that, on the legal objections raised at the trials, the lives of Frost, Williams, and Jones should be spared, was passed on to the Cabinet, and on that night, as Lord Granville Somerset tried vainly to discover the government's intentions, notice of the reprieve was sent to Monmouth. It was read to the prisoners on the following day, but they were given no intimation of the alternative arrangements being made for their transportation.

When news of the reprieve reached the rest of the population, attention switched to obtaining the free pardon which Pollock and Kelly had long demanded. Large meetings were held in many parts of Britain on 10 and 11 February, and even in South Wales there were a few brave interruptions to the round of balls, dinners, and teas celebrating the Queen's wedding.[95] Petitions signed by thousands arrived in London, where J. T. Leader and other politicians were trying to get a parliamentary debate on the subject. When Leader's motion in the Commons for an urgent address to the Queen had to be postponed he failed to secure promises that the Chartist prisoners would not be transported until the issue of a pardon had been formally discussed.

The Home Department and the authorities in South Wales had already acted with remarkable speed. About midnight on Sunday, 2 February, the three Chartist leaders were taken out of their cell and escorted, under heavy guard, through the pouring rain to Chepstow. There, in the early hours of Monday morning they stepped aboard a steamer bound for Portsmouth, and fifteen days later were transferred to the hulk *York.* The Chartists protested that because of this 'body-snatching' they had not taken leave of their families, and when, within a week, they put to sea in the convict-ship *Mandarin* there was an additional complaint that Parliament had still not discussed the petitions for a free pardon.[96] Five months later, after an appalling journey, the three Chartist leaders reached the shores of Van Diemen's Land. Australia was to be the home of Zephaniah Williams and William Jones for the remainder of their lives, but John Frost returned to Britain in 1856, still radical and weighed down with bitterness.

The trials of the Chartist rebels had thus come to a bloodless conclusion, though the sudden change in government policy at the end of January 1840 and the midnight 'kidnapping' from Monmouth gaol were not forgotten nor forgiven in the dining-halls of South Wales. The subsequent arrest and trials of half a dozen people suspected of participating in the rising had a distinct air of *déjà vu.*[97] They served, like the conflict over the legal costs and the confessions of Zephaniah Williams on board ship, only to disturb the mood of reflection and the search for a new beginning in this corner of Britain.

Conclusion

THE message in the months after the rising was 'enquire and secure'. Although the government turned down a request for a full parliamentary inquiry into the events of 4 November 1839, ministers of the Crown instructed Colonel Considine, Sir Edmund Head, assistant Poor Law commissioner, and his friend Seymour Tremenheere, inspector of schools, to report on the state of South Wales. The national press, too, sent their reporters to the area, and the local authorities, at their Quarter Session and Watch Committee meetings, entered into the spirit of self-analysis and reflection. Although the mood was generally one of pessimism, a few observers drew hopeful conclusions from the outcome of that November morning. 'There never was', commented a correspondent in the *Shrewsbury Chronicle*, 'in the history of the world a successful insurrection of mere working men.'[1] 'The strongly-compact framework of the English constitution will no more yield to the rude and ignorant assaults of the miners of Wales and Durham', agreed the *Birmingham Journal*, 'than it will yield to the frame-breakers of Nottingham, or the destroyers of agricultural machinery in Sussex.'[2]

Even before the Chartist rebel leaders left these shores, several private investigators, notably Edward Dowling and the Revd Evan Jenkins of Dowlais, published their own versions of the rising. In his definitive booklet, *The Rise and Fall of Chartism in Monmouthshire*, the proprietor of the *Monmouthshire Merlin* argued that the men who marched on Newport had no genuine grievances and therefore posed no lasting threat. 'Popular outbreaks, however mischievous in their immediate results, afford but little ground for permanent apprehension.'[3] Dowling, like Tremenheere, was pleased with the co-operation which he received during his inquiries, but many of the resident population soon grew tired of the persistent attentions of the army of reporters. Working people were said to have been incredulous at the interest shown in their lives, and suspicious of the purpose behind it.

The results of all these investigations were generally disappointing. This was a reflection of the secret and baffling nature of the evidence, and a tribute to the personal and political vendettas in which the inquirers were engaged. Some of the writers chose to relate the rising to the growth of Nonconformity, and others saw in it the spirit of the Celtic temperament. It was suggested that only in Wales, where the character and language of the people were different from the rest of Britain, was such a rebellion possible. The rising, together with the Merthyr insurrection and the Rebecca riots, proved that the Welsh had become as ungovernable as the Irish. Only the widest possible programme of Anglicization could effect a cure. Others, including Edward Dowling and other members of Welsh societies and the Welsh press, claimed that Chartism was 'a foreign implant', alien to the most loyal and least criminal of Victoria's dominions. These defenders of the Welsh character pointed out that a considerable number of those arrested had English origins or were, like William Jones, English-speaking.[4] This debate, however, which grew more intense during the next decade, obscured the essential fact that the rising was a mass movement, affecting thousands of people, Welsh and English, skilled and unskilled, miners, craftsmen, and town labourers. Even Irishmen can be found in the Chartist ranks, counterbalancing Daniel O'Connell's proud boast that Irish soldiers, specials, and workmen saved the British nation on that fateful day.[5]

The historian soon becomes aware that many contemporary investigations, both within and outside the Principality, were no more than excuses for recrimination. Just as *Yr Haul* attacked *Y Diwygiwr* so *The Times* and the *Morning Chronicle* fought each other through November and December. The rising was attributed variously to Whig tolerance of radical reform, to Tory antipathy towards the New Poor Law, and to the inadequacies of local magistrates. Only a few observers made fairly impartial inquiries, and these concluded that, as in the case of previous disturbances in Wales, the ingredients were neglect, demoralization, and ignorance. According to Tremenheere this bleak analysis fell like a bombshell on the world of 1840, but in reality people had grown tired of the battery of reports.[6] Everyone, it seemed, was to blame, and everyone had his own explanation and remedy. It was a classic recipe for inactivity.

Amongst the Chartists of Britain, some of whom had been genuinely shaken by Frost's adventure, post-mortem on the rising became a matter of curiosity and honour. As each piece of information came out of South Wales, so radical opinion swung wildly from one pole to the other. Initially, ideas of a premature rising circulated, and there was a suspicion, too, that the government had covered up the extent of the military casualities. Later, during the examinations and trials, the Chartist press began to doubt whether any violence had ever been intended, and the notion of a manufactured riot now gained credence.[7] Most radicals outside Wales, including William Lovett and Vincent himself, argued in public that the main objective of the demonstration had been to secure the release of the political prisoners in Monmouth. Inquiries revealed that people on both sides of the border expected Vincent to be freed on 5 or 6 November, but, as Zephaniah Williams pointed out, this was not the immediate aim of the Chartist marchers on Sunday night.[8]

One small group of radicals saw the rising as part of a massive Russian plot to undermine the integrity of western nations. William Cardo, Marylebone delegate to the Chartist convention, took this idea from the eccentric diplomat, David Urquhart, and on 15 November he arrived at Newport claiming to be on the track of a Russian agent. When detained by the magistrates he explained that Major Beniowski, Polish émigré and member of the London Democratic Association, had played an important part in organizing rebellion in South Wales. This only confirmed the contents of the letters which Lord Melbourne had recently received from the Marquis of Anglesey and Lt.-Col. Pringle Taylor. As we have seen, it is difficult to support this claim, although there are reports of 'strangers' and a foreigner on the coalfield in September and October. In fact, when Cardo was pouring his heart out to the Newport authorities, Beniowski had just reached Bristol from his London base. He was then keenly interested in the revolutionary possibilities of Frost's defeat and trial, as were some of his closest colleagues. So far as one is aware, none of them were in the pay of Russian officials.[9]

If most Chartists were sceptical of Cardo's grand theories, he won considerable support for his suggestion that the Queen's ministers were implicated in the rising. George Julian Harney, Robert Lowery, William Pattison, and other leading radicals told public meetings in the winter of 1839–40 that the 'Newport business' was all part of a government conspiracy to impose unpopular legislation and remove 'piece by piece the last vestige of [our] freedom'.[10] It was a claim which grew naturally from the Chartist view of history, their prejudice against central authority, and their estimation of the character of John Frost. Within a month O'Connor had labelled the rising 'a Whig trick', comparable with the manipulated Bristol and Nottingham riots of the Reform crisis, and he warned other districts of the dangers of *agents provocateurs*. In 1842 and 1848, when talk of revolution again filled the air, the Irishman was to return to the same theme. Meanwhile, in the months after the rising, other Chartist colleagues became convinced that the government, having suppressed public meetings, was seeking confrontation everywhere in order to crush their political movement and establish a police state. Perhaps, it was argued, ministers and magistrates had actually planned the Newport rising in order to establish an 'Irish despotism' in Wales.[11]

John Frost had indeed warned people of spies on the coalfield during September and October 1839, and there were suspicions expressed at the time of the trials about men like Matthew Williams and James Emery who had enrolled in Chartist clubs at the last moment, and had sometimes directed operations. The man who was called a deserter became a somewhat notorious figure in radical circles. He seems to have been one of the mounted guides on the march, and could have been the person who fired the first shot at the Westgate. What was never proved was that he acted on behalf of an outside authority. Another elusive character was the man with the glazed hat, who was identified as, or confused with, John Reynolds of Pontllanfraith. O'Connor, in a rather frenzied article in 1848, insisted that the man with the glazed hat, who had been an agent of the Newport authorities, was seen about Lancashire and Yorkshire some weeks after the rising, pleading for a second assault on the government's forces. Was this the foreigner, perhaps of French or Polish origin, who was sometimes mentioned as an *agent provocateur* in the Welsh and northern outbreaks? We shall probably never know the truth, for the Chartist movement lived on rumour and suspicion. In his last years O'Connor attributed much of the responsibility for the violence of 1839–48 to Dr Peter McDouall, and almost everyone, including George White, George Julian Harney, George Black, and Major Beniowski, was denounced as a spy.[12]

Of course, the idea of a government conspiracy was a convenient one for radical leaders, especially for those under criticism or

unable to explain a particular turn of events. William Jones, in a
letter from the convict ship *Mandarin*, claimed that the attack on
the Westgate hotel had been set up by magistrates' agents, and
Frost, too, retained his suspicions that some of the witnesses for
the prosecution, notably James Hodge and John Harford, had
always intended to 'shop' their colleagues. In a speech, delivered
in the year after his pardon, the Newport draper took up O'Connor's accusation about one of the leading (but sadly unnamed)
figures in the rising. 'I had a spy set on me in Wales, and never did
man labour more earnestly in his vocation to force on disturbances. . . . Some time ago I was informed that this fellow was
living at ease on the public money. . . .'[13]. Dr Price, as we have
seen, even wondered if Frost himself had been a carrier of information to the authorities. In the weeks of the examinations and
trials, as prisoners escaped full retribution because of 'favourable
circumstances' known only to the prosecution, and over the next
three years when genuine spies were identified in South Wales,
the natural reaction was to sound a note of betrayal. One would
certainly like to discover more about the roles of shy Job Tovey,
who was not called as a witness at the trials, of William Davies, the
converted Chartist, and of William Homan, the well-informed
police superintendent, and it is worth recording that by the end of
the century the idea of a government conspiracy had become
firmly lodged in a corner of the popular memory.[14] Yet a close
scrutiny of the evidence bears out the prosecution's denial that the
rising was a manipulated riot. The late defensive preparations at
Newport, the small number of troops in the area, the first instructions to Maule, and the recriminations afterwards, hardly suggest
careful planning by those in authority.

Historians, who always know more and less than contemporaries, have not been impressed with this conspiracy theory. In
general, they have seen the rising in two ways: either as a peaceful
demonstration or as part of a national conspiracy to overthrow the
government. Professor David Williams, who had a sneaking
regard for Zephaniah and John Frost, accepted all the defence
arguments except one: he did not believe that the purpose of the
march was to rescue Vincent. Being such a good historian, he
mentioned the alternative explanations and the 'revolutionary'
confessions of Zephaniah and Dr Price, but explained them away
with typical adroitness. 'It is safest to assume', he concluded, 'that

the only common purpose ... was a great demonstration of strength in Newport.'[15]

The weight of evidence in this book casts doubt on this assumption; the events were extraordinary both in design and execution. This rising was not like previous Chartist activities, as some moderates soon realized, and there was none of the defiant openness and publicity which characterized the wider movement. Even for this largely unpoliced 'Black Domain' the degree of secrecy was staggering. Many of those on the march were confused about what they were hoping to achieve at Newport: even William Ferriday appears to have died without knowing the ultimate destination of his earthly pilgrimage.[16] Intimidation, caution, secret oaths, and passwords all helped to make this mass movement one of the most elusive in modern British and Welsh history. The trials tell us much about the nature of Welsh industrial society and class relationships, but almost nothing about the rising.

Some historians, again following the Chartists' defence counsel, have suggested that contemporaries exaggerated the degree of impressment and arming involved in the affair. Many people, it is true, then and later found it advisable to deny willing participation, and some of the information about arming, especially in the spring and summer, is unreliable. Even so, the scale of intimidation and the preparations for self-defence were unique in the nineteenth century. 'Recollect that all of you that is not with us when the morning comes,' George Tillett of Gelligroes is supposed to have said, 'there will be a bright eye kept, and every one that is missing will be shot.'[17] As I have shown elsewhere, terror was almost a way of life on this Welsh frontier, and on this occasion it reached new levels of intensity.[18] Hundreds were taken from homes, meeting-houses, and works, and those families who fled and hid were remembered for generations. When companies of marchers moved on Newport, they were seen, and sometimes behaved, as an occupying force. Men of property took to their heels, and one dissenting minister spent the night in a pond. Even weeks after the rising he would converse with Seymour Tremenheere only under cover of darkness.[19]

If, as it is sometimes suggested, the Chartists behaved like a rabble at Newport and fled when fired upon, it must be remembered that the degree of planning and arming was still very considerable. Although the evidence is not complete, we know that the workmen marched down to the seaport town in large companies or brigades, and were collected and organized by 'captains', some of whom, like John Rees and deserter Thomas Kidley, had a dash of military experience. Almost all these leaders, with the possible and unduly emphasized exception of Zephaniah Williams, were armed to the teeth. If anything, I have underestimated the number of arms that were made, acquired, and stored in the days before the rising, and it is surely stretching credulity to believe that this was 'defensive arming', as recommended by the Chartist movement. Perhaps five or six hundred of the marchers had guns, and these were regularly tested on the journey and loaded at Newport. Alongside the gunmen were hundreds more with mandrels, pikes, and knives. Scouts and employers who met them on the last miles before Newport had no doubts of their willingness to use these weapons, and some of them bore the scars to prove it. The incident at the Westgate, when guns were cocked, levelled, and fired in unison, was a real battle, and had Thomas Phillips and the others been killed and not injured, history would have been written very differently. Almost every informed observer believed that the Chartists were within an ace of a dramatic victory, and the beginning of a possibly successful guerrilla war. Dr John Taylor, a student of revolution, remained convinced that this was the only way to defeat the most efficient and loyal force in Europe. 'If this [mode of proceeding] were to be done in many places,' wrote the Prime Minister on 6 November 1839, 'much mischief might happen.' On the same day he confided to the Queen: 'it might have been very dangerous'.[20]

By any standards this was an unusual form of protest, and so was the mood of expectation and danger that accompanied it. Workmen set off on Sunday night, leaving women and children crying in the streets, and there was a pervasive feeling that not all would return. 'I shall this night be engaged in a struggle for freedom,' George Shell, the 19-year-old cabinet-maker wrote to his parents, 'and should it please God to spare my life, I shall see you soon. . . .' David Lewis of the King Crispin, Brynmawr, told a new Chartist recruit that if the people lost they must 'be slaves' and if they won they would 'be comfortable'. A few of the marchers undoubtedly nourished the hope that the Charter would be the law of the land in a matter of days, or certainly weeks.[21] The frustration which they felt at the late arrival at Newport, and the recriminations and discussions in the following week, indicate that the rebels had much more than a co-ordinated moral gesture in mind. The long absence from work, the reaction of the authorities, and the instant knight-hood for Thomas Phillips, all confirm that the stakes were higher.

It is, nevertheless, difficult to say precisely what the rising was about. From a mass of confusing evidence one is left with the impression of several plans, last-minute decisions, and a divergence between intentions and execution. Part of the explanation is supplied by an examination of the Chartist movement throughout Britain. One of the main themes of early radical writing on the Newport rising was that Frost had been betrayed by his English and Scottish colleagues.[22] Joseph Crabtree, the imprisoned Barnsley Chartist, and William Lovett, Bronterre O'Brien, William Ashton, O'Connor, and many others believed that the events in Wales formed part of the plan for a national insurrection drawn up at the end of the Convention. Dr Price, in the Midlands during the autumn, and William Jones, lecturing in the west country, probably knew of the scheme, and Frost almost disclosed it to a public meeting at Blaina early in October. During this month, contacts, especially between Welsh, northern, Birmingham, and west-country Chartists, were strengthened by visits and correspondence, and in the last week the pace of such activity grew frantic. Amongst the messengers who passed through Blackwood and Newport in the days before the rising were some from Bath, the Forest of Dean, North Wales, and Bradford. According to William Davies and Job Tovey, the man from Bradford, who failed to persuade the Welsh to postpone their action, promised Frost that he would tell his friends to respond to the capture of Newport. David Lewis of Brynmawr, Jenkin Morgan, and many other people on the march talked in terms of a national rising, and Frost, above all, was keen to obtain maximum support. Even some of the rank-and-file Chartists, on the run from the Westgate soldiers, believed that comrades in England and Scotland would still rally to the flag.

A glance at the Home Office papers and at the reminiscences of men like Thomas Devyr and Thomas Frost reveals that radicals in a few areas had been warned at the last minute to expect news from Wales. The most militant of the Birmingham Chartists met daily from 24 October to 7 November, and talked of joining the defeated Welsh and declaring themselves part of the Chartist republic. At Trowbridge and at Newcastle delegates waited anxiously for 'the expected Proclamation by Frost' and there were desperately late attempts to organize men of the region under captains. In London a man was gaoled for calling on the people to assemble now that the insurrection had succeeded in Wales, and in some of the West Riding and west-country clothing towns there was much activity and arming in the first days of November. There was undoubtedly a sense of annoyance in certain places because the Welsh had jumped the gun, though the 'more combative' exclaimed: 'when they determined to start, what for did they no tak t' th' hills and stand it out like men?'[23] Others, including members of the conventions that were soon to meet, approved of Frost's initiative, and the risings at Sheffield, Dewsbury, and Bradford in December and January can be seen as belated expressions of solidarity.

It is unlikely, as Zephaniah Williams's confession shows, that the leaders in South Wales would have willingly taken up arms without some assurances of outside assistance. Yet, in the last resort the events of 3–4 November, like the actions of the Durham miners in August of the same year, only make sense in the community where they occurred. Despite Professor David Williams's denial, some form of local rising is the most satisfying explanation of what was intended. Dr Fletcher of Bury, in a speech on 25 September, had called upon rank-and-file Chartists to give a lead: 'if the working classes would fight, they must begin themselves, and the convention must not be the father of the act, but the child of it'.[24] South Wales, together with the West Riding and a few other areas, was an excellent place from which to launch a popular rebellion. As we saw in the first chapter, it was a unique industrial society, where the process of change was faster and the impact more socially divisive than perhaps anywhere else in Britain. It was a class society from birth, and the coexistence, in some districts, of a native workforce and an outside body of employers, tradesmen, and law officers helped to give its industrial relations a special character. Those who, in the shock of the rising, protested that rebellion had been alien to the Welsh since the reign of Henry IV, missed some of the point.[25] Since the 1790s the industrial valleys had been a culture of alienation, sedition, and violent protest, and June 1831 had seen one of the few genuine attempts at revolution in modern British history.

For some observers, like Henry Scale, the crusty ironmaster of Aberaman House, and an angry John Gwynne of Crickhowell, there was an umbilical cord between the two risings of 1831 and 1839.[26] They claimed that the Welsh industrial peasantry cast longing eyes at the property of their new masters and wished to divide it amongst themselves. At the dinners held to celebrate the military victory at the Westgate, men like Thomas Powell of the Gaer and Edward Dowling delighted the guests with descriptions of anonymous rebels who hoped to see the rich and poor change places. Yet the Newport rising, and that of 1831, were not workers' revolutions in the most complete sense. In the debates before the march one finds the common radical demand for a better return for labour and, less frequently, a desire for greater control at the workplace. There were also hints that unpopular employers should cut their own coal, a vague notion that times would be better after the Charter was granted, and one reference to making weapons in blast furnaces and foundries once Newport was taken, but that is all. We should remember, as Zephaniah Williams always did, that the rising was a general strike as well as a military adventure, but I have been unable to find Welsh Chartists who wished to use the occasion to take over the means of production. Their main objective was to obtain the political rights which were denied them.

The nature of the rising was formed by the environment, geographical and ideological, that was industrial South Wales. The idea of a people's army from the hills descending on established towns and fortifying them was not new in Welsh history. Henry Vincent had reminded his listeners of this fact, and disappointment with the radical leadership and frustration at the schemes and compromises of the National Convention kept the notion very much alive. The small number of troops, and perhaps a knowledge of Col. Macerone's views and the achievements of popular militias in America and France, had encouraged people to think in terms of a successful regional revolt. Xenophobic English newspaper correspondents later suggested that such a rising 'on the hills' was nothing less than a nationalist rebellion, and some of them talked, rather inconsistently, of Vincent being crowned 'King' of a self-contained Welsh republic.[27] It seems improbable, however, that the industrial workmen thought in terms of a nationalist revolt; they hoped to control and fortify an area, and, whilst waiting for other clashes between soldiers and the population, set up a provisional Chartist 'Executive Government of England', with Frost as its President. Zephaniah Williams wrote of a plan to overthrow the government and establish a British republic. The special nature of Welsh industrial society and Welsh Chartism helped to bring about a revolutionary situation on this side of the border, but, as Thomas

Phillips in his defence of Wales later remarked, the local rising was originally conceived as part of a general insurrection.[28]

There seem to have been several such plans, and it is quite possible, as the *Hereford Times* suggested, that discussions on the first of these were held by a delegate conference in either Tredegar or Dukestown shortly after the break-up of the Chartist Convention.[29] Zephaniah Williams, in his confession, described a scheme to attack Newport, Brecon, Abergavenny, and Cardiff, defeat the military stationed there, and collect guns and ammunition. Other people did not mention an assault on Cardiff, but claimed that after the three remaining towns had been sacked and fortified the Chartists would move on to Monmouth. In the last fortnight before the rising there was a strong feeling on the coalfield that Vincent would be released on 5, or possibly 6, November, perhaps with help from Lancashire or west-country Chartists.[30] Professor David Williams was doubtful about all this evidence, but the correspondence to and from government, the defence preparations of the authorities, and the movements of the Chartists after the morning of the rising, provide proof that an ambitious plan had been considered.

Whether it originated with Dr Price of Pontypridd, and whether it was discussed with William Jones and William David at their autumn meetings, is not clear, nor can we be certain about when it was rejected. Unfortunately, the dating of Dr Price's memoirs is imprecise and the accounts of the crucial delegate meeting of 28 October are most unsatisfactory. Already, at this Dukestown assembly, a note of caution was sounded, and we know that one of the main tasks of delegates who left that conference was to ascertain the level of support for 'ulterior measures'. All they told the rank-and-file Chartists was that a great torchlight meeting would be held, and that people should be armed and ready to do their leaders' bidding.

The role of John Frost in these last days before the rising was vitally important but difficult to understand. His relationship with the workmen of South Wales was an ambivalent one. He told Lovett and some of his English friends in October that his Welsh supporters were putting him under extreme pressure, especially to rescue Vincent, and, after his arrest, the Newport Chartist and his legal counsel continued to present a picture of a man who had been led to violence against his will. 'He was the last man in the Convention that I should have ever expected to be connected with such a proceeding', wrote Robert Lowery some years later, and this view has become the standard historical perspective.[31] It seems likely that the most aggressive leaders of the Welsh Chartist associations were, if necessary, prepared to act decisively on their own. 'So far from leading the working men of South Wales, it was they who led me,' recalled Frost in 1856; 'they asked me to go with them, and I was not disposed to throw them aside.' Yet he was more involved in physical-force argument and plotting than is sometimes suggested. On the very eve of the rising his speeches contained some of the anger and threats that had characterized his utterances in the late spring and early summer.[32] What Dr Price and, presumably his Rhondda colleagues, disliked in the last ten days before the march were Frost's criticisms of the bolder schemes of insurrection. The Chartist leader believed, perhaps justly, that a simultaneous attack on four or five towns was unlikely to succeed, and he proposed a modified plan. It seems that his arguments in the last week found a receptive audience, and there is even a little evidence to suggest that Frost actually persuaded some 'doubting Thomases' that a rising was feasible. It has to be remembered, of course, that there were people on the coalfield who believed, both before and after the rising, that their leaders were asking too much of them. So far as I am aware, there were few persons in the nineteenth century who accused Frost of selling the workers short. 'For many years', wrote William Adams of Cheltenham in 1903, '[Frost's name] was honoured and revered by the working people as no other name in England was.'[33]

In this book we have established the nature of the modified plan of insurrection. It included a full assault on Newport, though apparently some of the Chartists from Merthyr, Dowlais, the Rhondda, Rhymney, Brynmawr, and Blaenavon were to remain at their posts. From the comments and travels of those left behind, and from the concern of Josiah Guest and Charles Harford, it can be deduced that some of these reserve Chartists were required to hold the Brecon and Abergavenny soldiers at bay, and perhaps mount a full assault on instructions from the south. Significantly, the first newspaper correspondents who arrived at Newport and Bristol on 4–6 November claimed that large bodies of Chartists were marching on the Welsh military garrisons.[34] The other move was obvious: a forced march on Monmouth to release the political prisoners. Contrary, therefore, to the opinions of historians, William Jones was right when he said that the Chartists always intended to rescue Vincent, but the timing was critical and ultimately impossible. Undoubtedly the most interesting aspect of this modified strategy was the control placed in the hands of Frost. William Shellard of Pontypool, and many of those on the march, said that everything depended on what happened at Newport, and there, in his home town, the commander-in-chief would give them precise instructions on the course to follow.

Professor David Williams insisted that the march on Newport could not be regarded as a proper assault on the town.[35] It was not, he argued, conceived in a military fashion, and Zephaniah Williams, for one, had promised his men no bloodshed. What this book shows is that, in this respect, the Chartists were a victim of their own logic and changing circumstances. They had hoped to enter Newport in the early hours when the soldiers would be asleep, compliant, or afraid, and they knew that much of the local population would support them. Groups of Chartists had taken up strategic positions at all the entrances to their town, and others were congregated near the workhouse, by a powder warehouse, in a quarry, and on the bridge over the Usk. The leaders wished to obtain as much ammunition as possible and then fortify the town. Efforts were also to be made to prevent soldiers reaching Newport by land and sea, and to effect this the bridge was to be brought down, dock water-levels to be changed, and perhaps the river blockaded with trading vessels.[36] It was hoped that when the government inevitably ordered troops into Wales the population of the south-west would harrass them, and in a few places this was done. As a final touch, said William Jones, the Chartist flag would be raised above Newport church.

The workhouse on Stow hill was always the main target of the invading forces, and it was widely believed that 5,000 men would have no difficulty in capturing the soldiers and arms within it. In the last hours the Chartist leaders considered a simultaneous assault on the workhouse and the Westgate and ultimately on the hotel alone. William Jones said, on board the convict-ship, that the final decision was a mistake, and it is still virtually impossible to discover whether the Chartists at Court-y-bella wished to take over the town and avoid conflict with the soldiers, or whether—as seems less likely—they deliberately followed the small company of the 45th Regiment to the hotel for a final confrontation.[37] The Westgate, which was known to be the centre of the authorities' defences and which housed some of the Chartist prisoners, was always likely to attract the crowd. By marching down Stow hill and into the main thoroughfare the marchers also gave the impression to some by-standers that they were already in possession of the town. Had the Westgate fallen to them, hostages and arms would have been taken and the rest of the strategy carried out.

Those engaged in the task of defending the rebels in the trials, and historians at a comfortable distance, have argued that the Chartists on 3–4 November never seriously threatened persons and property, but no one facing them had any doubts of their inten-tions. This is a note from Thomas Phillips, written just before the moment of confrontation: 'It is said that the men's objects in com-ing here are first to possess themselves of arms & ammunition—to revenge themselves upon those who have taken part here in opposi-tion to the Chartists before they proceed to release them from Mon-mouth.'[38] Seven weeks later, having seen many of the examina-tions, the convalescing ex-mayor repeated his conviction: what was proposed was a massacre of the authorities and the release of prisoners.[39] 'The names of the prescribed gentry, and their homes,' said his colleague Thomas Prothero, 'were set down, and devoted to destruction.'[40] For weeks there had been talk of taking people like Thomas Powell of the Gaer, Lewis Edwards, the Revd Richard Roberts, William Homan, and other popular enemies, and secur-ing them in mines, churches, and makeshift barracks. At the Welsh Oak miners amused themselves in the early hours of Monday morning by choosing which pistols would dispatch 'Tom Phillips' and his Newport friends.[41] Some time later, crowds surrounded Lewis Edwards's home, and other groups of Chartists sought out Capel Hanbury Leigh and Police Superintendent Roberts of Pontypool. Had they been seized it was assumed that they would have been exchanged for political prisoners. The homes of these people, too, such as Tredegar House, Pontypool Park, and Malpas Court, would also have been occupied by successful Chartists as part of their attempt to secure the area. Moreover, in the opinion of those most threatened by the rebels, all this was simply 'a primary object'. 'Their ulterior one', said a rather smug Prothero, was to give a signal, 'and we should have heard of similar insurrections throughout the country . . . in places where they were much worse prepared than even we were here.'[42]

The last-minute decision to move troops to the Westgate, the appalling weather, and the lateness and confusion of the marchers, all helped to change the expected balance of power. When he came to the top of Stow hill John Frost knew that he had a real fight on his hands. 'I was not the man for such an undertaking,' he is reported to have said in gaol, 'for the moment I saw blood flow I became terrified and fled.' Such an 'errant coward' had, in the opinion of Lord Normanby, done a real service to his country, for he had effectively thwarted the grand design of a general insurrection.[43] Those resolute Welsh Chartists who stayed and fought, who waited on the outskirts of the town for further orders, and then met on the hills for days afterwards, presumably to demand some form of revenge, could not easily forgive leaders who were already miles away. History has, perhaps understandably, glossed over such bitterness.

The significance of the Newport rising becomes clearer once we know what was at stake on 4 November 1839. Contemporaries regarded it as one of the cross-roads of nineteenth-century political and social history. Within weeks of the event its impact on the Chartist movement, the government, and Welsh society was already discernible. The rising strengthened the convictions of certain radicals and changed the perceptions of others. George Black, from Nottingham, Major Beniowski, Robert Peddie of Scotland, the informer Joseph Fussell at Birmingham, and James Boardman of Sheffield said that people should act 'like men' and set out ideologically, and sometimes physically, to join the Welsh rebels. From Nottingham, Birmingham, Carlisle, East London, Trowbridge, and the West Riding came reports of radicals who were prepared to take up arms in the aftermath of the Newport insurrection, and the authorities of the border towns from Shrewsbury to Bristol quickly strengthened their defences. It seems likely that George Julian Harney and other determined militants were actually drawn back into the Chartist movement at this time, and, despite Feargus O'Connor's pleading, there were many ugly incidents and clashes with police and soldiers in December and January. Much of this was co-ordinated and known to the Welsh Chartists; apparently even Frost in Monmouth gaol anticipated a general rebellion about Christmastime. Had he been executed, it is quite possible that Britain would have experienced unprecedented popular violence. The government's decision, as Sir Charles Napier noted in his journal, was politically a very sound one.[44]

Although it would be wrong to think that this revolutionary tradition perished overnight, the events of 1839–40, the weakness of premature and partial risings, the publicity given to spies and informers, and the power of the government and the middle class, all entered the collective Chartist consciousness. 'What remains to be done? How SHALL THE CHARTISTS PROCEED?' asked the *Western Vindicator* on 23 November 1839. 'Moral force has failed. And alas! Physical force has failed likewise. We cannot fight against armed bodies of well organized butchers of mankind.'[45] Col. Macerone and Zephaniah Williams, with their talk of a popular militia and a timorous soldiery, had been too optimistic. Moreover, as Robert Hartwell told a London audience, those districts which, in August and November 1839, had declared themselves most in favour of general action, had been found wanting.[46] No wonder that some disillusioned men left the Chartist movement after the Newport rising, and that hunted and arrested rebels came to realize the strength of the government machinery which they had once mocked. William Edwards wrote from Oakham gaol, after twenty-one months' imprisonment 'I will not countenance any illegal proceedings.'[47] Ironically, therefore, one of the effects of the rising was to strengthen the constitutional strand in British radicalism.

Like his fellow inmate Henry Vincent, Edwards became even more convinced in gaol that the Chartists had to move forward under the banner of 'Peace, Reform and Religion'. Charles Jones, the elusive Mid-Walian, Edward Charlton of Newcastle, and many others believed that physical force was no longer an option, but 'let them apply their moral powers with unanimity, and they are irresistible'.[48] Some people, especially in Scotland, had long held such a view, and they contentedly supported the new ventures in self-help Chartism which had begun before the rising in some areas and which were such a marked feature of the next two years. Vincent, himself, became a prominent teetotal Chartist, and some of his friends were active in establishing radical schools, Chartist chapels, and co-operative stores. The months after the Newport rising also witnessed an accelerating drive towards a united Chartist movement, first in London, and, by the summer of 1840, across the whole country, culminating in the creation of the National Charter Association.

The rising became for years a point of reference in radical circles, guiding people towards the most effective methods of achieving progress. For example, the value of petitioning, which had been under a cloud since the summer of 1839, was reconsidered, notably by the Universal Suffrage Central Committee and by the various conventions and prisoners' aid societies of the early 1840s. At the same time Dr McDouall bemoaned the lack of organization amongst the working class generally, and called on Chartists to work more closely with the trade unions. The failure of the general strike and risings in 1839 had highlighted the different stages of economic development and trade consciousness amongst the workmen of Britain. Thus one member of the Swansea *Cambrian* staff criticized the miners of South Wales for their lack of vision, for until deference had been removed in other areas no revolution could be successful. Meanwhile, a numbrer of Chartists were seeking to widen support in other ways, chiefly by obtaining the middle-class help that was so evidently missing in November 1839. Soon after the rising, in his 'Address to the Middle Classes', William Carrier warned that popular radicals were not finished, and there were some bitter clashes with Corn Law repealers in the winter of 1839–40, yet the message was sometimes one of reconciliation. At a local level there were discussions with middle-class representatives who believed that their security demanded some measure of franchise reform, and important inter-class contacts were re-established in the battle over political prisoners.[49]

The campaigns on behalf of Frost and the other Welshmen did much to keep Chartism alive during the 1840s, and it also greatly helped to set O'Connor firmly at the head of the movement. Within days of the rising the Irishman and his *Northern Star* successfully called upon people to direct their immediate energies to the safety of the accused. From Huddersfield, Rochdale, and many parts of Scotland, people reported that the defence of Frost, and later attempts to get a free pardon, infused a new vitality into a lethargic movement. As we saw in the last chapter, this was probably the most extensive and satisfying aspect of radicalism before 1842. O'Connor, who had always talked in terms of 'liberty through martyrdom', quickly identified himself with the cause of the Welsh rebels. He attended protest meetings all over Britain, gave hundreds of pounds of his own money, and worked closely with the defence counsel at the Monmouth trials. Such was the revival in his popularity that those districts of Lancashire and Monmouthshire which since August had cursed him for his policy on the sacred month now looked to him as the only man who could lead them.[50] Even when Frost, Williams, and Jones were in Van Diemen's Land, O'Connor did as much as anyone to keep their memory alive. In May 1841, his friend, Thomas Duncombe, presented a huge petition calling for their return, and almost won over the depleted House of Commons. In 1844, 1846, and 1847–8 there were further popular campaigns on behalf of the rebels, and successful counterattacks by Octavius Morgan, Joseph Bailey, and some of the Welsh political establishment. Nor were the families of the 'exiles' forgotten; in spite of a few complaints, the National Charter Association and local workmen looked after their wives and children through a bewildering succession of victims' funds. Richard Rorke, the old United Irishman, regularly made public-house collections at Newport for his son, the 'persecuted Patriot' and other prisoners.[51]

The response of the government to the Newport rising was a mixture of surprise and embarrassment, determination and diplomacy. In August 1839 Lord John Russell had been replaced as Secretary of State for the Home Department by that casual bureaucrat, Lord Normanby. Russell's term of office had witnessed a change in official attitudes towards the Chartist movement, the initial tolerance being followed by the banning of public meetings, the arming of defence associations, arrests of leading radicals, show trials, and a series of Police Acts.[52] During the year the police forces of Birmingham, Manchester, and Bolton were reorganized, under the central direction of the Home Office, and in July and August the Counties Police Bill was rushed through the House of Commons. Disraeli, amongst others, queried the necessity for such innovations, but Russell and the leaders of the peace-keeping forces held firm. In the following weeks the reformed Whig government even indulged in a little self-congratulation, and Sir John Campbell, the Attorney-General, made the controversial statement that the slumbering Chartist movement had been smothered by legal and constitutional means.

The shock of 3–4 November, and the revelations of planned risings in other parts of Britain, put heavy pressure on ministers of state. Leading Tory politicians, and *The Times, Morning Herald*, and other organs of conservative opinion, berated the government for its poor information network and its lack of preparation. Rebellion in Canada had been unwelcome, but rebellion in the Principality was the result of criminal negligence. Lord Granville Somerset, the Monmouthshire representative in Parliament, pointed out that it was Lord John Russell who had originally allowed Frost's name to be placed on the commission of the peace, and he complained that the Whigs had deliberately ignored the publication of seditious tracts and other radical activities in South Wales. Like *The Times*, Somerset was highly critical of Normanby's early bid to play down the importance of the rising, and was prominent in demanding the minister's resignation. At the very end of January 1840 the government survived a vote of no confidence by only twenty-one votes. In fact, the Whig response to the rising had been prompt and decisive. South Wales was flooded with troops, and, as Sir Charles James Napier recommended, ministers hurriedly improved the military and police defences of other areas under threat. The legal response was also impressive: the swift appointment of a Special Commission, curbs on the sale of radical literature, and an initial determination to stand firm on executions.

The sudden change in the last policy confused a few of the militant Chartists and caused profound unease amongst Tories and Whigs alike, and the Attorney-General in particular received a severe buffeting. At the same time, Lord Melbourne came under fire from the radical press and from 'improvers' like Robert Slaney who wanted a Select Committee inquiry and measures to eradicate the so-called ignorance and alienation of the industrial working class. Instead, the government sanctioned a short investigation by Seymour Tremenheere and circularized some thirty gentlemen of South Wales on the need for more schoolrooms and teachers. Very soon, however, the Whigs were preoccupied with other matters and in the summer of 1841 crashed to spectacular election defeat.

Ironically, the next few years of Conservative government brought forth important reports and legislation on subjects directly relevant to industrial South Wales. Amongst the investigations of select committees and royal commissions at this time were those into the employment of women and children, the payment of wages, the truck system, and the state of the mining population and of Welsh education. In many of these inquiries the voice of Seymour Tremenheere was prominent, and the memory of Chartist rebellion was at the back of people's minds. It would be wrong to attribute too much of this social awareness, and of the factory and industrial legislation of the mid-century, to popular movements

like the Newport rising and the General Strike of 1842, but it is evident that a productive fusion of concern and self-interest had at last
begun to activate the governors of Britain.

On one matter, however, the politicians remained stubbornly
insensitive to public pressure. Despite the millions of signatures on
behalf of the three leaders of the Welsh rising, and despite the petitions from Australia about their good conduct, the Secretary of
State at the Home Department took fifteen years to authorize a free
pardon, and even then was reluctant to allow the rebels to return to
these shores. In the parliamentary debates on the subject, Sir
James Graham and other ministers claimed that the Newport
rising had been more dangerous than the Monmouth rebellion of
the seventeenth century and the more recent protests in Canada.
What had been contemplated in 1839—Macaulay reminded the
House of Commons in 1846—was 'a great war of classes in this
country. All the power of imagination fails to paint the horrors of
such a contest. It would produce a shock that would be felt to the
end of the civilised world, and that our grandchildren and posterity
far into the twentieth century would have cause to lament and
deprecate.'[53]

At the local level the impact of the rising can best be seen in
terms of the working class and those above them in the social scale.
It did not, as Edward Dowling and Josiah John Guest predicted,
kill off the Chartist movement in the industrial counties of South
Wales.[54] Although eighty prominent radicals from the area were
still in gaol at the end of 1840, there was still much campaigning
for the return of Frost, Williams, and Jones. 'I am convinced, by
what I heard and witnessed while in Wales, that no power on earth
can suppress the feeling which exists there in his [Frost's] favour,'
wrote one visitor in the 1840s, 'and that until the Government have
restored him and the other two to their families and to the land of
their birth there will be no pacifying of the Welsh.' By the end of 1841
there were signs of new radical life on the fringes of the coalfield, at
Llantrisant, Cardiff, Caerleon, Monmouth, and Abergavenny.
People greeted each release of a political prisoner as a minor
triumph, and news of the attempted escape of the Brynmawr Chartists, Kidley and Godwin, also gave a certain satisfaction. Chartist
lodges in the Aberdare–Merthyr district may even have increased in
size, and they became, after 1840, the hub of popular radicalism in
South Wales. Almost 14,000 signatures were collected there for

the National Petition of 1842, and by that time, the high point of the movement in Britain, associations had been re-established in Pontypool, Abersychan, Tredegar, Dukestown, Blackwood, and Newport.[55] In the last town the stubborn survival and recovery of Chartism owed much to the old guard of William Edwards, James Horner, Thomas and John Williams, plasterer and sailmaker respectively, Richard Rorke, Jenkin Morgan, and Robert Alexander. Alexander, still something of a political missionary on the coalfield, said that he had been in prison once for his beliefs and was prepared to return there. Richard Benfield and Thomas Davies, working amongst the Tredegar miners, William Shellard and Thomas Parry of Pontypool, and Charles Waters, resident in Caerleon, took similar risks. The last, who had carried a gun at the front of the Westgate hotel, said that he would repeat the gesture if called upon. Some of these men, including Waters and Rorke, were prominent in the Land Company adventure and the revival of Chartism in 1847–8.[56]

In the early 1840s Chartists in South Wales set up their own press and provision stores, dominated street politics, and kept the Anti-Corn-Law League at bay. They helped to organize various petitions and a community strike against high meat prices in 1841. Chartists at Merthyr and Newport also put forward candidates at the general election of that year, and made the first serious forays into local government. William Townsend senior, whose son had been imprisoned with Vincent in 1839, managed to get on to the Newport town council in November 1841 and turned his invective on Lewis Edwards, the new mayor.

In the years after the rising there were frequent references to 'bad feeling' in South Wales, and a few signs of renewed interest in revolutionary politics. On occasions English Chartist delegates, and itinerant militants like George Black, appear to have been sounding out Welsh opinion on another national rebellion.[57] The first anniversary of the Newport rising was marked by exaggerated fears of a second outbreak, whilst in the autumn and winter of 1841 there was evidence of arms being sold in Pontypool, Rhymney, and Merthyr.[58] In the following months, as the economy faltered, political and industrial agitation became more overt, and arms clubs were established, though it is significant that the General Strike of 1842 received limited support, mainly on the Glamorgan end of the coalfield. Perhaps the co-ordinated and ruthless policy of employers, police, and the military in the area intimidated the radical workmen. Nevertheless, the secret Chartist discussions in 1842--3 at the Coach and Horses in Merthyr have a special interest; at these David John, William Miles, and other militants rehearsed some of the very arguments that had been so common in the mining valleys two years before, and O'Connor actually wrote to them in November 1842 warning them of the folly of another premature Newport affair.[59] Even as late as 1847 the education commissioners detected barely concealed class hostility on the coalfield, but the fitful revivals of Chartist organizations in the industrial towns during 1847–8 and the 1850s were essentially peaceful ones. The last great Welsh demonstrations were in August 1856, when John Frost returned in triumph to his beloved Newport and was cheered to the echo outside the Westgate hotel. Not far away, up Stow hill, the graves of ten Chartist comrades were annually decked with flowers.

Despite considerable propaganda efforts from the local press, Chartism was, therefore, not destroyed by the defeat at Newport in November 1839. Yet the rising had some damaging consequences. Chartism in the smaller mining communities was never as lively again as it had been in this year, and disillusionment and divisions were a feature of 1840–1, as radical visitors sadly noted. Even Blackwood Chartists acknowledged in the autumn of 1841 that they had recently 'been apathetic', and a year later their members did not respond with any enthusiasm to the General Strike call.[60] Respectable observers, anxious to make the most of these changes in attitude, wrote much of a new appreciation of the power of government and of sustained Chartist anger against some of their leaders and colleagues. During the next decade informers like Israel Firman, James Hodge, and William Harris, and lesser-known characters in the Rhondda and Ebbw Fach valleys were abused and assaulted, and the lives of Thomas Watts, Barnabas Brough, and John Daniel, the foreman of the Monmouth jury, were made unbearable. These people, Edward Dorey, the Machan carpenter, and others who betrayed their Chartist brethren, received Scotch Cattle letters, and were prevented, by strike action in 1840, from working underground. As we have seen, families with something to fear disappeared from the Welsh mining communities, whilst other people, such as William Davies of Blackwood and Dr Price, returned months and years later, to be a constant reminder of the divisions that had existed in 1839. The surgeon remained in the Chartist movement until 1842, but he now had less influence and popularity outside Pontypridd. Bitterness over the execution of the rising continued for years afterwards and some Monmouthshire workmen, including Ebbw Vale colliers in 1842, told those who later sought their assistance that they had been 'left . . . in the lurch' on that famous night in November.[61] People who had been through the experience of the rising found it hard to forgive and adjust, and even, as Seymour Tremenheere noted in 1846, to recall their excessive hopes on that unique occasion.[62] In the mid-Victorian era of government concessions, piecemeal reform, and economic improvement, the very language and strategy of these old Chartists seemed strangely irrelevant.

The disintegration of the revolutionary tradition east of Merthyr did not mean the collapse of workers' solidarity and militancy. In some ways quite the reverse was true, though the correlation is not absolute. The early 1840s saw a guerrilla war on the coalfield as the decline of the coal industry brought attendant hardship and as the employers sought to remain competitive.[63] The latter were, in some districts, forced to retreat on a number of issues, in the face of prolonged resistance by their workmen. On four occasions all the sale-coal collieries in Monmouthshire came out on strike, and amongst their grievances were the severe wage-cuts, the iniquities of truck, and the growing practice of introducing cheap Irish labour and other outsiders to weaken the resolve of this group of determined men. There were a number of concerted and violent attacks on non-Welsh workmen in the mid-century, a fact duly noted in the commissions of the time, and immediately related to the now popular image of an inward-looking and bigoted native population. Resentment of the 'English devils' and 'dirty Irish' did exist, but criticisms of these popular attitudes came hard from those who did much to create them.

In 1841 and 1843, and later in some of the major strikes of the period 1847–53, the degree of combination amongst ironworkers and especially colliers reached union standards, and the masters needed the whole machinery of the courts, police, and military, and the loyalty of agents, overmen, and blacklegs, to break the men's will. In most of the smaller mining communities, and even in places like Blackwood, Blaina, and Blaenavon, the ultimate weapon on both sides was still one of physical force. 'Damn you, you must not send your coal down to Newport, or else you shall be burned, you and the trams and the coal, to Hell, you damned set of toads that you are' represents the threat behind negotiations.[64] Warning letters were sent to several employers and magistrates in the early 1840s, and the homes and persons of blacklegs in the Monmouthshire valleys were repeatedly attacked by crowds of men and women. Along the heads of the valleys Irish families were sometimes forced to pack their belongings and leave in a hurry. Increasingly, too, the Scotch Cattle directed their attention to the coal districts of Aberdare and the Rhondda, where Walter Coffin, Thomas Powell, and Thomas Prothero were making fortunes. There, until the comparative prosperity and tranquillity of the 1860s, were staged some of the most vicious and, on one occasion, fatal conflicts in our industrial history. 'Remember that the Bool is on the rode every night, he will catch you at last,' ran one letter found in this area in the winter of 1857, 'them strangers, poor men shal be kilt, every dam one . . . (then in Welsh) whosoever will be seen within this work shall die in his blood, either in his house or on the way. O madmen, how long will ye continue in your madness?'[65]

It would be a mistake, as John Owen of Monmouth, the 'Poor Man's Attorney', pointed out, to be hypnotized by the terror and counter-terror. There were, chiefly in the Merthyr Tydfil iron district, some peaceful and disciplined strikes in the mid-century, in which old radical artisans and shopkeepers acted as arbiters, and there were attempts to establish permanent trade unions on the coalfield. Regular visitors to the area noticed the change in atmosphere between the 1830s and the 1850s, and ascribed it to the new forms of control and education which we shall be discussing later. Yet, even when national unions achieved some success in the valleys, and peaceful bargaining became the norm, direct action was not completely forgotten in South Wales. Some of the longest strikes at the end of the century, and before and after the First World War, had their share of marching gangs and physical intimidation. Nor did political violence cease in 1840: in Monmouthshire, where the Conservative families of the Somersets, Morgans, and Baileys dominated the restricted world of mid-nineteenth century politics, elections in 1852, 1868, and 1874 were accompanied by furious rioting at Tredegar, Blaenavon, Abersychan, Pontypool, and Newport. South Wales, then, never quite lost the unflattering image which Lord Melbourne had given it in 1831.

What, finally, was the reaction of the employers and those in authority to the Newport rising? One response was to close ranks and defend their interests with all the resources and influence at their command. At meetings held across the three counties in November and December 1839, Anthony Hill, Samuel Homfray, Thomas Prothero, and other industrial and religious leaders recalled the success of united action in the past, criticized absent or maverick colleagues, and indulged in a great deal of self-praise. Messages of thanks from Queen and Westminster were returned with interest; the industrial gentry of South Wales now wished to carry the fight to the radical enemy, and called on ministers of the Crown and other representatives of local government to follow their example. Heavy punishment was inflicted on those Chartist rebels of 1839, like David Lewis and Ishmael Evans, who had not been tried before the Special Commission in Monmouth, and there were strong demands for new legislation to give magistrates greater powers to search premises and to close down Chartist lodges and beerhouses, the 'nuclei of sedition & hotbeds of treason'.[66]

The scale of the local assault on all aspects of popular radicalism was impressive. Boards of magistrates were set up in a few areas to deal specifically with the Chartist threat, and radical delegates and newsvendors were subjected to harrassment and arbitrary arrest. Elizabeth Edwards of Newport, for example, the wife of the imprisoned William, was one of those who suffered from the successful winter campaign against the *Western Vindicator*. 'The seizures of [her unstamped papers] were made [without a warrant] at a very late hour of the night', wrote Thomas Jones Phillips on 20 December 1839, '& it was considered better to risk the consequences of a little irregularity than to fail in putting a stop to the publication of Papers of such pernicious tendency.'[67]

Religion and the press were also called into service. For several weeks after the rising, sermons, lectures, and tracts were directed at those 'Misguided Men called Chartists'.[68] Clergy, notably those of the Anglican, Wesleyan and Calvinistic Methodist persuasions, lent their considerable support to the campaign of vilification and intimidation. The Revd Evan Jenkins of Dowlais and Thomas Thomas of Trosnant, Pontypool, matched each other in well-publicized denunciations of the 'evil of Chartism', whilst the Methodist James Etchall of the Abergavenny circuit and the Independent Richard Jones at the Sirhowy works excommunicated members who were prominent in the movement. Cheap addresses and tracts by educationalists, Conservatives, and newspaper editors buttressed this religious warfare, and the *Monmouthshire Merlin, Merthyr Guardian*, and *Cambrian* began a long and concerted policy of condemning, ridiculing, and increasingly ignoring popular radicalism in South Wales. Other institutions, too, especially the big friendly and temperance societies, were encouraged to denounce working-class politics and to proclaim their loyalty to the Queen and the British constitution. Thus the Christmas quarterly meeting of the Torfaen district of Oddfellows called on their branches to suspend or expel any members who had been on the march to Newport.[69] Naturally, not all of this propaganda battle had an effect; employers always found unity easier to preach than to practise, and clergymen and tradesmen who ostracized Chartist workmen often lost much of their custom.

No one in the area, with the exception of the philosophical Edward Dowling and William Crawshay, was over-confident, for there was a tendency in the early 1840s to regard every form of workers' action as Chartist-inspired or revolutionary. For over a decade the authorities kept firearms and lists of special constables close to hand, and soldiers were stationed around the coalfield. The rising also heightened the growing interest in police reform. 'Should a large district be left, with no effective guardians of the public peace or property?' asked Somers Harford at an Usk Quarter Sessions. 'During the Chartist meetings on the hills, they had no power of sending to know what was doing in that particular district. He sincerely believed, that had a constabulary force existed, there would have been no outbreak.'[70] The number of paid policemen at Newport doubled within weeks of the rising, and, despite the protests over costs and legality by Lord Granville Somerset and some agriculturists, Glamorgan established a county police force in 1841 and Monmouthshire sanctioned piecemeal reforms.[71]

The 'blue bottles' were heartily disliked by the Chartists, and with good reason. In their early days at Merthyr and other industrial towns these new policemen were used as spies, complementing the less efficient variety already employed by people like Samuel Homfray and Henry Scale. Superintendent Roberts and his Pontypool colleagues paid 'close attention' to every radical meeting in 1840, whilst Capt. Napier, the first head of the Glamorgan county police, actually directed anti-Chartist campaigns. In the autumn of 1842, for example, he successfully called on the ironmasters to dismiss radical workmen, and persuaded some employers of the wisdom of choosing more carefully their agents and overmen.[72] In the opinion of Napier, and many other observers, these key sources of information and authority had been responsible, directly and indirectly, for much of the bad feeling in 1839.

Perhaps the most fascinating response to the Newport rising was indeed in the area of social control. If nothing else, the 'little war' had shown that Welsh-speaking working people were outside the range of much respectable opinion and influence. It opened a window on to a landscape of Celtic 'barbarism' and 'irreligion'. 'Ignorance is the parent of violence' was perhaps the most common analysis of the rebellious nature of the industrial working class, and it was widely said that it was more important to 'change people's minds' than to surround them with soldiers. Anglican clergymen in Merthyr and Newport recalled earlier warnings of the Bishop of Llandaff: 'Schools and churches must be erected amongst them. Our own interest, scarcely less than theirs, requires that those steps should be taken immediately.'[73] The reports of Seymour Tremenheere and other commissioners and journalists in the 1840s reinforced the message. They described a race of greedy first-generation industrial employers, and the almost enclosed and alienated world of the dissenting Welsh. How to enter this world presented an immense problem: Thomas Phillips, Benjamin Hall, and others believed that it was vital to use the Welsh language for the purpose of education and religion, but Anthony Hill, anticipating the policy of School Boards forty years later, wanted to replace the vernacular with the tongue of the civilized imperialists.

The initial reaction to the call for greater social awareness on the part of the governors was hardly encouraging. On 20 March 1840 the Committee of the Privy Council on Education decided to send a circular to some thirty gentlemen connected with the iron and coal trades in South Wales, telling them of the desperate need for elementary education in the area and providing details of government financial aid. Almost all of them seem to have ignored the approach, and, in the colliery villages at least, life continued much as before. Perhaps the collapse of organized Chartism in some of these places removed any feeling of urgency, and the bad economic years that followed the rising, and the comparative decline of Newport as a port, hardly encouraged these employers to change priorities. Coalowners devoted much of their time to exploiting divisions in the workforce and, despite new legislation and public condemnation, resolutely refused to give up the one profitable organ of control, the truck system. For a decade after the rising, evangelical Anglicanism and the works school movement hardly touched the colliers. Education commissioners in 1847, and two years later, Sir Thomas Phillips, the hero of the Westgate, still spoke of 'neglected communities' and of people treated 'like cattle'.

At the great ironworks changes were more noticeable. In fact, there were towns where iron companies had already helped to build a few chapels and schools, and the comparative immunity of Dowlais and Blaenavon from violence on the night of 3–4 November 1839 was used to justify such philanthropy. After 1840 progress was more swift, and Bishop Copleston and Sir Thomas Phillips took much of the credit for this. Within a few years Anglican schools, churches, chapels, and Sunday Schools sprang up at Tredegar, Ebbw Vale, and Rhymney. In 1846 Tremenheere was able to document the emergence of a score of works schools on the coalfield, and was pleased by the improvements in 'moral and religious superintendence . . . and good and useful instruction'.[74] These schools, like the first Mechanics Institutes at Pontypool and Newport, were partly financed by the workmen themselves. Twenty years later, when the iron towns finally came of age, the coalfield was covered with day schools, Sunday Schools, libraries, institutes, and benefit and temperance societies, and mining families were at last having a little more time and money to enjoy these provisions.

The economic tide turned in the 1850s and 1860s, and the coalfield, especially the valleys above Cardiff, enjoyed an export-led boom in coal production. South Wales once again became the industrial El Dorado of Britain. The scale of company operations grew larger, and, with a new type of manager often at the helm, it became politic, and financially easier to increase the rewards, dependence, and loyalty of employees. Now that times were better, government regulations on female and child labour were more willingly executed, and middle-class lectures on the virtue of a good family life, so common after the Newport rising, grew faintly less hypocritical. A few works, such as those at Dowlais, Rhymney, and Abercarn, and further west, at Cwmavon and Maesteg, became over-praised models of community living. All this reminds one of

9. Lady Charlotte Guest giving an address in the Dowlais School, *c.*1855

the vision of George Kenrick, the teetotal master of the Varteg, at the time of the rising: the company was intended to be the centre of employees' lives, both within and outside working hours. The above works provided not only schooling and medical care, but also religious instruction for the young, lecture and reading rooms, playing fields, and facilities for choirs, bands, and a host of clubs and voluntary movements. The works' dinner and outing, as well as the orchestrated mass receptions for employers, managers, and their families, became, for newspaper editors at least, the symbols of improving class relationships on the coalfield. The retiring managing director of one of the first model companies, on receiving the present of a plate of silver from his workmen, recalled how he had spent 'much of my leisure time among you'. 'The Sabbath School' was, in his opinion, a special 'bond of union among us. . . .Keep the Bible in reverence among you, and you will never be troubled with Chartism, or any of its baneful consequences.'[75]

There was in South Wales, as in other parts of Britain, evidence that the economic changes and industrial paternalism of the mid-Victorian years had positive results in terms of workers' deference and the collapse of national labour politics. 'How rich as ever are the indirect and unlooked-for rewards of good actions' crowed the *Cardiff and Merthyr Guardian* in 1854. 'In all the mining districts of Wales, among the scores of thousands that at one time took an active part in public matters,' wrote John Frost three years later, 'it would at present be impossible to get a meeting.'[76] A great deal was made in respectable media of the lowered horizons of old Chartists, of the inter-class platforms of liberal and nonconformist reform, and of the changing nature of the lectures being delivered in the late 1850s and 1860s by those old heroes of 1839, Henry Vincent and John Frost. Even the popular memory of the rising was under threat from those creating the great cultural and historical myths of Welsh identity. 'The great bulk of Welsh people . . .', wrote Henry Richard in 1866, 'looked upon it with undisguised repugnance and horror.'[77]

The counter-trends in the mid-Victorian era rated much less attention in the local press and in the first books of Welsh history. There was still class bitterness and violence, and a general reluctance to accept the full range of the middle-class political and economic programme. Hostility to the Master and Servant law was common, working-class criticism of religious and political leaders never disappeared, and there was some support for doctrines savouring 'very strongly of Socialism'.[78] Few seemed to notice, too, that the memory of the Chartist rising was kept alive by the ordinary people of the valleys and nourished through later struggles for survival, dignity, and a new economic world. In the 1930s Aneurin Bevan and hungry miners recalled the heroic struggles of those Chartists who had marched a century before. This book shows why the rising deserved to be remembered by working people; for their downtrodden and unenfranchized forefathers of the industrial revolution it was 'the last chance . . . we should have', and they had been brave enough to take it.[79]

Sources

PRIMARY MATERIAL

The main sources for the history of the Newport rising are as follows:

British Library (BL), Francis Place, Additional MSS on the Working Men's Association and the General Convention

Cardiff Public Library (CPL), Bute Papers

Gwent Record Office, Quarter Sessions records, Depositions and Miscellaneous Papers

National Library of Wales (NLW), Tredegar Park MSS

Newport Public Library (NPL), Chartist Trials, and Miscellaneous Books and Pamphlets

Public Record Office (PRO), Home Office, Treasury Solicitor, and War Office Letters and Papers

Transport House, London, Vincent MSS

Windsor Castle Library, Royal Archives (RA), Lord Melbourne's Papers, and Queen Victoria's Journal

NEWSPAPERS

The Cambrian, 1839–40
The Charter, 1839
The Gloucestershire Chronicle, 1839
The Hereford Times, 1839
The Merthyr Guardian (MG), 1837–44
The Monmouthshire Beacon, 1839
The Monmouthshire Merlin (MM), 1832–44
The Morning Chronicle, 1839
The Northern Liberator, 1839
The Northern Star (NS), 1838–48
The Silurian, 1839–40
The Times, 1839–40
The Western Vindicator (WV),1839

The above newspapers can be consulted in the British Newspaper Library, Colindale, the Cardiff Public Library, the Monmouth Museum, the Newport Public Library, and the National Library at Aberystwyth.

The best source for the book is the legal record of the Chartist Trials, now located in the Local History Section of the Newport Public Library. References to this source have been set out thus: 'Chartist Trials, 15, W. Harris'. The number is that of the volume used, and the name that follows is that of the person examined.

Notes

Introduction

1. *Charter*, 10 Nov. 1839, and L. C. Sanders (ed.), *Lord Melbourne's Papers* (London, Longmans, 1899), pp. 407–8.

2. CPL, Bute Papers, xx. 92, and *Morning Herald*, 6 Nov. 1839.

3. T. Prothero, in the *Monmouthshire Merlin* (MM), 23 Nov. 1893.

4. T. Phillips, *Wales: the Language, Social Condition, Moral Character, and Religious Opinions of the People* (London, J. W. Parker, 1849), pp. 52–3.

5. Earl of Bessborough (ed.), *Lady Charlotte Guest. Extracts from her Journal, 1833–52* (London, J. Murray, 1950), p. 104.

6. Bute Papers, xx. 49.

7. PRO, Treasury Solicitor's Papers (TS), 11/500, deposition of J. Lewis, 2 Dec. 1839.

8. PRO, Home Office Letters and Papers (HO), 40/45, letter of 6 Nov. 1839.

9. TS 11/503, letter of 20 July 1839.

10. See e.g. J. E. P. Wallis (ed.), *Reports of State Trials* (London, State Trials Committee, NS iv (1892), repr. Biddles Ltd., Guildford, 1970), col. 418.

11. E. Dowling, *The Rise and Fall of Chartism in Monmouthshire* (London, A. H. Bailey, 1840), p. 3.

12. *Shrewsbury News and Cambrian Reporter*, 16 Nov. 1839.

13. e.g. the son of Thomas Rees, a leading Beaufort Chartist, said that his father refused to discuss the rising until his death. A. G. Jones, 'The Economic, Industrial and Social History of Ebbw Vale 1775–1927' (MA thesis, University of Wales, 1928), p. 122. For Frost, see *People's Paper*, 4 Oct. 1856, and W. E. Adams, *Memoirs of a Social Atom* (1903; London, A. Kelly, 1968), p. 198.

14. B. Harrison and P. Hollis (eds.), *Robert Lowery. Radical and Chartist* (London, Europa, 1977), p. 156. Lowery knew more about the affair than this remark suggests. See ibid., p. 155.

15. Quotation from T. F. Tout's edition of M. Hovell, *The Chartist Movement* (Manchester University Press, 1918), p. 190.

16. G. D. H. Cole, *Chartist Portraits* (London, Macmillan, 1965), p. 159. However, Cole's account is a most interesting one.

17. D. Williams, *John Frost. A Study in Chartism* (Cardiff, University of Wales Press, 1939).

18. A. Briggs (ed.), *Chartist Studies* (London, Macmillan, 1959), p. 241.

19. Since the above publication more information on the national

background has been given in A. J. Peacock, *Bradford Chartism 1838–1840* (Borthwick Papers, 36, University of York, 1969). A growing appreciation of the significance of the rising for government and radicals alike can be found in D. Thompson (ed.), *The Early Chartists* (London, Macmillan, 1971) and J. Epstein, *The Lion of Freedom* (London, Croom Helm, 1981).

Chapter One

1. Cited in Phillips, op. cit., p. 37.

2. H. Scrivenor, *History of the Iron Trade* (1854; London, Cass, 1967), pp. 124, 127, and 257–8.

3. A. Birch, *The Economic History of the British Iron and Steel Industry 1784–1879* (London, Cass, 1967), p. 130.

4. Cited in C. Davies, 'The Evolution of Industries and Settlements between Merthyr Tydfil and Abergavenny from 1740 to 1840' (MA thesis, University of Wales, 1949), p. 58.

5. J. H. Morris and L. J. Williams, *The South Wales Coal Industry, 1841–1875* (Cardiff, University of Wales Press, 1958), p. 8.

6. MM, 22 Feb. 1840. According to the census of 1841 the population was 8,305.

7. HO 40/58, letter of 23 Apr. 1840.

8. Ibid., letter of 10 Apr. 1840.

9. T. Jones, *Rhymney Memories* (Newtown, Welsh Outlook Press, 1938), p. 79.

10. All these quotations are conveniently cited in Phillips, op. cit., pp. 41, 39–40, and 35.

11. *Merthyr Guardian* (MG), 29 Mar. 1856. An excellent account of the story in one district can be found in I. G. Jones, 'Merthyr Tydfil: the Politics of Survival', *Llafur* 2 (1976), pp. 18–31.

12. I am grateful to the present incumbent of Bedwellty parish church for his assistance with the burial records.

13. B. Ll. James, 'John Hodder Moggridge and the Founding of Blackwood', *Presenting Monmouthshire*, No. 25 (1968), pp. 25–9.

14. H. Carter and S. Wheatley, *Merthyr Tydfil in 1851* (Cardiff, University of Wales Press, 1982).

15. T. Jones, op. cit., pp. 79–80.

16. MM, 4 May 1839.

17. Ibid., 27 Apr. 1839.

18. See e.g. the sarcastic comments in TS 11/502, letter of 6 Nov. 1839.

19. Quotation, changed into the first person, from MM, 4 May 1839.

20. Phillips, op. cit., p. 47. Compare the comment that all men with money flee to Cardiff, Swansea, and Neath. Bute Papers, xx. 75.

21. Cited in Phillips, op. cit., p. 34.

22. PP 1842, XVII, Commission on the Employment and Condition of Children in Mines and Manufactories (Children's Employment), Appendix, Part II, p. 550.

23. Paragraph based on close reading of above commission, of PP 1846, XXIV, Commission on the State of the Mining Districts (Mining Commission), and PP 1842, IX, Select Committee on the Payment of Wages. See also Bute Papers, xx. 75.

24. Earl of Bessborough, op. cit., p. 30.

25. PP 1847, XXVII, Commission into the State of Education in Wales (Education Commission), Part II, p. 293.

26. See e.g. A. G. Jones, op. cit., p. 137.

27. More on this later, but just compare the different claims and impressions in *Cambrian*, 21 Dec. 1839, Bute Papers, xx. 137, and Earl of Bessborough, op. cit., p. 100.

28. The age of Chartists committed to Monmouth and Brecon gaols ranged from 11 to 61 years. Keith Thomas is inaccurate on this, and several other aspects, of Monmouthshire Chartism: 'Chartism in Monmouthshire and the Newport Insurrection, 1837–39' (MA thesis, University of Wales, 1981), p. 60.

29. Letter from a Welsh Chartist in *Western Vindicator* (WV), 11 May 1839, and MM 27 Apr. 1839.

30. PP 1842, XVII, Children's Employment, Appendix, Part II, pp. 625, 514.

31. Ibid., pp. 601, 637. The figure for boys is higher than other contemporary estimates.

32. Ibid., p. 534. In such a situation it was feared that parental control vanished when children reached about seven years of age: PP 1840, XL, Minutes of the Committee of the Privy Council on Education (Tremenheere's Report), p. 212.

33. Note the strike in the Llanfabon area against an unpopular steward accused of partiality towards members of his own family in the distribution of work: PP 1842, XVII, Children's Employment, Appendix, Part II, p. 529.

34. E. L. and O. P. Edmonds (eds.), *I was there: the Memoirs of H. S. Tremenheere* (Eton, Shakespeare Head Press, 1965), pp. 37–8.

35. Phillips, op. cit., p. 55.

36. Ibid., p. 50.

37. MM, 16 Nov. 1839. Criticisms of the Baileys are in the *Cambrian*, 24 Oct. 1840.

38. See e.g. E. J. Davies, *The Blaenavon Story* (Blaenavon, Borough Council, 1975), p. 59.

39. MM, 24 Aug. 1839.

40. See e.g. A. G. Jones, op. cit., p. 133. Were these Blaenavon men originally deputed to attack Abergavenny?

41. PP 1840, XL, Tremenheere's Report.

42. Ibid., p. 212.

43. The records suggest that tradesmen and craftsmen had higher literacy skills. See HO 20/10, 40/45 (many depositions), and TS 11/502, letter from B. Richards. David Williams (op. cit., p. 148) also exaggerated William Jones's literacy problems. Several of his letters have survived in Home Office and Treasury Solicitor's Papers.

44. HO 73/55, Report of 14 Nov. 1839. *People's Paper*, 25 Oct. 1856.

45. MM, 4 May 1839.

46. The background to these paragraphs can be found in G. S. Kenrick, *The Population of Pontypool and Trevethin* (London, Simpkin and Marshall, 1840); O. Jones, *The Early Days of Sirhowy and Tredegar* (Tredegar, Local History Society, 1969); and I. G. Jones and D. Williams (eds.), *The Religious Census of 1851*, i (Cardiff, University of Wales Press, 1976).

47. Phillips, op. cit., p. 55.

48. A summary of the debate is in D. Williams, *John Frost*, pp. 323–6.

49. See e.g. Bute Papers, ii. 113 and 133; HO 52/42, letters from E. Thomas, 7 Mar. 1839, and from B. Byron, 22 Jan.1839; Earl of Bessborough, op. cit., p. 104 (exaggerated report).

50. *Silurian*, 11 May 1837, WV, 1 June, 15 June, and 6 July 1839.

51. *Silurian*, 15 June 1839.

52. Phillips, op. cit., p. 40.

53. Report of debate in MM, 22 Feb. 1840. Henry Scale claimed that the Beer Act turned hundreds of cottages into 'sedition shops'. Bute Papers, xx. 75.

54. Cited in Morris and Williams, op. cit., p. 209.

55. A useful article on this is W. H. Baker, 'Friendly Societies in Monmouthshire to 1850', *Presenting Monmouthshire*, No. 13 (1962), pp. 33–9.

56. *Silurian*, 2 Nov. 1839.

57. O. Jones, op. cit., pp. 82–7, and E. W. Evans, *The Miners of South Wales* (Cardiff, University of Wales Press, 1961),pp. 58–9.

58. PP 1840, XL, Tremenheere's Report, p. 216.

59. PP 1847, XXVII, Education Commission, Part II, pp. 298–300.

60. This paragraph is based on a study of the newspapers, and on D. J. V. Jones, *Crime, Protest, Community and Police in Nineteenth-Century Britain* (London, Routledge and Kegan Paul, 1982).

61. NLW, Tredegar Park MS 40/34, letter of 17 Feb. 1840.

62. HO 73/55.

63. Quotation from Somers Harford's speech in favour of a professional police force. MM, 4 Jan. 1840.

64. The most relevant secondary work is I. Bale, *Through Seven Reigns* (Pontypool, Hughes and Son, n.d.).

65. Cited in Phillips, op. cit., p. 35.

66. NPL, Chartist Trials, 14, E. Evans. See also William Jones's

hostility to J. Jordan, constable of Abersychan, ibid. 11, J. Emery. On Shell, see TS 11/500, letter from J. Roberts, 1 Dec. 1839.

67. A. Bainbridge and D. J. V. Jones,'Crime in Nineteenth-Century Wales', Social Science Research Council Report, 1975, Swansea, unpublished. See also Kenrick, op. cit., pp. 24–5.

68. Quotations from PP XVII, Children's Employment, Appendix, Part II, pp. 526 and 545.

69. K. Thomas, op. cit., pp. 54–5, provides some examples.

70. See the claim in PP 1847, XXVII, Education Commission, Part II, pp. 290–2.

71. NLW 16157B.

72. MM, 27 Apr. 1839.

73. Bute Papers, xx. 75.

74. PP 1842, XVII, Children's Employment, Appendix, Part II, p. 544.

75. Clifford Davies, and several other historians, have regarded employers' control and the company shops as an inevitable and necessary aspect of early industrial life: Davies, op. cit., pp. 99–104.

76. T. Jones, op. cit., p. 110.

77. Bute Papers, xx. 75.

78. By the present writer, *Before Rebecca. Popular Protests in Wales 1793–1835* (London, Allen Lane,1973), p. 104.

79. MM, 4 Jan. 1840. Tremenheere, originally such an opponent of truck, seems to have changed his position somewhat by 1846: PP XXIV, Mining Commission, Monmouthshire and Breconshire, p. 38.

80. MM, 16 Feb. and 4 May 1839.

81. PP 1840, XL,Tremenheere's Report, pp. 213–16.

82. *Northern Star* (NS),9 Feb. 1839.

83. See HO 20/10, and C. Godfrey,'The Chartist Prisoners, 1839–41', *International Review of Social History*, 24 (1979), pp. 201–2, and the reports of examinations in MM, Nov. and Dec. 1839.

84. Quotations from ibid., 23 Nov. 1839, and *Hereford Times*, 16 Nov. 1839.

85. Edward Dowling's interpretation is rather baffling. Op. cit., pp. iii–v, 1–3.

86. Edmonds, op. cit., p. 37, and Morris and Williams, op. cit., p. 209.

87. MM, 13 July 1839. This section is based on a close reading of the *Merlin* and the *Merthyr Guardian* of the 1830s and 1840s.

88. See e.g. T. Jones, op. cit., pp. 66–7.

89. WV, 6 Apr. 1839.

90. PP 1842, XVII, Children's Employment, Appendix, Part II, p. 533.

91. Note how the colliers supported themselves during a 14-week strike when they were denied the use of company shops, and how they begged at the ironworks: ibid., p. 546.

92. Cited in Phillips, op. cit., pp. 35–6.

93. E. W. Evans, op. cit.,pp. 25–6, and D. J. V. Jones,*Before Rebecca*, p. 100.

94. HO 40/45, letter from R. Blewitt, 6 Nov. 1839.

95. For background on combinations, see D. J. V. Jones,*Before Rebecca*, chs. 3 and 4, E. W. Evans, op. cit., chs. I–IV, and G. A. Williams, *The Merthyr Rising* (London, Croom Helm, 1978), chs. 4 and 9.

96. See e.g. *Cambrian*, 11 May 1839, and MM,29 June 1839. For Scotch Cattle-type activity in the year, see MG, 26 Jan. 1839.

97. NS, 23 Feb. 1839.

98. Letter in HO 52/21.

99. D. J. V. Jones, *Before Rebecca*, ch. 4, for this, and the Scotch Cattle generally. Add E. W. Evans, op. cit., pp. 48–52, and G. J. Williams, 'The Industrial Development of the Risca area in the early Nineteenth Century', *Presenting Monmouthshire*, No. 21 (1966), pp. 15–16.

100. See e.g. TS 11/497, cases against Pontypool prisoners.

101. MG, 1 Nov. 1834.

102. Ibid., 14 June 1834.

103. For some new detail on later Scotch Cattle activity, see A. Bainbridge and D. J. V. Jones, op. cit.,pp. 425–36.

Chapter Two

1. All this is set in context by I. W. R. David, 'Political and Electioneering Activity in South-east Wales, 1820–52' (MA thesis, University of Wales, 1959).

2. WV, 20 Apr. 1839.

3. On Frost's political education, see his own short account in NS, 28 Sept. 1839, and, of course, D. Williams, op. cit., chs. I and II.

4. J. Frost,*A Letter to the Reformers of Monmouthshire*(Newport,J. Frost, 1832), p. 35.

5. J. Frost, *A Letter to the Radicals of Monmouthshire*(Newport, S. Etheridge, 1822), pp. 47–8.

6. Homfray of Tredegar and Bailey also received threatening letters: MM, 4 and18 Dec. 1830.

7. See e.g. ibid., 11 and 18 Dec. 1830, and 1 Jan. 1831.

8. Ibid., 1 Jan. 1831–12 Nov. 1831, provides some fascinating local detail on the politics of the Reform Crisis.

9. J. Frost. *A Letter to the Reformers of Monmouthshire*, pp. 3, 50.

10. WV, 10 Aug. 1839.

11. See e.g. MM, 21 May and 1 Oct. 1831, and 23 June 1832.

12. G. A. Williams, op. cit., and D. J. V. Jones,*Before Rebecca*, ch. 6. For riots in the Pontypool area, and in Brecon later, see MM, 11 June,

2 July, and 19 Nov. 1831. Note the rare claim that Z. Williams took no part in politics until pressed to do so in 1839: NS, 6 July 1844.

13. In addition to the accounts in the MG and MM, see G. A. Williams, 'The Merthyr Election of 1835', *Welsh History Review*, x. 3 (1981), pp. 359–97.

14. MM, 29 July 1837.

15. WV, 5 Oct. 1839. Compare his comments ibid. 26 Oct. 1839, and MM, 3 Nov. 1838.

16. Ibid., 29 July 1837.

17. The association was formed on 3 July 1837, and not, as David Williams and others have claimed, January 1838: ibid. 13 July 1839.

18. For Edwards's account, see WV, 20 Apr. 1839, and NS, 28 Nov. 1840.

19. BL Add. MS 37773 (reference given in D. Williams, op. cit., p. 110). By April the number was at least 600. WV, 20 Apr. 1839.

20. K. Thomas, op. cit., p. 7.

21. Earl of Bessborough, op. cit., pp. 86 and 91, and HO 40/57, letter from Marquis of Bute, 4 Jan. 1840.

22. See e.g. Bute Papers, xx. 75.

23. Etheridge claimed that great efforts were made to get middle-class persons to join the WMA at Newport: Gwent Record Office, QSD 32.0016.

24. Chartist Trials, 14, J. Thomas.

25. Ibid., 11, S. Edmunds, and NLW MS 16157B.

26. WV, 4 May 1839, and HO 20/10.

27. e.g. TS 11/502, letter from J. Howard, 15 Dec. 1839.

28. NS, 15 Feb. 1840.

29. Compare I. Prothero, *Artisans and Politics in early Nineteenth-Century London* (London, Methuen, 1979).

30. Wells withdrew from the association well before the rising. His son, too, and his fellow tradesman, Edward Thomas, left the body three and five months before.

31. WV, 23 Feb. 1839.

32. Frost, like William Cobbett, was fascinated with taxation, and especially currency matters. See e.g. NPL, *The Welchman*, No. 1 (1832).

33. Quoted in O. Jones, op. cit., p. 94.

34. Royal Institution, Swansea, Address of the Swansea Working Men's Association, March 1839. I am indebted to Dr David Painting for this find.

35. *The Welchman*, No. 1 (1832), pp. 44–5.

36. WV, 29 June 1839.

37. See e.g. the speech of Mr Baldwin, reported in MM, 20 July 1844.

38. W. Edwards, *An Address to the Working Men and Women of Newport, and of the Monmouthshire Hills* (Newport, J. Partridge, 1839), p. 2.

39. TS 11/502, deposition of 2 Dec. 1839.

40. *Silurian*, 23 Feb. 1839, cited by L. Williams, 'Movements towards Social Reform in South Wales during the period 1832–50' (MA thesis, University of Wales), p. 37.

41. NS, 9 Feb. 1839 and 28 Nov. 1840. In the latter source, W. Edwards claimed that a petition of 1,165 signatures had been sent from Blackwood to request Frost's aid.

42. There are many versions of this meeting: see e.g. HO 40/45, depositions of J. Maggs and D. Jones, in the case of J. Llewellyn. The numbers at such meetings, and the content of speeches, were a matter of frequent controversy. I have tried to give balanced estimates and interpretations.

43. TS 11/502, undated note of James Price.

44. NS, 23 Feb. 1839.

45. Ibid., 9 Feb. 1839 and 28 Nov.1840; the venture cost Edwards £50. He took their petition to the Convention.

46. *Midland Counties Illuminator*, 20 Feb. 1841, cited in Godfrey, op. cit., p. 212, and WV, 20 Apr. 1839.

47. HO 52/42. Letters from E. Thomas, 7 Mar. 1839, and from B. Byron, 22 Jan. 1839.

48. Vincent's account of all this, in WV, 30 Mar. 1839. Cf. HO 40/45, report on the trial of the men at the Monmouthshire summer assize, 2 Aug. 1839.

49. Dowling, op. cit., p. 31.

50. WV, 6 Apr. 1839.

51. There are many reports of this meeting: see HO 40/45, report of 2 Aug. 1839, Bowling, op. cit., p. 31, and MM, 30 Mar.1839.

52. On Frost's views, see NS, 9 Feb. and 28 Sept. 1839.

53. WV, 11 May 1839.

54. HO 40/45. Letter from T. Phillips, 27 Apr. 1839.

55. NS, 9 Feb. 1839.

56. Estimating numbers is hazardous. For Z. Williams's estimate, see Tredegar Park MS 40/2, letter of 25 May 1840. Cf. the figures given in WV, 8 June 1839.

57. Ibid., 11 May 1839.

58. Chartist Trials, 5, statement of E. Pugh. The punctuation is my own.

59. MM, 20 Apr. 1839. For evidence of women and violence, see TS 11/502, undated note of E. Hopkins, and TS 11/497, examination of Mary Jones, in case of Amy Meredith.

60. To set this in context, see D. J. V. Jones, 'Women and Chartism', *History*, lxviii (1983), pp.1–21.

61. Chartist Trials, 15, T. Saunders and A. Thomas.

62. NS, 18 Jan.1840, and 16 Nov. 1839.

63. Chartist Trials, 9, M. Ferriday.

64. MM, 30 Nov. 1839.

65. TS 11/503, letter from E. Edwards, 14 July 1839.

66. For a selection of evidence on this, see examinations in the case of Z. Williams in MM, 30 Nov. 1839, and in Chartist Trials, 15.

67. MM, 30 Nov. 1839.

68. TS 11/503, letter of 2 November 1839.

69. Chartist Trials, 14, W. Edmunfds.

70. WV, 13 and 20 Apr. 1839.

71. MM, 13 Apr. 1839. Edwards and others were bitterly critical of the *Merlin*'s reporting in these months.

72. WV, 27 Apr. 1839.

73. There is some confusion between the events of 18 and 19 April. Amongst the best accounts are those in MM, 27 Apr. 1839, WV, 4 May 1839, and Dowling, op. cit., pp. 24–32. The quotations are from the last source, p. 30, and from HO 40/45, deposition of S. R. Jeffreys, 26 Apr. 1839.

74. Ibid. Letter of 20 Apr. 1839. Cross-examined by Roebuck at the subsequent trial, Phillips said: 'I felt no alarm till the 19th of April' (Dowling, op. cit., p. 27).

75. James Francis, *A Sermon to the Working Classes* (Newport, H. Webber, 1839).

76. I have changed the tense of the quotation: MM, 27 Apr. 1839.

77. All this was done with government advice, as the many letters in HO 40/45 and TS 11/502 show.

78. MM, 27 Apr. 1839. I have again changed the tense.

79. WV, 4 May 1839.

80. MM, 4 May 1839, and *Silurian*, 11 May 1839. (Note that Etheridge reported for the *Silurian*.) It is possible that the most hostile newspapers were trying to drive a wedge between Chartist leaders. Most of the latter called upon their followers to be orderly and disciplined (W. Edwards, op. cit., pp. 2–3).

81. MM, 4 and 11 May 1839, and HO 40/45, deposition of D. Jones, in the case of J. Llewellyn. Surprisingly, there are few other references to the 6 May meeting.

82. MM, 23 Nov. 1839, report of case of J. Llewellyn.

83. Bute Papers, xx. 4, 5, 7. Capt. Howells and Charlotte Guest were fairly optimistic about the chances of peace in their districts: ibid. 9, and Earl of Bessborough, op. cit., pp. 90–1.

84. WV, 29 June 1839, NS, 6 July 1844, and MM, 8 and 15 June 1839.

85. *The Times*, 23 Nov. 1839, and MM, 4 May 1839.

86. WV, 1 and 15 June, 7 and 14 July 1839.

87. J. Frost, *A Letter to the Working Men's Association of Newport and Pillgwenlly* (Newport, J. Partridge, 1839), pp. 3–7.

88. On these occasions, see MM, 13 Apr., 18 and 25 May, and 8 June 1839; see too the many letters in HO 40/45, and TS 11/502.

89. See e.g. WV, 27 Apr. and 8 June 1839, and NS, 22 June 1839.

90. WV, 4 May 1839.

91. MM, 4 May 1839.

92. TS 11/502, letter from Capel Hanbury Leigh, 21 Apr. 1839, and HO 40/45, memorandum of 10 May 1839.

93. Ivor Wilks is wrong about the arrival date: 'Insurrections in Texas and Wales: the Case of John Rees', *Welsh History Review*, xi. 1 (1982), p. 82 n. 96. The *Monmouthshire Beacon*, 11 May 1839, is a little confusing about this.

94. HO 73/55, notes of events at Newport, in the report of E. Chadwick, 25 May 1839. PRO, War Office (WO), 25/2917, record of desertions.

95. There are again many letters on the arrests in HO 40/45 and TS 11/502.

96. The story of the day's events has been reconstructed from many sources: see TS 11/502, letter from T. J. Phillips, 11 May 1839, and the attached depositions of M. Scard, E. Hopkins, W. Wilson, and J. Adye. For the Chartist view of Frost's role as peacemaker, see Wallis, op. cit., cols. 349, 353, and BL Add. MSS 27821, fos. 133–5, and 34245A, fol. 430.

97. See e.g. WV, 10 Aug. 1839.

98. TS 11/502, anonymous letter to T. Phillips, May 1839.

99. TS 11/503, letter from Capel Hanbury Leigh, 16 May 1839, and HO 73/55, notes of events at Newport, in the report of E. Chadwick, 25 May 1839.

100. TS 11/503, letter from J. Brown, 26 July 1839. Frost and Vincent were more interested, perhaps, in the problems of industrial workmen than has been suggested: see WV, 2 Mar. 1839, and MM, 27 Apr. 1839.

101. It appears that David Jones and James Emery kept very full notes of Vincent's speeches in their district: see Chartist Trials, 7, and HO 40/45, depositions of the two men.

102. Speech at Newport, MM, 27 Apr. 1839. I have altered the tense in this report.

103. On the awareness of Frost, and some of his enemies, of comparable events elsewhere in the world, see MM, 3 Nov. 1838 and 4 May 1839, and MG, 19 Oct. 1839.

104. WV, 11 May 1839.

105. See, for instance, HO 40/45, letters from T. Phillips, 9 and 12 Mar., and 30 Apr. 1839, from Capel Hanbury Leigh, 16 and 25 Mar., and 1 May 1839, and MG, 24 Aug. 1839. MM, 25 May 1839, has a report of two hawkers arrested. Alexander Somerville claimed that he countered Macerone's influence amongst the Welsh: *Cobdenic Policy: the Internal Enemy of England* (London, R. Hardwicke, 1854), p. 29.

106. See Bute Papers, xx. 3, and HO 40/45, letter from T. Phillips, 22 Apr. 1839. See also Lovett's request, in BL Add. MS 27821, fol. 278.

107. MM, 4 May 1839, HO 40/45, letter from Capel Hanbury Leigh,

19 Apr. 1839, with enclosure, and from R. Smith, 30 Apr. 1839, with enclosure. See too TS 11/502, letter from Leigh, 29 Apr. 1839, with enclosures.

108. HO 40/45, letter of 2 May 1839, and letter from Leigh, with enclosure, 19 Apr. 1839.

109. Dowling, op. cit., p. 34.

110. Reports on desertions and copies of anonymous letters, in TS 11/502 and WO 25/2917. It is extremely difficult to identify the deserter who was apparently killed at the Westgate. Note the interesting conversation with 'one of the 29th' in WV, 21 Sept. 1839.

111. W. Edwards, op. cit., p. 3.

112. J. Frost, *A Letter to the Working Men's Association of Newport and Pillgwenlly* (1839), pp. 4–5.

Chapter Three

1. BL Add. MS 34245A, fo. 445.

2. Earl of Bessborough, op. cit., pp. 90–1.

3. MM, 25 May 1839, and *Silurian*, 25 May 1839.

4. TS 11/503. Cf. HO 40/45, letter from C. H. Leigh, 21 July 1839.

5. NS, 15 June 1839.

6. See e.g. Bute Papers, xx. 69.

7. Evidence on fund-raising can be found in the columns of the *Northern Star* and the *Western Vindicator*. At the beginning of July Frost reported that £100 had been subscribed for the Defence Fund at Merthyr, and £50 from Newport and Pontypool: NS, 6 July 1839.

8. Chartist Trials, 11, W. Griffith.

9. Note the request for a public meeting on Aberdare Hill to petition against government measures to increase the size of the army and to introduce professional policemen: Bute Papers, xx. 20.

10. There is some confusion over the order and dates of these meetings: NS, 15 and 29 June 1839, and *Silurian*, 29 June 1839. See Henry Scale's delayed response, Bute Papers, xx. 69.

11. MM, 13 July 1839, and *Silurian*, 6 July 1839.

12. See e.g. Bute Papers, xx. 69.

13. Ibid., 18 and 19.

14. Dowling, op. cit., pp. 37–8.

15. Edition of 27 July 1839, cited in D. Williams, op. cit., pp. 174–5.

16. *Silurian*, 15 June 1839.

17. HO 20/8, Part 1, letter of 4 Aug. 1839.

18. WV, 4 May 1839.

19. Ibid., 23 Mar. 1839. Perceptive discussions of Chartism and the

language of violence can be found in D. Thompson, op. cit., and J. Epstein, op. cit.

20. WV, 8 June 1839.

21. NS, 3 Aug. 1839.

22. WV, 27 July 1839.

23. NS, 20 July 1839, and WV, 29 June, 20 July, 17 Aug., and 7 and 28 Sept. 1839.

24. Ibid., 29 June and 27 July 1839.

25. Bute Papers, xx. 16.

26. BL Add. MS 27821, fo. 283. A reading of the *Western Vindicator* gives the impression that Frost was more concerned at this time with the issue of political prisoners. Was, as the newspaper also suggests, Vincent more in favour of a strike than the Newport draper? WV, 27 July, 3, 10, and 17 Aug., and 14 Sept. 1839. See the interesting letter of 18 July in which Frost calls for deligates to agitate Wales on the strike. NS, 27 July 1839.

27. Bute Papers, xx. 56, 72, MM, 17 and 24 Aug. 1839, and BL Add. MS 34245B, fo. 91.

28. MM, 17 Aug. 1839. There are many other reports of this meeting, but at a later date.

29. *Charter*, 16 June 1839. Professor Williams mistakenly suggested that Frost's speech was the first occasion when the idea of taking hostages was mentioned. For Vincent, see MM, 27 Apr. 1839.

30. Cited in D. Williams, op. cit., p. 169. The idea of putting gentlemen down the pits was also discussed in other coalfields. HO 40/43, letter from Col. Wemyss, 1 Dec. 1839.

31. More of this in the story of the rising. The quotation is from Bute Papers, xx. 1, examination of D. Llewellyn. For the long list of nicknames, see the *Western Vindicator* in the late spring and summer of 1839.

32. Ibid. 6 Apr. 1839. Compare *The Times* and the *Gloucestershire Chronicle*, 9 Nov. 1839.

33. See e.g. WV, 11 May and 21 Sept. 1839, Earl of Bessborough, op. cit., p. 100, and Chartist Trials, 14, Jacob Thomas.

34. *Morning Chronicle*, 19 Nov. 1839. People asked the soldiers if they would fire on the Chartists. Note the October case involving S. Victory: *Hereford Times*, 23 Nov. 1839.

35. WV, 29 June 1839.

36. Ibid. 10 Aug. 1839, and BL Add. MS 34245B, fo. 137. Cf. WV, 24 and 31 Aug. 1839, and 7 Sept. 1839.

37. Quotation from ibid. 31 Aug. 1839.

38. For the discussion, or lack of it, at the Quarter Sessions, see MM, 19 Oct. 1839.

39. See the series of letters in NS, 21 and 28 Sept. 1839, and WV, 21 and 28 Sept. 1839.

40. Ibid. 31 Aug. and 5 Oct. 1839. We know that Dr Price organized his

men so, but did he, as suggested three years later, invent the plan? It seems unlikely. HO 40/57, fos. 1196–7.

41. Chartist Trials, 14, W. Davies. For Etheridge and the paper, see Gwent Record Office, QSD 32.0016.

43. MG, 19 Oct. 1839, and TS 11/497, deposition of J. Tovey, in the case of J. Frost. We will see that leaders in the rising wore white armbands. As always with Frost, one cannot be certain if he is referring to a peaceful plan of action. Epstein, op. cit., p. 195. Special constables sometimes wore white armbands.

43. Bute Papers, xx. 2. Information of 'A.B.'

44. Ibid. 21, and cf. 23 and 24. There was considerable debate about the level of arming in this area after the rising. See ibid. 61. On the right to wear swords, as was done in the rising, see NS, 7 Sept. 1839.

45. Bute Papers, xx. 33.

46. See e.g. Chartist Trials, 14, E. Evans.

47. TS 11/503, letter from S. Homfray, 7 Nov. 1839.

48. Ibid., letter from S. Etheridge to T. J. Phillips, Nov. 1839. Chartist Trials, 12, statement of D. Evans.

49. Ibid. 5, W. Davies.

50. Ibid. 15, T. Bowen.

51. Bute Papers, xx. 105.

52. His stated purpose was to obtain a printing press. Henry Scale and Capt. Howells believed that Williams knew more about the rising than was admitted: ibid. 75 and 87.

53. For this, and more, on the national background, see Peacock, op. cit., pp. 29–34, NS, 3–31 May 1845, Somerville, op. cit., pp. 28–30, and W. Napier, *The Life and Opinions of Sir Charles James Napier*, ii (London, J. Murray, 1857), p. 69. The letter from Pringle Taylor, 22 Sept. 1839, is in RA MP 38/28. David Williams was wrong about this. Op. cit., p. 249. On Beniowski, see N. Edwards, *John Frost and the Chartist Movement in Wales* (Abertillery, Western Valleys Labour Association, 1924), p. 41, and J. Epstein and D. Thompson (eds.), *The Chartist Experience* (London, Macmillan, 1982), p. 99.

54. W. Lovett, *Life and Struggles*, 1876 (London, MacGibbon and Kee, 1976), pp. 196–7, and Tredegar Park MS 40/2, letter from Z. Williams, 25 May 1840.

55. Quotation from Williams's letter.

56. The expression is that of the *Morning Post* correspondent, 16 Nov. 1839. See, too, the *Hereford Times*, 9 Nov. 1839. For a little on Dr Price, and Dr J. Taylor's belief in his prominent role, see J. Gule, 'The Eccentric Dr. Price of Llantrisant (1800–93)', *Morgannwg*, vii (1963), p. 108, and Birmingham Public Library, Lovett Collection, II, fo. 211, letter to W. Lovett, 10 June 1841. For one of Frost's visits to local lodges, see Chartist Trials, 9, G. Evans.

57. WV, 31 Aug. 1839.

58. D. Williams, op. cit., pp. 189–91. In addition, see TS 11/497, deposition of J. Tovey, and TS 11/502, detailed claim of T. J. Phillips for £881. 14s. 6d. Thomas Maddox dated the meeting on 11 or 12 Oct. 1839: Chartist Trials, 5.

59. *Silurian*, 16 Nov. 1839.

60. Chartist Trials, 5, T. Maddox, MG, 19 Oct. 1839, and *Silurian*, 8 Dec. 1839. Frost was not too apologetic for his language: *Monmouthshire Beacon*, 26 Oct. 1839.

61. MG, 15 Oct. 1839. Professor Williams was apparently mistaken about the place of this meeting, thus making his debate about Dr Price's accuracy rather less serious: op. cit., pp. 191–2.

62. *Cardiff Times*, 26 May 1888. One would like to be precise about the date of this meeting.

63. *Morning Chronicle*, 19 Nov. 1839, and *Shrewsbury News and Cambrian Reporter*, 9 Dec. 1839.

64. NS, 19 Oct. 1839. Cf. Bute Papers, xx. 69.

65. MM, 26 Oct. 1839. *Examiner*, 17 Nov. 1839.

66. TS, 11/501, examination of G. James, 2 Dec. 1839.

67. NS, 19 Oct. 1839, and Harrison and Hollis, op. cit., p. 155. Dr Peacock, op. cit., and D. Williams, op. cit., pp. 197–8, set out Frost's movements at this time.

68. WV, 26 Oct. 1839, MM, 2 Nov. 1839, Bute Papers, xx. 34, and HO 40/46, letter from the Marquis of Bute, 17 Oct. 1839.

69. Tredegar Park MS 40/2, letter from Z. Williams, 25 May 1840. See later chapters for more detail.

70. *Cardiff Times*, 26 May 1888. The role of Dr Price and William David in the last week of October was never fully explained. See e.g. Bute Papers, xx. 1, 103, 105. One report stated that Price absconded 'on account of his correspondence with Frost . . .': HO 40/57, letter from the Marquis of Bute, 10 July 1840.

71. David Williams pays little attention to this important meeting: op. cit., p. 204. See Bute Papers, xx. 72, *Silurian*, 16 Nov. 1839, and Chartist Trials, 11, James Emery.

72. Ibid., and 3, James Emery.

73. See e.g. HO 40/46, deposition of M. Morgan, 26 Nov. 1839.

74. According to Robert Edwards, however, Charles Jones was in London during the last week of October: HO 40/44, letter of 6 Nov. 1839. Jones seems to have passed messages between Frost, Dr Taylor, and possibly George White and Peter Bussey. The reference to Frost's companion is in Bute Papers, xx. 69.

75. Chartist Trials, 15, W. Howell. There are several references to the possible help of gentlemen. *Silurian*, 16 Nov. 1839.

76. Chartist Trials, 15, W. Davies.

77. Ibid., T. Thomas and R. Williams.

78. HO 40/46, deposition of M. Morgan, 26 Nov. 1839.

79. David Williams sets out the problems of timing such a meeting: op. cit., p. 207.

80. Paragraph based on many sources. For Rees, see Wilks, op. cit., and TS 11/502, letter from S. Homfray, 5 Nov. 1839.

81. Chartist Trials, 13, examination in the case of I. Phillips.

82. Ibid. 13, unsigned letter in the case of B. Richards. See also ibid. 15, W. Howell, and MM, 30 Nov. 1839.

83. Bute Papers, xx. 72, 97, 107, 109.

84. Chartist Trials, 7, letter from J. Roberts, 4 Dec. 1839, with enclosure.

85. Ibid. 10, L. Lloyd, and *The Times*, 29 Nov. 1839.

86. MM, 30 Nov. 1839.

87. HO 73/55, report of E. Head, 14 Nov. 1839.

88. Bute Papers, xx. 30.

89. TS 11/503.

90. Chartist Trials, 14, L. Lewis and J. Thomas.

91. Ibid. 15, H. Morgan and H. Davies. See also ibid. 8, evidence of H. Davies, in relation to 'captains'. The lodge usually met at the Ivy Bush. Cf. MM, 28 Mar. 1840.

92. Ibid. 30 Nov. 1839.

93. Chartist Trials, 15, T. Bowen.

94. HO 40/46, deposition of M. Morgan, 26 Nov. 1839. TS 11/500, depositions of D. Davies and D. Williams, 11 Nov. 1839.

95. The main sources for this meeting are Chartist Trials, 6, evidence in the case of W. Davies. Ibid. 4, W. Davies, and 5, E. Pugh, R. Pugh, and J. Tovey. TS 11/500; statement of W. Davies.

96. Bute Papers, xx. 105.

97. Chartist Trials, 5, E. Pugh. Esther Pugh was not always accurate with chronology.

98. According to Zephaniah, Frost also hoped that Chartists would seize soldiers as they trooped home from the public houses on Sunday night: Tredegar Park MS 40/2. Tovey's evidence can be found in Chartist Trials, 5, and TS 11/497.

99. On this, see D. Williams, op. cit., p. 202, Tredegar MS 40/2, letter from Z. Williams, 25 May 1840, Bute Papers, xx. 69, and several letters from Gloucestershire, Somerset, and Wiltshire magistrates in HO 40/42, 47, 48.

Chapter Four

1. The quotation from David Williams is in A. Briggs, op. cit., p. 237. The main sources for this part of the story are TS 11/497, deposition of

J. Tovey; TS 11/500, statement of W. Davies; Chartist Trials, 4 and 5, J. Tovey, S. Tovey, and W. Davies. Note also 'The Chartist Correspondence', *Free Press Serials*, xiii (1856), especially letters 1, 4, 5, and 8. The dating of these letters is very important. William Cardo claimed that he, and others, were surprised at Frost's speculative effort: *Examiner*, 24 Nov. 1839.

2. HO 40/46, deposition of M. Morgan, 26 Nov. 1839, in the cases of T. Giles and W. Owen.

3. Chartist Trials, 13 and 14, examinations of L. Lewis and M. Tachett, in the cases of L. Rowland and E. Williams.

4. TS 11/500, letter from T. Phillips, 14 Dec. 1839.

5. Chartist Trials, 5, M. Williams, and 14, W. Edmunds.

6. It was returned by his wife on Monday: *Hereford Times*, 9 Nov. 1839.

7. Chartist Trials, 15, B. James.

8. Ibid. 7, J. Coules.

9. HO 40/46, depositions of M. Morgan and R. Davies, 26 Nov. 1839.

10. MM, 7 Dec. 1839. Some of these were, possibly, an advance guard.

11. It was said that the Chartists had promised not to hurt women and children left behind. *Hereford Times*, 9 Nov. 1839.

12. Chartist Trials, 15, R. Williams.

13. TS 11/503, letter from S. Homfray, 2 Nov. 1839.

14. For some of this, see Bute Papers, xx. 34, 35, 72, David, op. cit., pp. 201–2, Earl of Bessborough, op. cit., p. 103, and C. Wilkins, *The History of Merthyr Tydfil* (Merthyr, J. Williams, 1908), p. 424.

15. PP 1840, XL, Tremenheere's Report, p. 208; the report in the *Silurian*, 9 Nov. 1839; and HO 40/45, letter from R. Blewitt, 6 Nov. 1839.

16. *The Times*, 14 Nov. 1839.

17. Earl of Bessborough, op. cit., p. 100.

18. See e.g. Bute Papers, xx. 61, 105. Walter Coffin claimed that both Price and David were at Friday's Blackwood meeting.

19. Apparently, David took Llewellyn's advice: ibid. 1. Compare Owen Morgan's account, in 'Morien', *History of Pontypridd and the Rhondda Valleys* (Pontypridd, Glamorgan County Times, 1903), pp. 202–5.

20. Bute Papers, xx. 85, and *Gloucestershire Chronicle*, 9 Nov. 1839.

21. Bute Papers, xx. 113, 133.

22. The main sources for this story are the depositions of R. Davies, 12 and 26 Nov. 1839, in HO 40/46 and TS 11/502.

23. Quotation from Chartist Trials, 6, letter from J. Watkins, 6 Dec. 1839, in the case of Joseph Davies.

24. Richard Pugh, perhaps inevitably, played down the amount of arming at his Coach and Horses. J. and T. Gurney (eds.), *The Trial of John Frost for High Treason* (London, Saunders and Benning, 1840), p. 396.

25. James Davies, *The Chartist Movement in Monmouthshire* (Newport, Chartist Centenary Committee, 1939), pp. 25–6.

26. Chartist Trials, 15, J. Lewis.

27. Chartist Trials, 7, E. and J. Walters, and MM, 30 Nov. 1839.

28. Thomas Watts claimed that on his return from Bedwellty House 300–500 men stopped him near Argoed: Chartist Trials, 5.

29. On Llewellyn, see e.g. ibid. 9, G. Evans, and 12, J. Hughes, M. Scard, and I. Venn.

30. The best sources for this paragraph are TS 11/497, deposition of J. Tovey; Chartist Trials, 4, W. Davies, 5, J. Tovey, and 12, M. Scard. Cf. MM, 30 Nov. 1839, and Tredegar Park MS 40/2.

31. Chartist Trials, 9, M. Ferriday. His brother Thomas was, to quote one source, 'a regular bad character' who had been in gaol and was a 'notorious Chartist': ibid. 4, notes in the case of J. Frost.

32. We shall be looking at the evidence of these, and of J. Harford and M. Williams, in a later chapter.

33. D. Williams, op. cit., p. 214. Chartist Trials, 15, W. Harris. James Hodge, however, could not positively identify the man in the glazed hat as Reynolds: Wallis, op. cit., col. 264. Wright Beatty, from Newport, also wore a glazed hat on the march, as did others. Gwent Record Office, QSD 34.0028.

34. See e.g. TS 11/497, deposition of Hodge. O. Jones, op. cit., p. 101.

35. D. Williams, op. cit., p. 214, and Gurney, op. cit., p. 396.

36. Chartist Trials, 5, second examination of W. Davies.

37. For some detail of the story at Pontllanfraith, see the accounts of examinations in *The Times*, 7 Dec. 1839, and MM, 30 Nov.1839. See, too, HO 40/45, depositions against E. Edmunds, in the letter from T. J. Phillips, 20 Nov. 1839.

38. Chartist Trials, 14, T. Morgan.

39. Something on the events at Cefn can be gleaned from the report of the trial in Wallis, op. cit., cols. 140, 278.

40. TS 11/497, deposition of Hodge, in the case against J. Frost. A number of people saw horsemen along the route. For example, Chartist Trials, 8, A. Thomas. See also ibid. 2, fo. 30.

41. Much of the Blaina story can be found in the examinations in ibid. 15.

42. Ibid. 13, J. Thomas. According to Charlotte Guest pikes were made at the Victoria works. Earl of Bessborough, op. cit., p. 99.

43. HO 40/45, depositions of C. Lloyd and O. Williams, enclosed in a letter from G. A. A. Davies, 12 Nov. 1839.

44. The 'hostile witness' mentioned in the text was W. Howell. Much of this, and the next paragraph, is taken from five sources: Chartist Trials, 15, examinations in the case of Z. Williams; MM, 30 Nov. 1839 and 18 Jan. 1840; NS, 30 Nov. 1840; *Cambrian*, 4 Jan. 1840; Wallis, op. cit., cols. 267–74.

45. Chartist Trials, 15, A. Thomas, and HO 40/45, letter from G. A. A. Davies, 12 Nov. 1839. Other parties, who did not go to the

mountain, set off early down the valley from Blaina: Chartist Trials, 2, fo. 4.

46. MM, 30 Nov. 1839.

47. Lloyd said that after several escape attempts he was thrown into a canal at Abercarn: Wallis, op. cit., cols. 267–71, and *Cambrian*, 4 Jan. 1840.

48. *Silurian*, 9 Nov. 1839 and 28 Mar. 1840; *Cambrian*, 4 Jan. 1839; HO 40/45, information and complaint of J. Powell and J. Thomas, in a letter from G. A. A. Davies, 12 Nov. 1839; and HO 40/46, note from J. Jayne, in a letter from J. Patten, 3 Nov. 1839.

49. For this, and the next, paragraph the best sources are TS 11/500, deposition of A. Walter and others in the case of W. Williams; TS 11/501, letter from G. A. A. Davies, 20 Nov. 1839, with enclosures; *Silurian*, 9 and 16 Nov. 1839; and *Cambrian*, 4 Apr. 1840.

50. Chartist Trials, 12, H. Lewis. TS 11/502, letter from Phelps, 22 Dec. 1839. TS 11/503, letter from S. Homfray, 10 Nov. 1839, and Briefs for the Crown, in the case of T. Morgan.

51. O. Jones, op. cit., p. 101, and Wilks, op. cit., p. 21. Clearly, many people came down the Sirhowy valley after Frost had left Blackwood: Wallis, op. cit., col. 301.

52. Cited in O. Jones, op. cit., p. 102. For a similar account of missing males and grieving females, see Earl of Bessborough, op. cit., p. 100.

53. Chartist Trials, 14, examinations and correspondence in the case of B. Richards. MM, 30 Nov. 1839, and *Monmouthshire Beacon*, 16 Nov. 1839.

54. Chartist Trials, 5, J. Morgan. For people meeting in the Rising Sun and other places in the Dukestown area, see *Monmouthshire Beacon*, 16 Nov. 1839.

56. TS 11/503, briefs for the Prosecution, in the case of T. Morgan. Chartist Trials, 12, T. Williams. *Hereford Journal*, 9 Nov. 1839.

57. MM, 16 Nov. 1839.

58. TS 11/500, deposition of D. Williams, in the case of W. Williams.

59. MM, 30 Nov. 1839. Chartist Trials, 15, J. Samuel. Wallis, op. cit., col. 272.

60. NS, 14 Dec. 1839, and Chartist Trials, 11, M. Thomas.

61. Ibid. 15, T. Saunders. Wallis, op. cit., cols. 276–8.

62. Chartist Trials, 13, R. Arnold. For some information on events at the Welsh Oak, see HO 40/45, depositions against E. Edmunds, in the letter from T. J. Phillips, 20 Nov. 1839.

63. TS 11/500, deposition of J. Lewis, in a letter from H. Lewis, 2 Dec. 1839. J. Lewis thought the leader was Beatty. Compare Gwent Record Office, QSD 34.0028.

64. The figures of crowd size, and number of guns, are taken from Thomas Evans, who kept the machine in the Park: Chartist Trials, 9.

65. The exact order of proceedings, like the information on leaders, is not absolutely clear. The main sources for this paragraph are MM and

NS, 30 Nov. 1839, and the *Shrewsbury Chronicle*, 15 Nov. 1839; Chartist Trials, 11, T. Pritchard, 12, R. Lewis, 14, T. Pritchard, and 15, examination of J. Davies, in the case of Z. Williams, and the examination of Margaret Davies, in the case of the man with the wooden leg.

66. See e.g. MM, 16 Nov. 1839.

67. Op. cit., pp. 41–2.

68. Chartist Trials, 11, J. Emery, and HO 40/45, letter from W. Wood, in one from R. Smith, 5 Nov. 1839. For related detail, see *Cambrian*, 16 Nov. 1839, and MM, 23 Nov. and 7 Dec. 1839.

69. Chartist Trials, 7, T. Maggs, and 14, J. Parry.

70. The evidence on Jones is confusing. See ibid. 11, statement of D. Jones, and examinations in the case of W. Jones; Gurney, op. cit., pp. 380–9; TS 11/497, deposition of G. Coles, against J. Briton and J. Davies. Did Coles refer to *the* William Jones or to another one? More than three gangs moved to Newport from Pontypool. Contrast the official version in Chartist Trials, 24, fo. 5, with the detailed recall in *South Wales Daily News*, 21 Apr. 1877.

71. Cited by A. Clark, 'Monmouthshire Chartists', in *Presenting Monmouthshire*, No. 39 (1975), pp. 19–20.

72. The last three paragraphs are based on TS 11/497, depositions in the cases of D. Williams, J. Charles, T. Keys, and others, and Chartist Trials, 2, fo. 5. Unfortunately, there appear to have been several prominent Chartists with the name 'William Jones' in the district. An old resident remembered that 'Roll up' had been the Chartist rallying cry in the area: *South Wales Daily News*, 14 Apr. 1877.

73. HO 40/45, letter from W. Wood, 3 Nov., enclosed in one from R. Smith, 5 Nov. 1839.

74. D. Williams, op. cit., p. 212. Chartist Trials, 11, J. Emery. MM, 16 Nov. and 14 Dec. 1839. Tredegar Park MS 40/2. Z. Williams said that placards were especially designed to induce soldiers to change sides.

75. The last two paragraphs are based on many accounts. The quotation is from HO 40/45, letter from T. Phillips. Amongst the best newspaper reports are those in MG, 9 Nov.1839, MM, 16 Nov. 1839, NS, 23 Nov. 1839, and *The Times*, 16 Nov. 1839. A man was committed in Pontypool for crying and selling papers giving a false version of events at Newport. MM, 23 Nov. 1839.

76. O. Jones, op. cit., p. 102.

77. MM, 23 Nov. 1839.

78. Jones's visit to the Royal Oak was sometimes presumed rather than firmly established. Benjamin Green, for instance, was told that the visitor on horseback was Jones: Chartist Trials, 15. Sarah Edmunds claimed that Jones was at Pontllanfraith 'a little before dark', and then went off towards Blackwood. Did he make two visits to the Coach and Horses on that night? It appears unlikely. HO 40/45, fo. 961, deposition of S. Edmunds.

79. Chartist Trials, 11, H. Davies, and MM, 18 Jan. 1840.

80. O. Jones, op. cit., p. 100. David Williams gave a typically cautious and critical judgement of Jones, op. cit., pp. 148, 221.

81. Note S. Briton's anger with Watkins, NS, 16 Nov. 1839, and Dowling, op. cit., p. 90 n.

82. Chartist Trials, 11, E. Dorey.

83. TS 11/497, deposition of J. Hodge, in the case of J. Frost. See also *South Wales Daily News*, 21 Apr. 1877, and HO 40/45, deposition of J. Phillips, in a letter from T. J. Phillips, Nov. 1839.

84. For the last part of this story, see especially Chartist Trials, 3, evidence in the case of W. Jones, and 11, examinations in the case of W. Jones; Wallis, op. cit., cols.299–300; MM, 9 Nov. 1839; HO 40/45, depositions in the case of J. Aust, in a letter from T. J. Phillips, Nov. 1839.

Chapter Five

1. Chartist Trials, 5, statement of T. Phillips.

2. On this paragraph, see HO 40/45, depositions in the case of J. Morgan, enclosed in a letter from T. J. Phillips, Nov. 1839, and MM, 23 Nov. 1839. Cf. Chartist Trials, 5, J. Tovey. Although annoyed by James's evidence, Jenkin Morgan pleaded guilty at the trial. His explanation for this is in HO 20/10.

3. MM, 30 Nov. 1839. For the background, sometimes confused, to this and the previous paragraph, see ibid., 30 Nov. and 14 Dec. 1839; Chartist Trials, 3, D. Herring, E. Brickley, and others, 10, examinations in the case of J. Gibby, and 13, examinations in the case of J. Palmer and P. Hickey.

4. See e.g. MM, 9 and 23 Nov. 1839.

5. Chartist Trials, 6, case against T. Davies, sawyer.

6. On Saturday the mayor was expecting trouble in four days' time: Wallis, op. cit., col. 217. On defensive preparations, see Chartist Trials, 5, statement of T. Phillips, and 13, E. V. Jenkins; Wallis, op. cit., cols. 204–18, and 227–34, Bute Papers, xx. 37, MG, 9 Nov. 1839, *The Times*, 16 and 30 Nov. and 5 Dec.1839, and MM, 16 Nov. 1839. Bale, op. cit., pp. 28–31, gives the police story.

7. Most of the prisoners were taken at Stow. There is a discrepancy over their numbers: MM, 16 Nov. 1839, *The Times*, 5 Dec. 1839, and TS 11/500, letter from R. Blewitt, 4 Nov. 1839.

8. See Phillips's account in Wallis, op. cit., cols. 206–8.

9. *Hereford Times*, 9 Nov. 1839, and MM, 30 Nov. 1839. Most historians have ignored the route-changes. There were also arms at the Westgate, and at the Court-y-bella machine. Jack the Fifer was, according to the unreliable John Rees, heard to say: 'they meant to have the "Westgate" by-and-by for themselves': Wallis, op. cit., col. 186.

10. The timing of all this is very difficult. For the two boys' evidence, see ibid., cols. 185–91.

11. Note the corrections of early accounts of the direction of the marchers: *Shrewsbury Chronicle*, 8 and 15 Nov. 1839. Those who argued, wrongly it seems, that a large party went up the Commercial Road claimed that it was led by various people, such as Henry Frost, Charles Waters, Jack the Fifer, and a deserter from the 29th Regiment: *Bristol Mercury*, 9 Nov. 1839, and D. Williams, op. cit., pp. 224–5.

12. Llewellyn for one denied that he was in the town. Chartist Trials, 3, case of T. Llewellyn, and 13, E. V. Jenkins. MM, 9 Nov. 1839. On Rorke, see Gwent Record Office, QSD 32.0015.

13. I am indebted for information on the chapel to Mr O'Leary, a research student at the University College, Aberystwyth.

14. Chartist Trials, 15, J. Davies, Margaret Davies, and T. Hignell. Daniel Evans said that Jack the Fifer was especially important at this point, but see Samuel Williams. HO 40/45, depositions of both men, in a letter of T. J. Phillips, 18 Nov. 1839.

15. It was not, however, firmly established in court that the Chartists knew that soldiers were located, out of sight, in the hotel, though it was admitted that they knew about the Chartist prisoners inside: Wallis, op. cit., cols. 335–9. Note how Pollock, for the defence, cleverly used, or perhaps misused, the matter of timing.

16. Compare the evidence of S. Simmons, T. B. Oliver, H. Evans, and D. Evans, in ibid., cols. 157–67, and 191–203.

17. See also Dowling, op. cit., pp. 41–2, MM, 9 Nov. 1839, and Wallis, op. cit., cols. 157–67, 191–203, 354–66, 375–9, and 383-8.

18. Ibid., col. 192. Some argued that it was impossible to tell who fired first, but most observers blamed the Chartists. See the defence witnesses, J. Wilton, B. Gould, and E. Patten, in ibid., cols. 347–52, 354–66. These argued, possibly accurately, that the special constables were in an aggressive mood, but their picture of a pacific mob is overdrawn.

19. *Silurian*, and *Northern Liberator*, 9 Nov.1839, *Cambrian*, 19 Sept. 1840, and Chartist Trials, 15, Margaret Davies.

20. The bill for damage inflicted was £86. 15s. 9d. TS 11/500, bill of S. T. Hallen.

21. For personal accounts of all this, see evidence of T. Phillips, B. Gray, and J. Daily, in Wallis, op. cit., cols. 204–27.

22. The official version of cautious and limited firing is in ibid., cols. 221–2.

23. MG, 9 Nov. 1839, for this version. Radicals claimed that the conflict lasted longer, and the casualities on the authorities' side were greater, than the press admitted. NS, 23 Nov. and 7 Dec. 1839, and the *Champion*, 17 Nov. 1839.

24. Bute Papers, xx. 37.

25. Brief accounts of deaths in ibid., and Wallis, op. cit., col. 201.

26. TS 11/500, deposition of D. Davies, in the case of W. Williams. Chartist Trials, 15, W. Harris.

27. Ibid. 14, W. Powell.

28. TS 11/502 and 503, letters from S. Homfray, 5 and 7 Nov. 1839. Homfray said that, contrary to reports, David Jones was not dead, a cautionary story for historians. Isaac Thomas, one of the wounded, is included in the lists of deaths given by some writers: James Davies, op. cit., p. 37.

29. MM, 9 Nov. and 14 Dec. 1839, and Chartist Trials, 16, list of prisoners, 30 Nov. 1839.

30. NS, 7 Dec. 1839, *Champion*, 17 Nov. 1839, and *Northern Liberator*, 9 Nov. and 7 Dec. 1839.

31. Chartist Trials, 14, S. Smith.

32. Moses Scard gave him a sip of water just before he died, MM, 18 Jan. 1840.

33. Ibid., 16 Nov. 1839, *Cambrian*, 23 Nov. 1839, *Morning Herald*, 7 Nov. 1839, and Bute Papers, xx. 57.

34. *The Times*, 9 Nov. 1839.

35. A fact confirmed by *Morning Chronicle*, 7 Nov. 1839, and TS 11/500, letter from T. Phillpotts, 5 Nov. 1839.

36. Gurney, op. cit., p. 228.

37. According to Watkins, the deserter was killed by Lt. Gray. Bute Papers, xx. 37. He had a lot of well-prepared ammunition on his person: ibid. 69, and Dowling, op. cit., p.79.

38. Chartist Trials, 15, A. Thomas.

39. Register of deaths, located in the church. The burial of these men caused a 'sensation'. MM, 9 Nov. 1839.

40. Useful sources include: MM, 9 Nov. 1839, *Silurian*, 9 Nov. 1839, and *Hereford Times*, 9 Nov. 1839.

41. MM, 16 Nov. 1839.

42. TS 11/502, letter from J. Brown, 7 Nov. 1839.

43. Other names mentioned include Robert Lansdown, and 'John the Roller'. See, for instance, Chartist Trials, 5, J. Morgan, and 8, evidence on 'captains'. *Silurian*, 9 Nov. 1839, and MM, 9 Nov. 1839. There were also a few unnamed victims. One, for example, had recently been dismissed from Insole's colliery: Bute Papers, xx. 59.

44. Chartist Trials, 15, W. Whitson.

45. On Rees and Jones, see ibid. 6, J. Wright, and 11, letter to J. Coles, 6 Dec. 1839, in the case of W. Jones.

46. Ibid. 8, C. Rogers, and *Salopian Journal*, 11 Dec. 1839. For a somewhat different version of the 10 o'clock attack, see HO 40/57, declaration of W. Reid, 16 Jan. 1840.

47. TS 11/500, deposition of D. Davies, in the case of W. Williams.

48. Chartist Trials, 4, T. Duffield, and 14, information of A. Thomas, in the case of J. Saunders.

49. Earl of Bessborough, op. cit., pp. 100–1, and Chartist Trials, 14, letter, in the case of B. Richards.

50. TS 11/500, deposition of H. Lewis, 2 Dec. 1839. Compare the *Cambrian*, 7 Dec. 1839, and TS 11/501, letter from T. J. Phillips, 24 Nov. 1839. For evidence of continuing distrust of leaders, see ibid., letter from S. Homfray, Dec. 1839.

51. Chartist Trials, 15, examinations, especially that of W. Harris, in the case of Z. Williams.

52. See Frost's comment in *Shrewsbury News and Cambrian Reporter*, 9 Dec. 1839.

53. TS 11/502, deposition of R. Davies, 12 Nov. 1839, in a letter from L. Lewis, 15 Nov. 1839, and Chartist Trials, 11, letter from L. A. Homan, 27 Nov. 1839, in the case of D. Jones.

54. *The Times*, 7 Dec. 1839. Davies claimed that Frost ordered him to stay behind because he was unwell: ibid. 4.

55. *Shrewsbury News and Cambrian Reporter*, 9 Dec.1839, and NLW, MS 16157B. It is difficult to establish the truth of these remarks.

56. *Cardiff Times*, 26 May 1888, Dowling, op. cit., pp. 46–7, and Bute Papers, xx. 37. Z. Williams also believed that had affairs been handled better 'it would have been a difficult matter to defeat us': Tredegar Park MS 40/2.

57. MG, 9 Nov. 1839.

58. See e.g.*Morning Herald*, 6 Nov. 1839, and MM, 7 Dec. 1839. For criticisms of reports and press exaggerations, see ibid., 9 Nov.1839, and Dowling, op. cit., pp. 55–6.

59. HO 40/47.

60. See the prosecution of such constables in MM, 16 Nov. 1839.

61. Dowling, op. cit., pp. 45–6, and TS 11/500, letter from R. Blewitt, 5 Nov. 1839.

62. Some believed that the Chartists were seeking to rescue Frost: Bute Papers, xx. 37. Cf.MG, and *Hereford Times*, 9 Nov. 1839.

63. The examinations had begun on Tuesday morning. See the next chapter for details.

64. *Hereford Times*, 16 Nov. 1839, and Edmonds, op. cit., p. 39, for the atmosphere of the town a few weeks later.

65. *Hereford Times* and *Monmouthshire Beacon*, 9 Nov. 1839, *Hereford Journal*, 13 Nov. 1839, MM and NS, 9 Nov. 1839, and TS 11/500, letters from T. Dyke, with enclosure, 4 Nov. 1839, and from T. Phillpotts, 5 Nov. 1839.

66. *Hereford Times* and *Monmouthshire Beacon*, 9 Nov. 1839, *Silurian*, 9 Nov. 1839, and TS 11/503, letter from E. Hopkins, 16 Nov. 1839. See the recollections in Gwent Record Office, D. 992.5, and HO 40/45, letters from W. Powell, 4 and 6 Nov. 1839.

67. *Morning Chronicle*, 5 and 6 Nov. 1839, *Hereford Times, Monmouthshire Beacon*, and *Silurian*, 9 Nov. 1839. For a little on the defences at Caerleon, see Dowling, op. cit., pp. 44–5. Quotation from HO 40/46, letter from town clerk of Brecon, 5 Nov. 1839.

68. Bute Papers, xx. 56, and PP 1840, XL, Tremenheere's Report, p. 208.

69. Earl of Bessborough, op. cit., p. 104, and MG, 9 Nov. 1839. Others suggested that Aberdare, Merthyr, Dowlais, and Rhymney men were peaceful, even moral-force, Chartists, but see the report which suggests that they were actually considering a repeat performance of the Merthyr insurrection of 1831: *The Times*, 26 Dec. 1839.

70. The story at Merthyr is based on Earl of Bessborough, op. cit., pp. 99–104; TS 11/502, letter from S. Homfray, 5 Nov. 1839; Bute Papers, xx. 32, 35–9, 41–3, 45, 50, 52–3, 56–7, 62, 69; MG, 9 Nov. 1839; and *The Times*, 26 Dec. 1839.

71. The authorities wanted more police and soldiers: Bute Papers, xx. 62, and Earl of Bessborough, op. cit., p. 104.

72. There was, apparently, a major invasion-scare on Tuesday and a lesser one on Wednesday: Bute Papers, xx. 50, 57, 65, and 137. For concern in the area, see also ibid. 41, 61, 63, and 85; *The Times*, 26 Dec. 1839; and HO 40/46, letter from W. Bird, 6 Nov. 1839.

73. On Cardiff, see e.g. Bute Papers, xx. 32, 36, 38, 40, 46–7, 50–2, 57–8, 60, 66–7, 137.

74. Ibid. 57.

75. Ibid. 44 and 54, and MM, 16 Nov. 1839. There was also concern at Carmarthen over events: NS, 23 Nov. 1839. Melvin's letter of 9 Nov. is in HO 40/52.

76. TS 11/502, 503, and *Monmouthshire Beacon*, 16 Nov. 1839.

77. *Hereford Times*, 9 Nov. 1839.

78. For something of the secrecy and anxiety that characterized these days on the coalfield, see TS 11/502, letters from S. Homfray, 5 and 6 Nov. 1839; Bute Papers, xx. 49; HO 40/45, letter from C. Bailey, 5 Nov. 1839.

79. TS 11/502, letter from S. Homfray, 6 Nov. 1839, Earl of Bessborough, op. cit., p. 100, and *Monmouthshire Beacon*, 9 Nov. 1839.

80. TS 11/503, letters from S. Homfray, 7, 10, and 12 Nov. 1839.

81. On 12 Nov. magistrates at Newport reported that all was well in the area, but 'excitement' still existed at Merthyr. Tredegar Park MS 10/13. See, too, HO 40/45, letter from T. J. Phillips, 14 Nov. 1839.

82. Bute Papers, xx. 69, 75, 76.

83. *The Times*, 20, 21, 26, and 29 Nov. 1839; HO 40/45, letters from Considine, 25 Nov., and from C. H. Leigh, 26 Nov. 1839.

84. Bute Papers, xx. 62, 75, 76, 77, 83, 87.

85. Ibid. 78, 80, 85, 87, 92–4, 97–8, 101.

86. The best source for reports on these military manœuvres is HO 41/15.

87. TS 11/502, letter from S. Homfray, 22 Dec. 1839. Quotation cited by K. Thomas, op. cit., pp. 132–3. Note the confidence of Considine, HO 40/45, letters of 23 and 26 Dec. 1839.

88. MM, 23 Nov. 1839. Cf. Dowling, op. cit., pp. 50–1, *The Times*, 23 and 29 Nov. 1839, but note the delayed thanks from some places: *Hereford Times*, 23 Nov. 1839.

Chapter Six

1. On the pattern of arrests and committals, see Tredegar Park MS 40/3, 4, 6, 8, 74, 77; Chartist Trials, 16, list of prisoners. For the general policy of government in this area, see Godfrey, op. cit., p. 193.

2. For some of this story along the heads of the valleys, see TS 11/502, letter from James Brown, 14 Dec. 1839; TS 11/503, letters from S. Homfray, 10, 12, and 13 Nov. 1839; *Gloucestershire Chronicle*, 16 Nov. 1839.

3. Bute Papers, xx. 93.

4. Ibid., 78, 105.

5. TS 11/501, letter from T. J. Phillips, 24 Nov. 1839.

6. For some of this, see Wilks, op. cit., and R. Boston, *British Chartists in America, 1839–1900* (Manchester University Press, 1971), p. 27. The Treasury Solicitor's Papers have been surprisingly neglected: TS 11/502, letter from J. Brown, 7 Nov. 1839; 11/503, letters from E. Hopkins, 13 and 16 Nov. 1839. See, too, the report of David Jones's capture in 1844, NS, 16 Mar. 1844.

7. Again, there is additional information on Jones, Williams, and others in the above papers: TS 11/503, letters from S. Homfray, 7 Nov. 1839, from M. Groves, 15 Nov. 1839, and from J. Brown, 'Wednesday, November 1839', to T. Phillips. W. David was said to have been driven to America partly because of his poor financial situation: Bute Papers, xx. 85. Jenkins apparently hid in a coal-level for six months before going to America: Gwent Record Office, D. 849, scrapbook.

8. The mayor of Cardiff suspected that Zephaniah and other Chartist leaders had planned to flee the country on the *Vintage*. He was obsessive about the suspected collusion of the Portuguese consul in the affair: Bute Papers, xx. 108, 118.

9. Ibid. 103, 85.

10. Ibid. 93, 105, and see Chartist Trials, 24, letter from S. Homfray, 1 Dec. 1839.

11. TS 11/500, deposition of D. Davies, 11 Nov. 1839. For trouble over arrests in the Pontypool area, see NS, 7 Dec.1839.

12. TS 11/503, letter of Dec. 1839, to T. J. Phillips.

13. Ibid., letter from Phelps, 19 Dec. 1839.

14. Chartist Trials, 9, examination of J. Williams, and letter from W. Churchey, 3 Dec. 1839, in the case of W. Jones. There are several anonymous letters in ibid. 6 and 11.

15. Ibid. 14, letter from R. Smith, 12 Dec. 1839, in the case of D. Thomas.

16. The quotation is from TS 11/502, letter from S. Homfray, 22 Dec. 1839.

17. MM, 30 Nov. 1839. For a little on Homan and friends, see *Monmouthshire Beacon*, 16 Nov. 1839, and Chartist Trials, 24, letters from S. Homfray and W. Homan, 1 and 8 Dec. 1839.

18. Wallis, op. cit., col. 382.

19. TS 11/503, letter of 2 Mar. 1840.

20. His own description. Tredegar Park MS 40/59, letter from T. Watts, 18 Apr. 1842.

21. One cannot be certain about the figures; most were based on the list in ibid. 40/8.

22. TS 11/501, letters from Maule, 10 and 11 Nov. 1839. Cf. *Northern Liberator*, 23 Nov. 1839, and RA MP 10/84 and 85.

23. Phelps's charges totalled £2,777: Tredegar Park MS 40/12.

24. Chartist Trials, 6, evidence in the case of W. Davies.

25. TS 11/502, claim of T. J. Phillips, in his letter of 3 June 1840.

26. See e.g. TS 11/500, letter from T. Phillips, 28 Nov. 1839, and Tredegar Park MS 40/40, letter from T. J. Phillips, 18 Mar. 1840. Benjamin Hall estimated that the whole affair would cost not far short of £20,000: ibid. 40/25. There is a prodigious amount of material on finances in the Treasury Solicitor's Papers, the Tredegar Park MSS, HO 40/55, Chartist Trials, 25, and in the Quarter Session records at the Gwent Record Office.

27. For a little detail on these, and similar, prisoners, see MM, 9, 16, and 23 Nov. 1839.

28. Ibid. 16 Nov. 1839. The other cases mentioned can be found in ibid. 9, 23, and 30 Nov. 1839.

29. Ibid. 16 Nov. 1839.

30. Ibid. 23 Nov. 1839.

31. TS 11/503, letter from S. Homfray, 12 Nov. 1839.

32. MM, 23 and 30 Nov. 1839, and TS 11/503, letter from S. Etheridge, Nov. 1839, to T. J. Phillips.

33. It was reported that Phelps did not wish to press the charge. MM, 30 Nov. 1839. For other cases mentioned in this paragraph, see ibid. 9–30 Nov. 1839.

34. Ibid. 16 Nov. 1839.

35. Ibid. 23 Nov. 1839. See also TS 11/503, letter from W. P. Roberts to T. J. Phillips, undated.

36. TS 11/502, letter from B. Richards, 4 Dec. 1839. HO 20/10, interview with J. Morgan. NS, 27 July 1844. See the angry letter from W. Jones,

26 Nov. 1839, in HO 20/8, Part II, and the protest about over £300 expenses faced by the family of E.Edmunds.NS, 21 Mar. 1840.

37. HO 40/45, depositions, enclosed in a letter from T. J. Phillips, 18 Nov. 1839.

38. This paragraph is based on the reports of examinations in MM and NS, 16–30 Nov. 1839.

39. TS 11/502, letter from J. Howard, 15 Dec. 1839. TS 11/503, letters from T. Phillpotts, 15 Nov. 1839, and from Geach, 12 Dec. 1839. Chartist Trials, 10, cases of B. Gould and J. Thomas.

40. See e.g. ibid. 5, E. Pugh. Note Coles's treatrment of Mary Ferriday. NS, 9 Nov., and MM, 16 Nov. 1839. T. Phillips thought that the wounded Lovell could be offered his life for information. TS 11/500, letter of 14 Dec. 1839.

41. MM, 23 Nov. 1839.

42. For evidence, at a later date, on the consequences of being a witness, and living at Blaina, see TS 11/503, letter from J. Brown, Dec. 1839, to T. J. Phillips; TS 11/500, letter from J. Brown, 20 Apr. 1840.

43. See Phillips's anxiety about the scope of evidence; ibid., letter of 28 Nov. 1839.

44. TS 11/500.

45. TS 11/500, 502, letters from T. Phillips, 11 and 14 Dec. 1839, which reveal his fear of witnesses breaking down under pressure.

46. *The Times*, 16 and 19 Dec. 1839. People 'on the inside' were less enthusiastic, except in the case of T. J. Phillips, writing on 24 Nov. 1839, TS 11/501.

47. NS, 16 Nov. and 28 Dec. 1839, and 18 Jan. 1840.

48. Analysis of the list in Chartist Trials, 17.

49. MM, 30 Nov. 1839.

50. Chartist Trials, 15, J. Brown.

51. Note the interesting advice on mass arrests, in Tredegar Park MS 40/15.

52. Lists of prisoners and witnesses in Chartist Trials, 16 and 9 (case of J. Fisher and others). For Firman, and hostility to him, see *The Times*, 2 Dec. 1839, NS and MM, 7 Dec. 1839.

53. TS 11/500, letter from Phelps, 4 Dec. 1839.

54. TS 11/501, letter of 24 Nov. 1839.

55. NS, 30 Nov. 1839.

56. MM, 30 Nov. 1839, and 18 Jan. 1840.

57. Ibid. 14 Dec. 1839, and Chartist Trials, 10, case of J. Gibby.

58. TS 11/500, letters from T. Phillips, 11 and 23 Dec. 1893.

59. Tredegar Park MS 40/18, and Bute Papers, xx. 112.

60. Cited in D. Williams, op. cit., p. 256.

61. *Charter*, 1 Dec. 1839, NS, 28 Dec. 1839, *Morning Chronicle*, 25 Nov. 1839, and HO 40/45, letter from Geach, 6 Dec. 1839.

62. A few individuals feared at an early date that the Chartists would be lightly punished: Bute Papers, xx. 73.

63. HO 40/45, letter of 25 Nov. 1839.

64. Indictments for conspiracy were also sustained against Etheridge and Partridge, and No Bill was found against one other person. The events, and Tindal's charge, can be found in Dowling, op. cit., pp. 61–71.

65. *The Times*, 5 Dec. 1839, and *Shrewsbury News and Cambrian Reporter*, 9 Nov. 1839.

66. At least two of these soldiers were 'seduced' by Chartists. NS, 30 Nov. 1839, MM, 7 Dec. 1839, and *Gloucestershire Chronicle*, 30 Nov. 1839.

67. *Shrewsbury Chronicle*, 6 Dec. 1839. Cf. Chartist Trials, 24, Risca letter of 17 Dec. 1839.

68. TS 11/502, letter from J. Brown, 14 Dec. 1839.

69. TS 11/500, letter of 24 Dec. 1839. TS 11/502, letter from Phelps, 22 Dec. 1839.

70. Ibid. There are many fascinating letters in TS 11/500–2 concerning the determination of the authorities to get an anti-Chartist Grand and Petty Jury. On the Chartist claims about Welsh-speaking C. John and the packed jury, see NS, 15 Nov. 1845, and *People's Paper*, 27 Sept. 1857.

71. NS, 7 Dec. 1839.

72. HO 40/42, letters from P. B. Purnell, 6 and 11 Dec. 1839, NS, 3–31 May 1845, and *The Times*, 26 Dec. 1839.

73. HO 40/45, letter of 26 Dec. 1839.

74. Bute Papers, xx. 138. Cf. HO 40/51. Note from two magistrates of Bradford, 16 Dec. 1839.

75. Bute Papers, xx. 144. NS, 28 Dec. 1839, and 4 Jan. 1840. HO 41/15, letters to Considine and others, 24 Dec. 1839–1 Jan.1840. HO 40/45, letters from Phelps, 19 Dec., and from Considine, 20 Dec. 1839.

76. MM, 28 Dec. 1839, and TS 11/501 and 502, letters from S. Homfray, Dec. and 22 Dec. 1839. Bute Papers, xx. 146.

77. NS, 4 Jan. 1840. Cf. HO 40/45, letter from Considine, 23 Dec. 1839.

78. On Geach and the legal objection, see D. Williams, op. cit., pp. 274–5.

79. Wallis, op. cit., cols. 139 and 145.

80. David Williams was clearly much influenced by the defence counsel, and accepted much of their case, especially in relation to Z. Williams.

81. Wallis, op. cit., col. 431.

82. David Williams, who rightly condemned these witnesses, was inclined to forget this point. Op. cit., pp. 278–9.

83. Wallis, op. cit., col. 447.

84. The reason for the recommendation is unclear. L. Strachey and R. Fulford (eds.), *The Greville Memoirs 1814–60*, iv (London, Macmillan, 1938), p. 229.

85. HO 20/8, Part I, letter from J. Campbell, 19 Feb. 1840. HO 20/10, interview with J. Morgan. Tredegar Park MS 40/23.

86. Dowling, op. cit., p. 90.

87. Tredegar Park MS 40/29. But see Wallis, op. cit., col. 479. W. J. Linton, like many radicals, was convinced of the importance of public pressure at this time. *Memories* (London, Lawrence and Bullen, 1895), p. 44.

88. NS, 28 Dec. 1839.

89. NS, 14 Dec. 1839–25 Jan. 1840, and MM, 18 Jan. and 1 Feb. 1840.

90. NS, 11 Jan. 1840, for one of O'Connor's messages.

91. Ibid., 22 Feb. 1840.

92. For this paragraph, see Tredegar Park MS 40/23–36, and the replies in HO 41/15. See also HO 40/57, letter from the mayor of Cardiff, 14 Feb. 1840, and HO 40/55, letters from Somerset, Jan. and Feb. 1840.

93. The beleaguered government survived a vote of confidence by 21 votes. See next chapter.

94. David Williams, op. cit., pp. 293–4. For some of the feelings in Wales about a possible and actual reprieve, see *The Times*, 23 Dec. 1839, Dowling, op. cit., p. 87, *Cambrian*, 15 Feb. 1840, and *Western Mail*, 30 July 1877. Modern writers have perhaps exaggerated the degree of government cunning and care. D. Thompson, op. cit., p. 27, and K. Thomas, op. cit., p. 142. See particularly Lord Brougham (ed. J. C. Hobhouse), *Recollections of a Long Life*, v (London, J. Murray, 1911), pp. 241–5, and RA Queen Victoria's Journal: 30 Nov. 1839.

95. MM and NS, 15 Feb. 1840.

96. NS, 15 and 22 Feb. 1840, MM, 20 July 1844, and Tredegar Park MS 40/1, letters from J. Frost, 4 May 1840. Leader's motion for a free pardon was heavily defeated on 10 Mar. 1840. He was criticized in the radical press for the delay. For his defence, and the debate, see Hansard, LII (1840), cols. 1133–50.

97. Tredegar Park MS 40/34.

Conclusion

1. Edition of 8 Nov. 1839.

2. Quoted in MM, 14 Dec. 1839.

3. Op. cit., p. 57.

4. See e.g. *Silurian*, 16, 23, and 30 Nov. 1839, *Morning Chronicle*, 6 Nov. 1839, *Charter*, 24 Nov. 1839, and Dowling, op. cit., pp. 55–6.

5. MM, 14 Dec. 1839.

6. Edmonds, op. cit., p. 39.

7. See the changing views in NS, 9 Nov.–14 Dec. 1839, and 4 Jan. 1840.

8. Wallis, op. cit., col. 278.

9. D. Williams, op. cit., pp. 246–50, Harrison and Hollis, op. cit., pp. 157–68, NS, 14 Dec. 1839, and HO 40/45, letters from T. Hawkins, 16 and 17 Nov. 1839. Note the Chartist response to the publication of David Urquhart's correspondence, in *People's Paper*, 26 Jan. 1856.

10. *Northern Liberator*, 16 Nov. 1839, and NS, 9 Nov. 1839.

11. Ibid. 7 Dec. 1839.

12. Ibid. 16 Sept. 1848. Compare Hansard, XCVII, 1848, col. 1372. See also e.g. NS, 21 Mar. 1840.

13. MM, 25 July 1840. D. Williams, op. cit., p. 320, and *People's Paper*, 26 Apr. 1856.

14. Matthew John, a leading Welsh Chartist, expressed such a view in 1844. MM, 20 July 1844. *The Scottish Vindicator*, of 30 Nov. 1839 claimed that the confusion of the marchers and the calculated lack of preparations by authority were clear proofs of a conspiracy.

15. D. Williams, op. cit., pp. 288–9.

16. See e.g. Chartist Trials, 5, T. Smith, 9, M. Ferriday, and 13, R. Arnold.

17. MM, 7 Dec. 1839. Note that the source is I. Firman.

18. D. J. V. Jones, *Before Rebecca*, pp. 109–10.

19. Edmonds, op. cit., p. 38.

20. See e.g. Lovett Collection, II, fo. 211, letter from J. Taylor, 10 June 1841, and RA MP 14/79, and Queen Victoria's Journal: 6 Nov. 1839.

21. MM, 23 Nov. 1839. David Williams was not fully convinced that Shell wrote this letter. Op. cit., p. 230. The Lewis quotation is cited by K. Thomas, op. cit., p. 107. Note the debate in the trials about how often the rebels mentioned the Charter. Wallis, op. cit., cols. 408, 434–5.

22. NS, 24 Oct. 1840, and 9 and 16 Sept. 1848.

23. Harrison and Hollis, op. cit., p. 156. For a little on preparations elsewhere, see Lovett Collection, II, fo. 211, letter from J. Taylor, 10 June 1841; MM, 23 Nov. 1839; T. Frost, *Forty Years' Recollections* (London, Sampson Low, 1880), p. 115; T. A. Devyr, *The Odd Book of the Nineteenth Century* (New York, T. A. Devyr, 1882), pp. 193–209; and HO 40/42, 47, 48, 50, and 51. But note the denial of a link between Welsh and Birmingham Chartists in RA MP 10/86 and 87.

24. Cited in A. Briggs, op. cit., p. 49.

25. *Morning Herald*, 6 Nov. 1839.

26. Bute Papers, xx. 69, and *Monmouthshire Beacon*, 30 Nov. 1839.

27. The border-county newspapers were especially keen on this version: e.g. the *Hereford Times*, 16 Nov. 1839.

28. Tredegar Park MS 40/2, and T. Phillips, op. cit., p. 53.

29. *Hereford Times*, 9 Nov. 1839.

30. Tredegar Park MS 40/2, *The Times*, 6 Nov. 1839, *Morning Chronicle*, 6 Nov. 1839, *Hereford Times*, 9 Nov. 1839, NS, 9 Nov. and 7 Dec. 1839, and *Gloucestershire Chronicle*, 9 Nov. 1839.

31. Harrison and Hollis, op. cit., p. 137. Compare the interesting dream story in WV, 16 Nov. 1839.

32. *People's Paper*, 25 Oct. 1856. Chartist Trials, 12, M. Scard.

33. Ibid. 4, W. Davies, and Adams, op. cit., p. 196. The anger remained, despite some talk of his becoming a government agent: Gwent Record Office, D. 992.5, scrapbook, p. 116. His friend Zephania was also more aggressive than some writers have claimed. See his anger later in *South Wales Daily News*, 28 Apr. 1877.

34. See e.g. *The Times*, 6 Nov. 1839, and the *Morning Chronicle*, 6 Nov. 1839.

35. *John Frost*, pp. 288–9.

36. In addition to the evidence cited in earlier chapters, see Z. Williams's letter in Tredegar Park MS 40/2, Chartist Trials, 8, T. Lisle, and HO 40/58, report of Col. Considine, 23 Apr. 1840.

37. W. Jones's remark is in MM, 25 July 1840.

38. TS 11/500.

39. Ibid., letter of 23 Dec. 1839.

40. MM, 23 Nov. 1839.

41. Chartist Trials, 15, J. Davies, saddler.

42. MM, 23 Nov. 1839. Historians have, perhaps, like the defence counsel, spent too much time discussing the communication of this 'signal'. Job Tovey, William Davies, and Zephaniah Williams talked of stopping the traffic and the mail from Newport, thus supporting the claims of more doubtful court witnesses. For the defence's counter-arguments, see, for instance, Wallis, op. cit., col. 408.

43. *Shrewsbury News and Cambrian Reporter*, 9 Dec. 1839, and RA MP 10/82.

44. This paragraph is based on NS and *Northern Liberator*, Nov. and Dec. 1839, HO 41/15 and 52/42, and D. Thompson, op. cit., p. 27. Frost's comment is in HO 40/46, letter from A. Hill to the Marquis of Bute, 22 Dec. 1839.

45. Compare the *Charter*, 10 Nov. 1839. Not everyone accepted this view of government strength. HO 40/57, fo. 1200, report of a Chartist meeting, 26 Sept. 1842.

46. NS, 23 Nov. 1839.

47. *Midland Counties Illuminator*, 20 Feb. 1841, and NS, 28 Nov. 1840.

48. NS, 25 Jan. 1840.

49. WV, 9 Nov. 1839. I have tried to set these developments in a wider context in *Chartism and the Chartists* (London, Allen Lane, 1975). For the criticism of the miners, see 'One of the People', *Riots in South Wales* (Swansea, Cambrian Press, 1840), pp. 3–4.

50. NS, Nov. and Dec. 1839, and Jan. 1840.

51. Godfrey, op. cit., pp. 210–15, MM, 9 May 1840, and NS, 12 Sept. 1840. Mrs Frost was treated well, but Charles Waters and Jenkin Morgan

ran into debt. John Llewellyn vainly tried to join the 'victims': ibid. 6 Dec. 1845. Note that millions signed the petitions for a free pardon, including some of the jurymen of Dec. 1839. Hansard, LXXXIV, 1846, cols. 867–921.

52. See the excellent summary by F. C. Mather, in A. Briggs, op. cit., pp. 375–86.

53. Hansard, LXXXIV, 1846, cols. 894–5. Cf. J. Foster, *Class Struggle and the Industrial Revolution* (London, Weidenfeld, 1974).

54. For Chartist protests against this picture, see WV, 7 Dec. 1839, and MM, 20 July 1844.

55. Altogether, at Merthyr, Aberdare, Tredegar, and Pontypridd, some 36,000 signatures were collected. D. Williams, op. cit., p. 335. The quotation is from NS, 2 Jan. 1841.

56. Chartism in South Wales after 1840 can be studied in A. John, 'The Chartist Endurance: Industrial South Wales, 1840–68', *Morgannwg*, xv, 1971. See the copy of a letter from your 'still Radical son', in Gwent Record Office, D/144, Misc. MS 234.

57. And possibly receiving support from people like James Moore, of the Pontypool district, who had been arrested in the winter of 1839–40, and Matthew John of Merthyr. See the many Welsh letters in HO 45/OS 265, and 45/54, and the reports of secret meetings in HO 40/57. Capt. Napier anticipated a rising early in 1842: HO 45/OS 265, letter of 5 Feb. 1842.

58. See ibid., NS, 3 Oct. 1840, and HO 40/57, letter from R. Smith, 2 Nov. 1840.

59. For the background, see D. J. V. Jones, 'Chartism at Merthyr', *Bulletin of the Board of Celtic Studies*, xxiv. 2 (1971), and for O'Connor, see HO 45/OS 265, letter from Napier, 30 Nov. 1842.

60. So we are told: Tredegar Park MS 40/62, and 73, letters from H. Marsh, 17 Aug. and Sept. 1842.

61. HO 45/OS 265, letter from Napier, 6 Sept. 1842.

62. PP 1846, XXIV, Mining Commission, Monmouthshire and Breconshire, p. 32.

63. E. W. Evans, op. cit., ch. V.

64. MM, 11 Feb. 1843.

65. MG, 26 Dec. 1857.

66. Quotation from Tredegar Park MS 40/18.

67. HO 40/45.

68. Quotation from an Address of 27 Nov. 1839: Tredegar Park MS 57/148.

69. MM, 4 Jan. 1840. Note this newspaper's policy to ridicule and ignore Chartism after June 1840: HO 40/55, letter from R. B. Dowling, 17 June 1840.

70. MM, 4 Jan. 1840. Compare the anonymous letters of 23 and 29 Dec. 1839, in HO 40/52.

71. One can follow the debate over the Glamorgan police, which pre-dated the rising, in many of the letters in the Bute Papers, xx.

72. See, for example, NS, 12 Sept. 1840, and HO 40/57: minutes of magistrates' meeting, 6 Nov. 1840, and Bute Papers, xxii. 20, report of Napier, 6 Sept. 1842.

73. Quotations from the *Morning Chronicle*, 8 Nov. 1839, 'Amicitia' in MM, 7 Dec. 1839, and *The Times*, 23 Dec. 1839.

74. Quotation given in D. C. James, 'Hugh Seymour Tremenheere and Educational Provision in South Wales, 1839–61' (M.Ed. thesis, University of Wales, 1978), p. 37.

75. *Cambrian*, 15 Feb. 1840. This is an unusually early example of a close employer–employee relationship from the Margam–Maesteg area.

76. Quotation given in E. Havill, 'The Respectful Strike', *Morgannwg*, xxiv (1980), p. 80. Compare P. Joyce, *Work, Society and Politics: the Culture of the Factory in Later Victorian England* (London, Harvester Press, 1980), and I. G. Jones, *Explorations and Explanations* (Llandysul, Gomer Press, 1981), p. 290. Frost's words are in the *People's Paper*, 14 Nov. 1857.

77. H. Richard, *Letters and Essays on Wales* (1866; London, James Clarke, 1884), pp. 81–2. Frost, in fact, still had a sharp radical tongue: *Star of Gwent*, 23 and 30 Aug. 1856.

78. E. W. Evans, op. cit., p. 72.

79. MM, 18 Jan. 1840, which has a report on the evidence in the trial of Z. Williams. Compare H. Francis and D. Smith, *The Fed* (London, Lawrence and Wishart, 1980), pp. 194, 250.

Index